CW01654503

MODERN AND

JUNE to
SEPTEMBER
1931

LONDON
TO
DUNDEE

(The Gateway to the Scottish Highlands)

EVERY WEDNESDAY AND SATURDAY

DUNDEE TO LONDON

EVERY WEDNESDAY AND SATURDAY

THE DUNDEE, PERTH & LONDON SHIPPING COMPANY LTD.

LONDON OFFICES

CITY OFFICE

61 MARK LANE, E.C.3

Telephone—**ROYAL 3166**

Telegrams—**"DEPEEANEL, FEN, LONDON."**

WHARF OFFICE

DUNDEE WHARF
THREE COLT STREET
LIMEHOUSE, E.14

Telephone—**EAST 0658**

HEAD OFFICE: 26 EAST DOCK STREET, DUNDEE

Telephone—**3075**

Telegrams—**"COWPER, DUNDEE."**

Captain William Speedy *McManus Galleries, Dundee*

DP&L

A History of the Dundee, Perth & London Shipping Company Ltd and Associated Shipping Companies

by
Graeme Somner

Published by the World Ship Society
Kendal LA9 7LT
1995

CONTENTS

LIST OF APPENDICES

ISBN 0 905617 63 0

PREFACE

My interest in the Dundee Perth and London goes back many years — to be exact the mid-1930s. As a school boy I used to "haunt" Leith Docks and often watched LOUGA, KILDRUMMY and LOCHEE (II) load up and sail from Edinburgh Dock. Eventually in the spring of 1939 I obtained permission from Dundee to make a round trip on the nearly new LOCHEE if I "signed articles" — LOCHEE had no passenger certificate though there were two spare cabins. I "signed-on" at Leith as "Captain's Steward" my pay being one shilling per month (which incidentally I never saw!). My accommodation was quite impressive for those times — a two berth cabin with hot and cold running water. The master was Sandy Campbell, the 1st mate John Murray and 2nd mate George Wood.

The voyage took me from Leith where the ship had loaded everything from whisky to coal, to Dundee where she loaded up with yet more general cargo, whisky (mostly for the North American market) and also potatoes for the Royal Navy. The weather was pleasant and I soon found myself part of John's watch — a call at 3.45 a.m. (with a mug of tea) was my introduction to watch keeping. Arriving in the wheelhouse 15 minutes later, I found we were just passing Dover but I did not have time to look around for long — John soon put me on the wheel to earn my keep! Some hours later with Sandy on the bridge (he held a Solent Pilot Licence) we were making our way up the Solent towards Southampton. I was back at the wheel, the morning was still and fine with a low mist covering the water when I was suddenly confronted with the appearance above the mist of two funnels and masts ahead — Sandy put my mind at rest when he said they belonged to the liner EDINBURGH CASTLE (13,326/10) laid-up and at anchor. We tied up at a berth just astern of the Cunard liner QUEEN MARY (81,237/36). Sandy very kindly arranged for me to visit this huge ship during our stay. After unloading the cargo for Southampton, we moved round to nearby Portsmouth to discharge the coal for the local utilities and the potatoes for the Navy, and then sailed for the Thames, almost empty, to load bagged cement.

In pre-war days ships had to queue up off either Greenhithe or Swanscombe cement works to load their cargo. When we arrived in the early hours one morning there were three or four ships already anchored there awaiting their turn to load. The day was pleasant so John Murray organised the bosun and the four seamen to paint the numerous samson posts with which LOCHEE was equipped. This work was well underway when a decision was made that LOCHEE should top up her fuel tanks at Purfleet, some four miles up-river. Sandy did not want to disturb the routine of the ship nor waste a good morning's painting, so decided that rather than call the men down from aloft, he would get the two mates to raise the anchor and to take the bridge himself with myself as helmsman. We were soon underway on a flood tide and found the river fairly busy with not only ships of various sizes moving up and down stream but also tugs with strings of lighters doing likewise. Steering the ship was fairly routine until we came to the point where we had to turn to get alongside the wharf at Purfleet — with a single screw vessel this meant using the engine and helm, hard-a starboard, full astern, hard-a-port, full ahead and so on until we had turned 180°, and all this with other vessels passing round us. To Sandy it was all in the day's work but I was somewhat relieved when the lines to the wharf were secured and I could have a spell away from the wheel. We had soon topped up the tanks and then off we went back down river to our original anchorage lower down the Thames.

It was a trip I will always remember and one that I had hoped to repeat in August 1939 by going to Portugal to load cork, but it was not to be — war intervened. I never did sail on LOCHEE again but did "run into" John Murray quite by chance in early 1941 on a crowded train travelling South from Scotland — I was on an Army posting to London, he was on his way to Liverpool to rejoin LOCHEE (as master) after having been blown off the bridge some months earlier when the vessel struck a magnetic mine. John left the Company in 1954 (and died some years later). George retired in January 1962 and Sandy did the same (finally) in August 1969. George still lives in Dundee but Sandy died in July 1993 in his 92nd year. Happy days!

Graeme Somner
Christchurch, Dorset.
June 1995.

FOREWORD

It is easy to be infected by Graeme Somner's enthusiasm for his subject, and this is the more so if you are familiar with the Company over many years as I am, formerly as an interested observer and latterly as a manager and director. I am pleased to say that Graeme Somner has produced an account of historical record in this volume, and has captured something of the spirit that has driven the Company onward since 1826, a combination of restlessness, adaptation and high standards. The book has been the result of a considerable effort of research, compilation and hard work and it has turned out to be an entertaining and enjoyable read. I hope you will enjoy it as much as I did and that you can dip into it again and again, not only as a work of reference but also as a very good story.

Alasdair D. Chalmers,
Managing Director.

The Company's first office — 5 Shore Terrace, Dundee

CONTRACT OF COPARTNERY

Historically Tayside has always looked to the sea. A hinterland of hills and mountains made land travel difficult before the development of roads. With the Firth of Tay penetrating deep into Central Scotland and the Scottish Highlands from the North Sea, it allowed trade links to be established from the principal town of Dundee, at the entrance to the Firth, not only with the ports and towns on the upper Tay, such as Newburgh and Perth, but other ports in the adjacent Firth of Forth. The Firth of Tay's geographical location was also convenient for sailings to such major ports as Newcastle, Hull, London, Glasgow and Liverpool to be introduced, as well as to the Baltic Sea, northern Russia, the Low Countries and northern France.

Companies came into being from early times to provide sailings to the various destinations and amongst them was the Dundee, Perth & London Shipping Co. This company was the direct descendant of an amalgamation of the Dundee & Perth Shipping Co. and the Dundee & Perth Union Shipping Co., fierce rivals on the important Dundee to London route.

The Dundee & Perth Shipping Co. itself was established in 1798 as the Dundee Shipping Co. to provide a service to London. Little is known of the first ships it employed but on 2nd October 1806 the company purchased the fleet of another rival, John Richardson & Co. of Perth, and formed the Dundee & Perth Shipping Co. They advertised that they would dispatch two sailing smacks each week to London, and also that two lighters per week would load at Dundee for Perth, a distance of about 22 miles up the Tay. To cope with Napoleon's privateers which attacked shipping in the North Sea, all the company's smacks were armed with carronades and small arms. In the following year the Dundee & Perth Shipping Co. had to cope with competition from the newly formed Tay Shipping Co. which placed smart new smacks on the London sailings but this company only lasted a short while when two of their three vessels were purchased by the Dundee & Perth Shipping Co.

Subsequently in 1819 another company, the Dundee & Perth Union Shipping Co. was formed also to trade between Dundee and London, Glasgow and Leith, with also a lighter service to Perth.

By 1824 the two companies had 12 smacks engaged trading between Dundee and London, too great a number for the quantity of goods on offer and the number of passengers wanting to travel. In addition they had eight sloops trading to Glasgow and six on the river trade. The cut-throat competition between the two companies ended on 3rd July 1826 when a contract of copartnery was signed, not however, before the Dundee & Perth Union Shipping Co. had advertised their fleet for sale in the Dundee, Perth & Cupar Advertiser. Presumably this action pressured the Dundee & Perth Shipping Co. into making a move to come to some sort of agreement with their rival rather than let further rivals enter the trade.

The objects and the business of the new company, to be designated as the Dundee, Perth & London Shipping Co., was defined as "the conveyance of goods and passengers between the Tay and London, Glasgow, and Liverpool". Vessels could be employed "in such other trades as the committee of management might judge beneficial to the company". The first business was to get the ships of the two original companies valued. This was arrived at by a committee of three independent shipowners and three shipbuilders, who in pairs gave a separate valuation of each vessel, with the average figure of the three estimates being accepted as the value of the vessel — see

Appendix A, numbers 1-23 for the details. The value of the 23 vessels came to £33,580. The properties of the two companies were treated in the same manner, and the capital of the Dundee, Perth & London Shipping Co. was fixed at £38,045 split into 1,200 shares of £31/14/1d each, with the stipulation that no individual partner or company could hold more than 20 shares.

With both companies having offices in Dundee and Perth, it was no easy task to sort out which officials should undertake the combined functions. It was decided that a committee of management of 20 would be formed, 10 from each company of which two members would represent the merchants of Perth, and that Thomas Matthew and James Nicholl would be appointed joint managers at Dundee. Prior to the amalgamation of the two companies, Dundee & Perth Shipping Co. had used Downe's Wharf at London, whilst the other company had used Hore's Wharf. It was agreed that for political reasons neither wharf could be dispensed with, so they were to be used alternately. This was soon found to be impractical and it was then decided that inward to London should be landed at Hore's Wharf, whilst loading for the north would be undertaken at Downe's Wharf. The difficulties of amalgamation were present even in those days!

THE SAILING SHIP ERA 1826-1868

Of the 23 vessels taken over by the new company, 13 were smacks which were principally employed on the London sailings, departing twice weekly on Tuesdays and Fridays so as "to avoid sailing on the Lord's Day". The average passage time was 5 days 17½ hours southbound and 6 days 12 hours northbound. The master of such a vessel was paid £50 per year plus commission of 7½% on the passage money received, and an allowance of 10/6d per round voyage for expenses. He also received commission of 5% on the nett profit of the ship (after deduction of "charges on business"). Sailings by sailing smack to Liverpool round the North of Scotland were introduced but trade did not develop as expected so from 1827 goods were shipped to Glasgow from where they were carried to their destination by steamer. As a result three of the smacks became surplus and were sold, BRIDPORT PACKET (1793) for £560, OSNABURGH (1800) for £750 and DEFIANCE (1807) for £450.

Of the 10 sloops taken over, four were employed in the river trade whilst the other six were engaged on the sailings to Glasgow via Grangemouth, a port on the Firth of Forth, where the vessels entered the Forth and Clyde Canal (opened in 1790) and made their way through 40 locks to Port Dundas on the River Clyde.

In 1828 two new vessels, the smack SOVEREIGN and the sloop ROSE (II) joined the fleet. The goodwill, together with a schooner and two sloops, of the Dundee to Leith trade were acquired in 1829 from the local shipowner George Clarke at a cost of £2,000.

Whilst no further smacks were built for the company after 1828, between 1830 and 1838 the company had built 11 sloops to replace older vessels of this type.

Railways, which had developed extensively in the 1840s, brought serious competition to the trade between Dundee and Glasgow, so much so that in 1844 agreement was reached with the Glasgow & Edinburgh Railway Co.

for goods for Glasgow and Liverpool to be transferred at Leith, the port for Edinburgh, on to the railway. Canal dues also rose during the same period because of the reduction of traffic passing through and in 1849 the Company decided to pull-out of the Glasgow and Liverpool trades. All the sloops in service were sold except the three involved in the river trade, SWAN (1830), TAY (II) (1830) and LARK (1831).

Between 1838 and 1847 no new sailing vessels were brought into service. However, in 1847 the Company's faith in sail came to the fore again with the launching of the first and only iron hulled schooner CLEOPATRA. At the same time, the traditionally wooden built schooner ZENOBIA came into service. These fast vessels were employed in the Baltic and White Sea trades carrying flax and timber, and on occasions were placed on the London berth to supplement the steamers — of which more later.

A further five schooners were built or purchased between 1849 and 1857 but the days of sail were drawing to a close. SOLICITOR (1849) and ZENOBIA (1847) were sold in 1856 and 1861 respectively, GEORGE DUNCAN (1847) and QUEEN (I) (1842) were wrecked in 1860 and 1861 respectively and the last three schooners were sold in 1863, VICTORIA (1849) for £1,000, FALCON (1854) for £800, and CLEOPATRA (1847) for £2,000. The iron-built CLEOPATRA finished her days in Australian waters some 50 years later.

The Company then only retained the three sloops employed in the river trade but in 1868 these last members of the sailing ship fleet were sold out of service. Steam was now all conquering.

During the whole era from 1826 until 1868 only three of the vessels were lost, GEORGE DUNCAN and QUEEN (I) as mentioned in an earlier paragraph and the sloop FORFARSHIRE (1823) in 1832. This vessel should not be confused with a steamer of that name built in 1836 and owned by the Dundee & Hull Steam Packet Co., but mistakenly claimed as owned by the Dundee & Hull Shipping Co., which was taken over by the Dundee, Perth & London Shipping Co. only in 1857. This steamer ran ashore on the Farne Islands off north-east England in 1838, and this incident is best remembered for the heroic action of Grace Darling in helping her father rescue the passengers and crew of the vessel in a gale then blowing.

EARLY STEAMERS 1830-1854

The Company's venture into steam ship ownership came in 1830 when delivery was made of the wooden paddle tug SIR WILLIAM WALLACE. Before placing the order for this vessel, the Board had chartered the small tug ATHOLL (1828), owned by Tay Steam Packet Co., to tow lighters between Dundee and Perth. The charter cost £23 per month, which the Board considered excessive so the decision was made to build a tug of their own. Tenders were invited from three local shipyards and David Calman quoted a price of £1,200, D. & W. Brown £897 whilst Thomas Adamson (the successful builder) came up with a price of £700. SIR WILLIAM WALLACE not only towed the Company's lighters but would also tow other sailing vessels to and from Perth at a charge of £4/10/- if under 100 tons, and up to £5/10/- for a vessel of 150 tons. Passengers were also carried at a fare of 2/- per head.

Other coastal shipowners were by now operating steam ships but the Board bided their time as many of these early steamers were not successful. However, in the summer of 1832 a Glasgow company placed two paddle steamers, LIVERPOOL (330/30) and GLASGOW (280/28), on the Dundee to London route and this very quickly convinced the Board that they too would have to operate such vessels to meet this competition. Initially they chartered the paddle steamer LONDON MERCHANT (320/31) in 1833 having meantime placed an order for two vessels. The order for two wooden paddle steamers had been placed in August 1832 with the famous Clydesdale engineer, Robert Napier, at a cost of £18,000 each, with the hulls to be constructed by John Wood, also of Port Glasgow. Early in their construction the French Government offered to buy them, but the Company would only agree to this if Robert Napier could replace them on equally favourable terms by April 1834, with the Company also receiving a bonus of £10,000 per ship. Nothing came of this offer.

The first vessel, named DUNDEE, was the second vessel of this name in the fleet, the earlier vessel having been a smack built in 1818 for Dundee & Perth Shipping Co. Launched on 19th August 1833, she arrived at Dundee from the Clyde on 26th March 1834 after a stormy passage round the North of Scotland. She was a splendid vessel with a figure-head of Neptune mounted on the clipper bow, had three masts, and was schooner rigged. She sailed on her maiden voyage to London on 2nd April 1834 making the passage in 38 hours.

The sister ship, PERTH (III) sailed from Greenock on 9th May 1834 for Dundee carrying some 90 passengers who had paid the sum of £3/3/- for the voyage. Good time was made on the passage through the Gulf of Corrievrechan, the whirlpool near the northern point of the island of Jura, through the Sound of Mull, past Skye and on round Cape Wrath and John o' Groats reaching the mouth of the Tay on 12th May after a passage of 66½ hours. PERTH (III), with a figure head representing the Fair Maid of Perth, sailed from Dundee on her maiden voyage on 6th June 1834.

During the summer months of 1834 to 1836, the vessels used to call occasionally at Great Yarmouth and Scarborough to land passengers but these calls were subsequently discontinued to improve timekeeping.

Initially each of these vessels carried a Commander (pay £15 per month) as well as a Sailing Master (£8 per month) as it was deemed the complications of a steamer were too great for one man, but this style of manning was soon dropped, with the sailing master becoming the first mate.

DUNDEE (II) and PERTH (III) were the most luxurious and fastest steamers on the East coast, and their masters took a great pleasure in outpacing their Leith and Aberdeen rivals. The travelling public and merchants were well pleased with this new service (despite the fact that the steamers were laid-up in the winter months and sailing vessels substituted) and this enabled the Company to order a third steamer, again from Robert Napier, but now costing £22,000. LONDON (II) arrived at Dundee on 10th July 1837 from the Clyde, sailing via the North of Scotland and carrying 60 passengers who had paid a fare of £3/3/- for this voyage.

Wages to the crews in July 1843 are recorded in the Minutes book of the period. A master of a steamer (when in service) received £14 per month but this dropped to £9 when the vessel was laid-up. A master of a sailing vessel received £7. In the engine room the Chief Engineer received £8, a second engineer £6, a fireman 18/- and a coal trimmer 15/- per month, whilst a seaman got 12/-, with a cook receiving 20/-, somewhat higher than a second mate who only received 16/4d.

The three paddlers settled down to a period of long service on the London sailings but now and again performed other tasks with PERTH (III) acting as a pilot ship to the Royal Yacht on the occasion of the visit of Queen Victoria to Dundee in September 1844 and LONDON (II) being despatched on a cruise to Hamburg in July 1845 with 66 passengers — fare 1st class £4/4/-, 2nd class £3/3/-. The return voyage embarked in addition 126 head of cattle and 14 sheep but there is no record of any complaints from the cruise passengers!

In March 1838, James Nicoll, one of the original managers, resigned and Thomas Matthew carried on alone until his death in 1842. Over the next three years first Thomas Mearns and then George Mills took over as interim managers until Robert Marshall was appointed in August 1844. He had been manager of the Dundee & Arbroath Railway Co. and under his managership the Company advanced steadily until he resigned in 1852 to become manager of West India Royal Mail Steamship Co. in London. He was succeeded by Thomas Couper who had been the manager of the Dundee & Hull Shipping Co. from 1844.

Trade with Glasgow had progressively become more difficult with the development of the railways over the years, and whilst agreement had been reached with the railways over the transfer of goods from sea to rail at Leith in 1844, the use of sailing vessels on the sea sector was more and more uncompetitive. Consideration had been given in September 1835 as to the use of a steamer but nothing had been done about ordering one until December 1847 when two small steamers, MARS and NEPTUNE, were ordered. They took over from the sailing vessels in the summer of 1848 operating between Dundee and Leith and also Grangemouth on the upper reaches of the Forth. During the winter of 1850/51 the services were altered to avoid relying on the railway for forwarding goods to Glasgow from Leith. MARS was rescheduled to sail twice-weekly direct to Grangemouth where the goods for Glasgow were transhipped to the track-boats on the Forth and Clyde Canal. NEPTUNE served Leith only twice a week and did not carry passengers or cargo destined beyond the Edinburgh area.

On Friday 2nd May 1851 MARS was very late in departing from Grangemouth and by the time she was off the east Fife coast it was a very dark, calm, moonless night. About 11.30 p.m., slightly off course, she struck a reef at Roonieness, about a mile east of Crail, and was badly holed below the waterline. She turned and ran for Anstruther harbour, but it was so dark that the entrance could not be identified. The captain dropped anchor in four fathoms and launched a boat with the intention of locating the entrance to the harbour. However, he still could not find it, but fortunately returned to his ship just in time to save those on board, as the vessel was by this time rapidly going-under. One young woman was drowned. Over the next week the cargo was gradually discharged but despite repeated salvage attempts, MARS remained underwater and eventually a gale at the end of the month broke her up.

After the loss of MARS, NEPTUNE's sailings were altered to serve Grangemouth once a week, and Leith twice a week. NEPTUNE was lengthened during the winter of 1851/52 and remained on these sailings until 1854 when the services were discontinued altogether — the railways had won!

As well as introducing steam to the inter-Firth sailings, Robert Marshall set-up a towage service in 1849 when delivery was taken of the wooden paddle tug HERCULES (I). She gave the Company good service for four years before she was sold to Australian speculators for use in connection with the gold rush then sweeping that country. With her engine unshipped, she sailed from Dundee on 11th April 1853 for Melbourne. A new tug HERCULES (II) was delivered some months later.

HERCULES (I) was not the only Company vessel to sail to the other side of the world. The 16 year old LONDON (II) was also sold to Australian owners in the same year at a handsome price of £20,000 (only £2,000 less than what she was built for) and set sail (her engine unshipped for the passage) from Dundee on 8th June 1853 carrying 58 passengers. She arrived 118 days later at Sydney, New South Wales, where she had her engine re-installed and was then employed on sailings between Sydney and Melbourne.

PADDLE TO SCREW 1854-1880

The Company took delivery of its first screw steamer in 1854. LONDON (III), iron built and engined by Napier, did not however stay with the Company long as within three months she had been sold to London owners who sent her out to the Black Sea, where there was a great demand for steamers to support the troops fighting in the Crimean War. To replace her the Board ordered a larger steamer from the newly formed local yard of Gourlay Brothers & Co. and LONDON (IV) was delivered in 1856. She proved to be one of the most successful vessels to fly the Dundee, Perth & London flag, remaining with the fleet for 53 years, latterly named HULL. Initially the vessel served the London run but also inaugurated the Company's first sailings outside the North Sea. With peace between Russia and Britain now established she was sent to Cronstadt, the port of St. Petersburg (for many years known as Leningrad) in the summer of 1857, loaded mainly with machinery and cured fish, returning with flax (for Dundee's staple industry), tallow, caviare, cranberries, manna-croup (a grain) and hams. The experiment did not pay off because there was insufficient cargo on the outward voyage, so after 1859 these sailings were discontinued. It demonstrated, however, the possibilities of using a fast steamer on longer distance runs.

Between 1859 and 1875 LONDON (IV) was extensively used in the fruit trade from Greece and Spain and became a regular vessel to load the first of the currant crop at Patras each year, and as she was knots faster than most of the other steamers in the Mediterranean trade, she could be relied upon to be first into London where her cargo fetched the best prices. Even when she was 19 years old in 1875 she still won the race from Patras to the Thames. Oranges from Spain were also carried. On one occasion she loaded at Valencia some 4,500 boxes of this fruit and in order to achieve the maximum load, used the bunks in the passenger cabins as additional stowage space.

Early in 1857 the Company acquired the goodwill and the vessels of the old established Dundee & Hull Shipping Co. This firm (see Appendix F for a list of vessels) had been formed in 1824 and using smacks and schooners, served the two ports until delivery of their first steamer QUEEN (II) in 1854. The Company acquired this steamer and also a schooner of the same name, QUEEN (I) (1842) which must have caused confusion from time to time! A "running mate" for QUEEN (II) was ordered and the Company took delivery of EAGLE in 1858.

Late in 1857 the Company started a fortnightly sailing to Hamburg with their new steamer of that name, but this venture proved to be unprofitable and HAMBURG was soon switched to Bordeaux sailings instead. As this service in turn did not prove very profitable either she was sold in 1863 to London owners for £8,400.

To replace the last two paddlers, the Company ordered two new screw vessels from Gourlay Brothers & Co., SCOTIA (I) was completed in September 1861 but early in 1862 an offer of £20,000 was made for her by an Italian owner who wanted her to operate sailings between Naples, Messina and Ancona. Despite the fact that the paddle steamer PERTH (III) had already been sold, this offer was taken up as it was considered that the volume of London trade could be managed by the paddle steamer DUNDEE (II), together with the screw steamers LONDON (IV) and HAMBURG until a replacement vessel could be built. SCOTIA (II) was delivered later the same year. Another new steamer, ANGLIA, was delivered in September 1863 after which the last coastal paddle steamer, DUNDEE (II) was sold. The traditional names of Perth and Dundee disappeared from the fleet for a time.

Both SCOTIA (II) and ANGLIA, like LONDON (IV), were often employed in the Mediterranean currant and fruit trades. Between April and June 1870 SCOTIA (II) made several voyages to Archangel in Northern Russia to load flax and it was on a voyage to Cronstadt in August 1870 that she was run-down in the Baltic and sank within 15 minutes. ANGLIA loaded telegraph cable in February 1869 for Corfu and in November of the same year was chartered to carry a French party from Marseilles to view the newly opened Suez Canal.

On 18th November 1865 LONDON (IV) was in collision with the steamer HARVEST QUEEN (562/60) in the Tay off Monifieth and sank. The local shipbuilder, Henry Gourlay, agreed to raise her after several other attempts had failed. To raise her, the pumps of QUEEN (II) were utilised and LONDON (IV) was again afloat on 22nd December 1866, some 13 months after she had sunk. She was taken to Gourlay Brothers' yard nearby and repaired — the total bill came to £11,000.

Two additional vessels were put into service during 1865, HIBERNIA and GALLIA. HIBERNIA was built, at a cost of £19,700, for the London sailings whilst GALLIA was purchased from Gourlay Brothers & Co., who had built her as a speculation. GALLIA was fitted out to accommodate 24 passengers with the intention that she would open a service to Dunkirk, but as prospects on this route seemed doubtful she was switched to Rotterdam instead. However, neither service proved profitable so she was sold out of service after only three years.

Competition on the London route appeared in the summer of 1867 when a company calling itself Tay-Thames Shipping Co. placed the iron screw steamer BRIGADIER (444/55) on the route. However, as the Dundee vessels could make the passage about four hours quicker than she could, she was soon withdrawn.

Another new vessel, CAMBRIA, joined the fleet in 1868 to serve the London route, bringing the number in the fleet up to eight for a short time, although GALLIA was sold a few months later.

Commencing in the autumn of 1869, the Company undertook the lengthening and refitting with compound engines of their five larger vessels at a cost of between £10,000 and £14,000 per vessel. The work on SCOTIA (II) was carried out in 1869, that on ANGLIA in 1871, on LONDON (IV) and HIBERNIA in 1872 and CAMBRIA in 1874, the latter vessel also having electric light installed, the first ship in the fleet to have this form of lighting.

After 24 years the Company in 1873 discontinued its involvement with towage. HERCULES (II) built in 1853 had been joined in 1857 by SAMSON, and in turn the former vessel had been replaced in 1865 by ATLAS. ATLAS was now sold, and with SAMSON having already gone in 1869, the fleet was now entirely screw propelled.

During the winter of 1875/76 both ANGLIA and HIBERNIA ran ashore on Holy Island off the coast of Northumberland. ANGLIA, whilst making for the inner passage through the Farne Islands on her way to London, came too close inshore to Holy Island and struck a rock. She was subsequently refloated and towed to Dundee for repair but the wisdom of her master in taking such a course was questioned. Just six weeks later HIBERNIA, bound for Dundee on her way through the inner passage through the same islands, ran ashore near the inner lighthouse. She came off under her own power, and because she was leaking made for the shelter of Holy Island harbour but unfortunately ran aground on the harbour bar. Six days later she broke in two and was declared a constructive total loss. Her master had his certificate suspended for three months.

The Hull trade had been served by QUEEN (II) and EAGLE for many years, but the volume of trade now required larger vessels. The new SCOTIA (III) was placed on the sailings in 1875. It had been the intention of the Company to replace QUEEN (II) with the larger LONDON (IV) but this had to be delayed as the result of the loss of HIBERNIA as LONDON (IV) was needed to maintain the thrice weekly sailings to London during the summer months of 1876. To make good the loss of HIBERNIA an order was placed for a new and larger passenger ship, and BRITANNIA joined the fleet in March 1877. LONDON (IV) eventually took over the Hull sailings in conjunction with SCOTIA (III), and was to remain on this route until 1909, latterly named HULL, so as to release her original name for another new vessel. SCOTIA (III) by 1880 was not considered suitable for the Hull trade and was sold.

To assess the potential of a service between nearby Arbroath and London, the Company chartered the small iron steamer FAIRPORT (353/77) of Arbroath from October 1879 until March 1880 but this venture proved to be unsuccessful.

In August 1879 Thomas Couper was forced to resign as manager because of ill-health, and was succeeded by James W. Kidd, who had been in charge of the Company's London office since 1869.

BOARD OF DIRECTORS 1881
(Standing) George Gray, Melville Jamieson, Wm. Lowson, Jas. W. Kidd (Manager), Robt. A. Mudie, Wm. Cox
(Seated) Jas. Soote, Jos. Garland, Wm. Harris, John Leng, Peter Stuart, Robt. Guild, John Ewan

EXPANSION AND CONTRACTION 1881-1901

The larger ships that now served the London route were no longer used on the seasonal fruit trades as in the past. So as to retain the Company's deepsea connections two medium sized (and later a third) tramp steamers were ordered. The sister ships, NORTH SEA and WHITE SEA, were delivered by the Dundee yard of Alexander Stephen & Sons in the spring of 1881 and traded to the Mediterranean, Baltic Sea and Black Sea until 1895. Some eight years later in 1889 the larger RED SEA joined them.

Until 1883 the largest ship on the Thames run had been BRITANNIA (938 gross tons), which despite her modest size still holds the Company's passenger carrying record of 360 persons embarked for London during the Dundee Holiday Week in 1886. In 1882 however, an order was placed with Gourlay Brothers for a large passenger vessel of over 1,500 tons at a cost of £40,000. To offset some of this amount, ANGLIA, which had been on charter to George Gibson & Co. of Leith for the winter of 1882/83, was sold to them for £10,250 in July 1883. The new vessel re-introduced the traditional name of DUNDEE, the third ship of this name in the fleet. She was capable of a speed of 16½ knots, and had accommodation for 112 passengers. She proved to be a very "tender" ship and despite being refitted with lighter masts in November 1884, was not considered suitable for all-the-year round service so was placed on the sale list. She was sold early in 1885 for £36,000 to the Italian Government who converted her into a troopship for service between Naples and Massowah, Eritrea, where the Italians were setting-up a colony.

An order had already been placed with Gourlay Brothers & Co. for a replacement vessel and she came into service in January 1886. DUNDEE (IV) was the first ship in the Company's service with the first-cabin — with berths for 65 — located amidships, with a further 60 berths for second-class under the poop, and fitted throughout with electric light. She could also carry 75 deck passengers, and her triple expansion engine (again a first in the fleet) gave her a speed of 15 knots.

Having "seen-off" competition on the London route in 1867, another company entered the field at the end of 1886. This time it was a local company, the Arbroath & London Shipping Co., who advertised that their steamer ST. THOMAS (473/82) would call at Dundee on her way to London. However, just one month after advertising the sailing the vessel foundered on 8th November 1886 while on her way to London, and again competition faded away.

Another passenger ship was placed on the London sailings in the summer of 1890. She was PERTH (IV), somewhat larger than DUNDEE (IV), and capable of carrying up to 350 passengers. She replaced BRITANNIA which had been sold for £31,700 to George Gibson & Co., Leith in early 1889 and now joined ANGLIA, sold some six years earlier to the same owners, on the service between Leith and Rotterdam.

During the winter months of 1890/91 when only two vessels were needed to maintain the London sailings, CAMBRIA was chartered to The Carron Co., for service between Grangemouth and London. Whilst on one of her voyages to Grangemouth she was in collision with the steamer KILLINGWORTH (527/55) on 14th May 1891, and although beached on a sandbank, became a total loss, fortunately without loss of life.

A sister ship to PERTH (IV) was ordered and LONDON (V), costing £40,000, with a passenger certificate for 280, was delivered for the summer season of 1892. LONDON (IV) had previously been appropriately renamed HULL to make the name available. The London sailings were now maintained by three modern steamers, DUNDEE (IV) (1885), PERTH (IV) (1890) and LONDON (V)

(1892) the like of which was not to be repeated.

The Company were forced gradually to pull-out of the tramp trade because of the depression that hit the industry in 1892. RED SEA was sold at the end of 1892, and WHITE SEA and NORTH SEA followed in early 1896, so that at the turn of century the fleet was reduced to four vessels.

For some years the Board had been considering the need to have a new wharf in London to replace that at Wapping. Their attention was drawn to a site at Limehouse and construction of ''Dundee Wharf, Limehouse'' was started in 1897. The berth was ''opened'' by the arrival of LONDON (V) on 19th December 1901 with 887 tons of cargo.

CAPTAIN WILLIAM SPEEDY

One of the many colourful and loyal servants of the Company was Captain William Speedy, who served at sea from 1840 until 1900.

Born at Brechin, Forfarshire on 16th July 1824 he moved with his family to Aberdeen where he found employment in a mill at an early age. Shortly afterwards the family moved to Dundee where his parents died, leaving him an orphan with the shaping of his career in his own hands.

His ambition was to be a sailor and at the age of 16, with a fresh complexion, brown hair, grey eyes and nearly 5′ 7″ in height, he secured a berth as a boy on the Company's paddle steamer DUNDEE (II) on 5th July 1840. This vessel was commanded by Captain James Kidd who took a fatherly interest in him. After nearly four years service on DUNDEE, William Speedy now promoted to able seaman, was advised by Captain Kidd that a deep-sea voyage would widen his experience, so he joined the Dundee owned brig VERA (186/42). As an able seaman he sailed on her from Liverpool on 19th July 1844 bound for Valparaiso. He signed-off at Liverpool on 28th April 1845.

He joined the Dundee-owned snow GRATITUDE (155/17) as an able seaman in May 1845 sailing on her to the Baltic, before returning to the Company's service in October 1845 when he joined the sloop TAY (II), remaining with her for five months, when he transferred to the sloop ROE as mate. Having served as mate for a year, he then left the Company for four months and between August and December 1848 became master of the local sailing vessel MARY & ANN.

However, in December 1848 he returned to the Company as mate of the recently completed schooner ZENOBIA and remained with her until April 1851. He had passed as master (Home trade) at Dundee on 8th March 1851 and on his merits was promoted to 2nd mate of the paddle steamer PERTH (III) in May 1851 (later becoming mate). A year later he returned to his first ship DUNDEE (II) as mate, and stayed with her until July 1856, when he transferred to the newly built screw steamer LONDON (IV) in a similar capacity, becoming relief master of her for a few months at the end of 1857.

In January 1858 he took command of the steamer QUEEN (II) on the Hull sailings, but subsequently in May 1858 transferred to HAMBURG. As he had passed for master (Foreign-going) in February 1858 he now regularly took his ship to such ports as Hamburg and Bordeaux, but when HAMBURG was sold in January 1863, he found himself for a short time back as master of the sloop TAY (II) until another steamer command became vacant.

His next steamship was SCOTIA (II) in September 1863, which was employed on the London sailings, as was ANGLIA to which he transferred in April 1865. As well as trading to London, ANGLIA made voyages to the Mediterranean calling at such ports as Valencia and Corfu to load fruit. In November 1869 Captain Speedy arrived at Port Said just a month after the Suez Canal had been opened, carrying a party of French passengers to view the Canal. He returned to SCOTIA (II) in January 1870, this time sailing to the Russian ports of Cronstadt and Archangel. It was while on a voyage from Newcastle to Cronstadt in August 1870 that he had the misfortune to have his ship run-down in fog by the steamer MAGNA CHARTA (964/65) off Sweden. SCOTIA (II) was struck amidships in the engine room and sank in 15 minutes. This was the one and only time that Captain Speedy lost his ship.

He then found himself without a command until May 1874 when he returned to ANGLIA and he stayed with her until July 1874 and then transferred to the re-engined CAMBRIA. When the newer and larger BRITANNIA came into service in May 1877, Captain Speedy took command of her and in turn moved to DUNDEE (III) in July 1883 when she was handed-over by the builders. Unfortunately this latter vessel proved to be rather "tender" so was subsequently sold in April 1885. Captain Speedy then joined LONDON (IV), the Company's first screw steamer, before transferring once again to CAMBRIA. On the commissioning of the new DUNDEE (IV) in January 1886, Captain Speedy, by now Commodore of the fleet, took command of her and in turn moved to PERTH (IV) on 17th July 1890, and then to LONDON (V) on 5th May 1892.

In 1890, after 50 years at sea and at the age of 66, a presentation was made to him. Most would have thought of retirement after half a century of arduous service, but not Captain Speedy. With the full consent of the Board he continued to sail as Commodore until the end of the summer season of 1900 when he left LONDON (V) and finally "swallowed the anchor". In his 60 years of service he had served six years as a seaman, some 11 years as a mate, and as master for a remarkable 43 years. During the period 1857 to 1900 he had commanded all but one of the 11 ships usually employed on the Thames service (the exception being HIBERNIA) from LONDON (IV) built in 1856 to the fifth vessel of the same name built in 1892. He had served under six managers — two years under Mr. Thomas Matthew, one under Mr. Thomas Mearns, two under Mr. George Mills, seven under Mr. Robert Marshall, 27 under Mr. Thomas Couper and 21 years under Mr. James W. Kidd, son of the master of his first ship.

He died at his home in Madeira Street, Dundee after a short illness on 21st June 1901 just before his 77th birthday.

CONSOLIDATION 1902-1914

For the first nine years of the century the Company's four vessels maintained the London and Hull sailings more or less uneventfully. With the faster and larger ships now in service, the bunker requirements became greater. The high cost of transporting the coal to Dundee had originally come to the attention of the Board in 1890. Until then coal had been carried by rail from Fife but in 1890 the Company purchased the ex sailing vessel CAROLINE, which had recently been fitted with a steam engine, and employed her carrying coal from Tayport, just across the water in Fife, to the ships docked in Dundee. By 1903 CAROLINE was worn out, so an order was placed in May of that year for a new steel steamer. CARBON, as she was appropriately named, and costing £1,925, was delivered in the spring of 1904, when CAROLINE was broken up. Whilst the Alloa Coal Co., with mines in the upper reaches of the Forth, could by rail supply coal "alongside at Dundee" for 11/9d per ton (and did so for a while, until CARBON came into service), with a monthly requirement of 600/700 tons, the Company found a better price of 9/8d per ton could be achieved by railing the coal to Tayport and then loading it into CARBON for delivery to the ships in dock at Dundee.

Despite now having three large steamers available on the London run, in some years during March it was found necessary to charter other vessels to help uplift the large amount of Scottish seed potatoes moving to the South.

During June 1908 a periodic valuation of the fleet was undertaken with DUNDEE (IV) being then assessed at £10,000, PERTH (IV) at £14,000, LONDON (V) at £16,000, HULL at £1,000 and CARBON also at £1,000.

In January 1909 consideration was given to replacing the 53 year old HULL. A price of £24,700 was quoted by the local Caledon yard but this price was subsequently reduced by £1,480 when it was agreed the new vessel would not have any passenger accommodation. GOWRIE (I) was delivered in the late summer of 1909. HULL was sold to shipbreakers for £1,500 and sailed from Dundee on 28th October 1909 for the last time under her own steam bound for Bridgeness near Bo'ness on the Firth of Forth.

During January 1909 DUNDEE (IV) collided with the barge GOOD HOPE off Caister, Norfolk. The latter sank with the loss of her four crew. The Board sent a contribution of 100 guineas to the Mayor of Yarmouth's Dependants Fund. Unfortunately this was not the only loss of life as during the subsequent task of dispersing the wreck by a crew from a Trinity House tender, seven men were killed as a result of a premature explosion — the cargo included 15 tons of gelignite.

After a period of 18 years without a loss, DUNDEE (IV) was involved in a collision in 1909 with The Carron Co.'s THAMES (1,327/87) in the Thames. To prevent DUNDEE sinking she was run ashore but later slipped off and sank in deep water. Raised five months later, it was found that her cargo of jute had swelled and split her hull, so she was declared a constructive total loss and sold for £1,875. She was towed to Felixstowe, Suffolk for demolition.

An order was then placed with the Caledon yard for an even larger vessel to replace DUNDEE (IV) and the fifth ship of that name was completed at a cost of £50,019 at the end of 1911.

Some upsets to the sailings took place in February 1912 when there was a miners' strike in the Fife coalfields. To conserve coal, sailings had to be reduced to a minimum as supplies were hard to come by. However, the Company did find coal (some 750 tons in February and a further 500 tons in March) but the price that they had to pay was 27/6d per ton. Fortunately the strike was settled in April and prices dropped back to what they were previously.

With PERTH (IV) now 24 years old, an order was placed in early 1914 for a replacement but she was still on the stocks when war broke out.

The Company was incorporated under The Companies Act in March 1914 with a total capital of £280,000, a rise of £80,000 since 1903 in anticipation of having to pay for the latest steamer ordered.

THE WAR YEARS 1914-1918

All sailings were initially suspended on 4th August 1914 on the outbreak of war. However, limited sailings, without passengers, were resumed on 20th August. Already the value of the major vessels in the fleet had risen considerably with DUNDEE (V) now valued at £50,000, PERTH (IV) at £24,000 (previously £14,000 six years earlier), LONDON (V) at £27,000 (previously £16,000), GOWRIE (I) at £24,000 (built five years earlier for £23,270), whilst the new steamer (to be named PERTH and still on the stocks) was to be insured against war risks for the sum of £80,000.

The new PERTH (V) was launched in February 1915, the previous vessel of that name having been renamed ARBROATH (I). However, before PERTH (V) could enter service with the Company, she was requisitioned on 27th August as an Armed Boarding Steamer and, fitted with three 4.7″ guns, sailed from Dundee on 15th November 1915 for Perim and service at the entrance to the Red Sea. Nearly three years later on her way back to northern waters she was acting as the sole escort to 13 merchant ships on passage from Gibraltar to the English Channel, when on 1st October 1918 a U-boat was sighted in the Bay of Biscay. The convoy was immediately ordered to zigzag but after stalking the ships for two hours, the U-boat surfaced and PERTH (V) engaged her with her starboard 4.7″ gun, the U-boat replying with her rather heavier 5.9″ gun. PERTH (V) was holed above the waterline but beat off the attack. Some three hours later the U-boat repeated her attack but again PERTH (V) drove her off and the convoy arrived in home waters without loss.

PERTH (V)

The Company's present office — 26 East Dock Street, Dundee

In May 1915 the Company moved its offices from 5 Shore Terrace, where they had been since 1826, to 26 East Dock Street as the Dundee City Council had acquired the original site on which to erect the Caird Hall. At first only the ground floor of the new building was rented, but ultimately in 1918 the whole building was acquired by the Company.

During August 1915 the Company received an offer to buy ARBROATH (I) ex-PERTH (IV) for £20,000 from London & Edinburgh Shipping Co. Ltd. of Leith, who had earlier lost their FINGAL (1,582/94), a near sister ship and built also by W. B. Thompson & Co. Ltd., Dundee. The offer was rejected.

CARBON and DUNDEE (V) were both requisitioned in September 1915. The latter, having arrived at Dundee on 9th July 1915 from London, was laid-up until October 1915 when she was taken up as an Armed Boarding Steamer. Fitted with two 4" guns, she sailed from Dundee on 21st January 1916 for service with the 10th Cruiser Squadron, which had the task of enforcing a blockade north of the Shetland Islands to detect the movement of enemy vessels between Iceland and the Norwegian coast. The patrol was normally a cruiser and an Armed Boarding Steamer and in March 1917 this was made up of the armoured cruiser H.M.S. ACHILLES and DUNDEE (V) under the command of Captain Selwyn M. Day, R.N.R.

DUNDEE (V) sighted a strange steamer on 16th March 1917 which had the name RENA painted on her, but suspicions were aroused because the letter 'N' was reversed. The action that followed is described in a letter written three days later by an unknown member of DUNDEE's crew.

"We were engaged on patrol duties in company with ACHILLES I believe something like 280 miles due North of the Shetland Islands, having left our base at 11.20 p.m. Sunday February 11th having fairly moderate weather although it was extremely cold and altogether wintery. We intercepted one or two steamers before the 15th. On that date we intercepted and put an armed guard on board a Norwegian steamer and sent her into ———— (Lerwick?). On the morning of the 16th at 11.40, a vessel was sighted a long way off and we set off in pursuit doing our utmost speed. The weather was misty and rainy at times. Occasionally the vessel was in view and at other times obscured in the mist and rain. We apparently could not reduce the distance between the two vessels and the ACHILLES which had so far kept company with us increased her speed and apparently got within signalling distance of the strange vessel, stopped her by signal to await our arrival. At 2.40 p.m. our "Action Station" bells were sounded and the ship's company rushed to their respective stations. A good deal of signalling was done between the pursued vessel and ourselves which however failed to convince our Commander that the ship was what she pretended to be. We were then fairly close to her and I could plainly read her name RENA NORGE painted on her side and with the Norwegian colours on her bow and quarter. Our Commander not being satisfied as to the vessel's identity, lowered our gig and sent away a boat's crew with Lieut. F. Lawson in charge, to investigate her. These poor chaps never returned nor were they ever seen again after they were obscured from our view in going alongside (the) strange vessel on the side opposite to us.

The strange vessel then commenced to manoeuvre by working her propeller, and to draw their attention that he saw this, our Commander at different times with perhaps a few minutes between, fired two blank shots. The stranger, however, continued to manoeuvre, every move of which appeared to be skilfully countered by DUNDEE. At last, however, he appeared to have been in a favourable position, the vessels being then lying at something like an angle to each other with a distance of perhaps 500 yards between them. Suddenly, doors in her (the raider's) side were seen to fall down, and torpedoes were fired at DUNDEE. At least four torpedoes were observed at different places and almost simultaneously. One crossed our bow, another crossed close astern, one ran up alongside a few yards off and I myself are of opinion that the first one of all launched, passed clear underneath us, we being then so close that the impulse given in the launching caused the torpedo to dive and before it could recover its normal depth had passed underneath us. That instance the raider's sides dropped so our after gun let go. The shell raked the enemy's port battery, knocking it out of action. The second shot fired was from our forward gun and was practically simultaneous with the first shot. This second shot I saw exploded between the funnel and the engine room and must have wrecked things. I saw a column of steam rush upwards and the dust and smoke of a heavy explosion was plainly visible. We continued to fire as long as we possibly could, every shot telling and every shot being directed at some vital spot. Our gun layers did excellent work indeed and controlled their guns crews with a calm precision and skill which was really admirable, and this without the guidance of officers, we then being two officers short (one officer being sent in with the prize crew and another being of the boarding party which was lost).

We commenced firing at 3.40 p.m. but the promptitude in hitting so effectively combined with the missing of their mark by the many torpedoes must I think for the time being have thoroughly demoralised the enemy for a few minutes elapsed before he got his guns to work. Meanwhile we had been going full speed manoeuvring the ship to extract ourselves from torpedo range, continuing to fire not a second being lost. So effective was our fire that the enemy was soon ablaze forward and aft and virtually a wreck. He was blazing so that the fire never could have been controlled although he continued to fire salvo after salvo and indeed keep on firing till the very (end) when even he was blazing all over and sinking.

It was not before the raider was blazing forward and aft that the ACHILLES came into action. I don't know why. When the action commenced I am told by those that know that ACHILLES was seven miles away from us and that at least eight minutes elapsed from our commencement until ACHILLES took a hand and as I said by that time we had the enemy beaten completely. We continued to fire however, until our ammunition was nearly expended, firing some seventy from our larger guns and forty odd from our small ones. Shells and shrapnel screamed over us but we were never hit. Some pieces of shrapnel were picked up around the decks when things quietened down. We had no casualties on board. The actual action lasted about 40 minutes. Everyone on board was as calm, some calmer, than they were while at drill, a queer kind of calm particularly dangerous and effective. No words were uttered only those words of command which were necessary. The crowd below behaved splendidly, sprang to carry out every order with no hesitation and with no attempt to abandon their posts. Simpson handled the main engines with no excitement whatever but as I thought a bit white about the gills.

ACHILLES did the last of the firing and signalled to us to steer a certain course. We asked permission to return and look for our boat hoping that some of the poor chaps that left in her might be wounded in the boat. This permission was granted and we got within a short distance of our boat and saw there was no one there but just then we sighted the conning tower and good part of the hull of a huge submarine pretty close to us, and between us and the ACHILLES. We dodged at once eluded the sub entirely and I suppose thinking we had had enough, got on a clear course. The ACHILLES steamed round the scene of the action but they say they saw no survivors but I rather think there would have been some surely. That however, I don't know but men couldn't survive long in the extremely cold water. Latterly we set course to resume our patrol and when well clear ACHILLES steamed up close alongside us with their men ranged along the decks and gave DUNDEE a rousing cheer. It is almost unbelievable to know what we did in knocking our enemy out. The ship was I judged four times our size, our armament and complement, besides being fitted with four torpedo tubes which we were not. How we escaped without any injury passes my comprehension when one considers what we were up against. How the ACHILLES did not come to our rescue sooner I cannot understand, there may be some information on the subject later.''

The raider LEOPARD turned out to be the converted British merchant ship YARROWDALE (4,652/12) of Glasgow. YARROWDALE, on passage from New York to Savona, was stopped on 11th December 1916 when 540 miles SE¾E from Cape Race by the German raider MOWE. The cargo on board was considered to be of such value that it was decided that the ship should be taken by a prize crew of 19 to Germany, round the north of Iceland and down through Scandinavian territorial waters to Swinemunde, where she arrived on 31st December 1916. YARROWDALE was taken in hand and converted into the raider LEOPARD, fitted with five 5.9" guns, four 3.4" guns and two torpedo tubes. With a crew of 400, disguised as the Norwegian steamer RENA (4,686/11) she sailed from Germany in early March 1917 to endeavour to break out into the Atlantic so as to attack Allied shipping.

The writer of the letter (possibly the Chief Engineer) queries why ACHILLES stood off such a distance. This was to safeguard the cruiser from a surprise attack. While the small DUNDEE was able to stay under the stern of the raider, and get some protection, the much larger ACHILLES could not have hoped to do so, being less manoeuvrable and a much larger target to hit.

DUNDEE (V) was later switched to convoy escort duties, and whilst carrying out these duties in the English Channel on 3rd September 1917, she was torpedoed and sunk with the loss of eight lives.

The Board enquired of the Caledon yard of the possibility of a replacement, to be told that the yard had already 12 ships on order and that such a replacement was years away!

On 10th October 1917 just over a month after the loss of DUNDEE (V), GOWRIE (I) which had been requisitioned in June 1917, was also torpedoed and sunk NE of Cherbourg while carrying supplies from Newhaven.

To add to the Company's problems, ARBROATH (I) was requisitioned (despite strong protests) in November 1917, which left LONDON (V) only to maintain the sailings. Various other vessels were allocated by the Ministry of Shipping from time to time to ''help out'' during 1918 including the Dutch steamer ZEUS (1,504/01) for a period of three months from March 1918, and single voyages by the Swedish LILLY (1,773/83) and the City of Dublin Steam Packet Co. Ltd.'s LOUTH (1,229/94). LONDON (V) herself was torpedoed and sunk on 23rd June 1918 leaving the Company with just LOCHEE (I). The Company were fortunate to find, at a high price of £81,500, the British & Irish Steam Packet Co. Ltd.'s LADY GWENDOLEN (2,163/11) which had recently returned from northern Russian waters and she took over the London sailings. In the first month of her service she was attacked by a U-boat on the surface off Whitby, Yorkshire but fought off the attack with her single gun.

A proposal was made in the winter of 1917/18 that the Company should amalgamate with the London & Edinburgh Shipping Co. Ltd. and The Aberdeen Steam Navigation Co. Ltd. to run joint sailings to London under the title of the Union Steam Navigation Co. Ltd. of Scotland but nothing came of this idea.

CARBON, which required a new engine and boiler, was ''released'' during November 1917 for this refit to be carried out. It was the intention that such a refit would then allow her to trade to Newcastle, but unfortunately the new machinery was lost at sea on its way to Dundee, so the refit had to be held over until the end of the war.

With the compensation received for the loss of DUNDEE (V) of £75,000 and GOWRIE (I) of £40,000, the Company were able to buy in January 1918 for £75,000 a new engines aft steamer from Charles Hill & Sons, Bristol, which was named LOCHEE (I). She immediately came under the direction of The Ministry of Shipping and remained so until December 1920.

When the war finished in November 1918, the Company found itself with no vessels to maintain the sailings, LADY GWENDOLEN, PERTH (V), ARBROATH (I) and CARBON were still under the control of The Ministry of Shipping and were not released until 1919, the first two having been employed since the autumn of 1918 in carrying prisoners of war between Hull and Rotterdam.

ARBROATH (II) during World War 1

ACQUISITIONS 1917-1920

Before the end of the war the Company had begun a policy of expansion by the acquisition of other coastal liner companies sharing their general field of operations.

On 25th January 1917 the Company was approached by the Dundee & Newcastle Steam Shipping Co. Ltd., with a proposal that the Dundee, Perth & London Shipping Co. Ltd. should purchase the goodwill and business of the firm, together with their vessel TAY & TYNE (556/09). Dundee, Perth & London Shipping Co. Ltd. offered the sum of £22,000 for the vessel and a further £500 for the goodwill of the business. This offer was accepted and the transaction was completed in March 1917.

The Dundee & Newcastle Steam Ship Co. Ltd. (as the original title was) had been established in 1861 when the new steamer DALHOUSIE introduced sailings between Dundee and Newcastle on 17th April of that year. Unfortunately in her fourth year of service she was wrecked on the Abertay Sands, a dangerous shoal at the entrance to the Firth of Tay, with the loss of her crew of 13 and 20 passengers. To replace her the firm acquired the Clyde Shipping Co.'s PLADDA (397/61).

After running "single handed" for over 20 years, PLADDA was joined in 1885 by the small steamer TAY, but this situation was to last only some four years before the latter was sold. This was unfortunate in many ways as just over a year later, PLADDA was wrecked whilst in bound for Dundee. Until a replacement could be found, the Clyde Shipping Co. Ltd.'s new steamer TUSKAR (1,185/90) was chartered.

A replacement for PLADDA was purchased in April 1891, when at the same time the title of the firm changed to the Dundee & Newcastle Steam Shipping Co. Ltd. The new acquisition was the London & South Western Railway Co.'s ALDERNEY (422/75) and she maintained the Newcastle sailings until sold in May 1910. Prior to her sale, the firm had taken delivery of a smart new steamer named TAY & TYNE, which had accommodation for 39 passengers, and this vessel remained on the sailings until war intervened.

Within months of the take-over, TAY & TYNE was requisitioned by the Admiralty, subsequently being bought by them for £33,750, a profit of over 50% in just six months of ownership.

As it turned out, TAY & TYNE was to have an exciting war, being fitted out as a special service ship at Lowestoft, armed with "visible" 6-pounder and 3-pounder guns (as expected of a merchant ship) but in addition was fitted with three "hidden" guns (one 4-inch and two 12-pounders) as well as a 14-inch torpedo tube.

She sailed from Lerwick, Shetland Islands of 19th February 1918 for an area south of Narvik to look for German ore carriers. On 22nd February she sighted two vessels just south of the Vigten Islands, one going south, the other (in ballast) going north. TAY & TYNE converged on the former which was obviously loaded with iron ore, but this vessel failed to respond to a "Stop Immediately" signal and only a shot across her bows made her stop. TAY & TYNE passed under the vessel's stern and found she had captured DUSSELDORF (998/09). A boarding party was sent over whereupon the German master protested that he was within Norwegian territorial waters while on passage from Narvik to Emden. Manned by nine Royal Navy prize crew together with two German engineers and three firemen to work the engines, DUSSELDORF set sail for Scotland. The prize had no sextant, no proper chart and the compass deviation chart was missing — with the holds full of iron ore, the compass would be subject to considerable deviation. The vessel encountered vile weather with a strong westerly gale allowing her to make only 30 miles on one day. She broke down three times and more by good luck than by exact navigation, the Bell Rock Lighthouse (east of the Firth of Tay) was sighted on 1st March, and she finally dropped anchor in the Firth of Forth. In June 1919 when the case came before the Prize Court, it soon became apparent that the ship indeed was within Norwegian waters by 200 yards at the time of her capture. She had meantime been renamed POLDORF but in December 1919 she was returned to her German owners and resumed her original name.

TAY & TYNE made a second capture on 21st March 1918 off Oxnaes Lighthouse of the Hamburg registered steamer VALERIA (1,216/13) bound from Narvik to Hamburg. A prize crew was put on board and both vessels (accompanied by an armed trawler) set sail for Lerwick. Bad weather struck again, and with VALERIA short of bunkers, by the 23rd she had run out of fuel and came to a stop. The crews were taken off and VALERIA was sunk by gunfire. Subsequently when her case came before the Prize Court VALERIA was also found to be within Norwegian waters at the time of her capture (this time by only 50 yards) so compensation had to be paid for her loss.

TAY & TYNE was later despatched to the White Sea to support British forces during their evacuation from that area and arrived back at Lerwick on 3rd December 1918. She then sailed for Lowestoft arriving there on 7th December, finally paying off on the 12th. She subsequently became the Royal Fleet Auxiliary storeship INDUSTRY until she was sold to Norwegian owners in October 1924. She was broken up in 1952 after 43 years' service.

On 31st October 1918 the Company purchased for £500 the goodwill and business of the Kirkcaldy Steamship Co. Ltd., the latter firm having gone into voluntary liquidation. Kirkcaldy, often known as "the lang toun" because of the length it stretched along the northern shore of the Firth of Forth, was (and still is) a prosperous town, highly industrialised and became the centre of the linoleum industry by the end of the 19th century. Linoleum requires for its manufacture large quantities of jute (imported from India) cork (from the Iberian peninsula) and linseed oil (oil extracted from flax), and these raw materials had to be shipped into Kirkcaldy from such major ports as London, Hull or Dundee, where they had been landed from overseas. Kirkcaldy was also a centre of linen manufacture which depended on a regular supply of flax. There was therefore a need for a regular steamer service to bring these raw materials into the town, and at the same time to carry away the manufactured goods for distribution in other parts of the country, and also for shipment overseas. The Kirkcaldy Steamship Co. Ltd. was formed to meet this requirement and in the latter part of 1899 took delivery of their newly built steamer RAVENSCRAIG (the name of a local castle built in the 15th century), and she was placed on regular sailings between Kirkcaldy and Hull.

As trade increased there was a need to acquire another steamer so that additional ports of call could be introduced. The Dundee built ROSYTH (409/03) was acquired from her builders in December of the same year and sailings were then offered from Hull, Tees and Tyne to Arbroath, Montrose, Inverness, Invergordon and other Moray Firth ports, with Berwick-on-Tweed being included on the Kirkcaldy-Hull sailings.

The outbreak of war in 1914 reduced the amount of raw materials being imported from abroad so the services of the two vessels became more varied, and eventually as the prices offered for secondhand vessels rose upwards, the owners decided to sell both ships to Sunderland owners and suspend the sailings. The link between Kirkcaldy and Hull was not resumed until 1919 on the acquisition by the Company of GOWRIE (II) (1909), when a call at Kirkcaldy was introduced on the Hull-Dundee sailings.

GOWRIE (II) at Dundee *Struan J. F. Robertson*

In November 1919 the Company acquired for £5,000 the goodwill of Thomas Cowan's sailings from Leith and Dundee to Southampton and Treport, together with the tall funnelled steamer LOUGA (945/98) for a further £42,500.

Thomas Cowan had received little formal education but acquired by hard work a good working knowledge of shipping matters in the port of Grangemouth. He joined in 1886 a group of local businessmen who had decided to enter the Baltic trade, and was appointed Managing Owner of the group's first steamer ITUNA (408/84). This vessel was bought whilst lying in London at a very keen price of £5,000, her owners having just gone into voluntary liquidation. Having established her in the trade, it was not long before Thomas Cowan acquired a second vessel, BRUGES (576/84), and then an even larger vessel, CAIRNGORM (1,108/83) to meet the demand of increased trade.

Up until 1894 Thomas Cowan had depended on second-hand tonnage, but in that year he took delivery of the new steamer NAROVA. She came into service on 28th May 1894 to join the other three vessels in the fleet but unfortunately within a few months BRUGES was lost. An order was placed for another new vessel and RASONA came into service during 1896, but unfortunately was herself lost within a year.

By 1897 only NAROVA remained, the other two having been sold, but an order was then placed for another new vessel, though not for the Baltic trade. Thomas Cowan had his sights on trade other than coal outward with timber, pit props and flax inwards — that of carrying manufactured goods made in industrial Central Scotland and whisky distilled in the Scottish Highlands to the port of Southampton where they would be transhipped principally to the Royal Mail Steam Packet Co.'s vessels sailing to South America but also to vessels sailing to South Africa and North America. The return cargoes would be primarily wine from northern France using the port of Treport situated on the River Bresle some 20 miles NE of Dieppe.

The first fortnightly sailing was made from Dundee on 8th April 1898 by LOUGA but trading conditions were such that by November NAROVA was taken off her Baltic sailings to permit a weekly service to be offered. In order to maintain weekly sailings throughout the year it was necessary to charter tonnage from time to time; so as to overcome this problem another steamer was ordered. PLOUSSA left on her maiden voyage to Southampton on 16th May 1905 and the three vessels maintained the sailings between them until 1910 when the newly built KOOLGA was delivered, after which NAROVA was sold.

The outbreak of war in August 1914 caused Thomas Cowan first to have to abandon calls at Treport because of the nearness of that port to the battle front, and second to have to move his operation from Grangemouth to Leith because the Admiralty closed off the upper part of the Forth to all merchant shipping. PLOUSSA was sold during 1916 leaving Thomas Cowan with just two ships at the war's end. With trading conditions very poor, Thomas Cowan decided to retire from business and to sell the firm which he had virtually controlled since the beginning of the century. KOOLGA was sold in 1918 to the Aberdeen Steam Navigation Co. Ltd. and in the following year the Company took over the sailings, together with LOUGA. However, until the volume of trade to Southampton improved, initially LOUGA was used on the Dundee to Ghent sailings of her new owners, but eventually resumed working the Southampton sailings and remained doing so until sold in September 1937. The first sailing of this new trade was undertaken by LOCHEE (I) on 4th November 1919, the vessel still being under the direction of The Ministry of Shipping.

The Company acquired in 1919 for £2,000 the goodwill and trade of the Leith-Dundee-Perth sailings previously operated by A. F. Henry & MacGregor Ltd. of Leith, a route the Company had last served in 1854. Also purchased for £5,000 was Henry & MacGregor's "puffer" GARMOYLE (100/04) which was renamed NORTH INCH (the name of a park at Perth). She was later joined on this service by CARBON which, having been released from war service in June 1919, was then sent for re-engining and came into service again as FAIR CITY in 1920. The re-introduction of this service was not a success and was made even more difficult by NORTH INCH becoming stranded on Carr Rock near Fife Ness on 2nd May 1921, resulting in repairs costing £2,800. After two years the sailings were discontinued, with NORTH INCH being sold and FAIR CITY left to maintain the sailing between Dundee and Perth.

An attempt by the Company to acquire The Aberdeen Steam Navigation Co. Ltd. failed in early 1920 after negotiations had been underway for 18 months. This would have given the Company a virtual monopoly of sailings between north-east Scotland and London.

BETWEEN THE WARS 1919-1939

When the war ended there was a mad scramble to find ships to re-open sailings. Not only was the Company looking for ships but other owners were approaching the Company to sell them their ships.

To re-open the Dundee to Kirkcaldy and Hull sailings as well as the Dundee to Newcastle sailings, the Company considered purchasing in January 1919 the steamers SPORTSMAN (572/14), GOLFER (377/91) or CAPE WRATH (330/00) but none of them met the Company's requirements or the price asked was too high. In turn during May 1919 the Company was offered £77,750 for ARBROATH (I) and £82,500 for LADY GWENDOLEN but both offers were rejected at that time.

The Company did eventually acquire three ships in 1919. In June they took delivery for the sum of £90,866 of DUNDEE (VI), which had been laid-down by the Caledon yard as WAR WENSUM. She made her maiden voyage from Dundee to the Tyne and Dunkirk and in the following years made many and varied voyages, in 1919 being seen both at Lisbon and Seville loading cork for Kirkcaldy, in 1920/21 carrying coal from Grangemouth to Antwerp and also from Swansea to Benisaf, Algeria, and then in 1922/23 trading between Middlesbrough and Barcelona and Valencia. In July the Company bought the Hull-owned HALLER for £32,250 and renamed her GOWRIE (II), placing her initially on sailings between Aberdeen and Antwerp via Grangemouth outward, but latterly she was employed on the Newcastle/Hull sailings. In December the small coaster ROSYTH (I) joined the fleet and spent most of her time on the Hull sailings but also visited such ports as Fraserburgh during the herring season loading fish for the south. ROSYTH (I) had been owned between 1903 and 1917 by Kirkcaldy Steamship Co. Ltd. prior to the acquisition of that firm in 1918. She had been sold in November 1917 by her original owners for £20,000 but when the Company came to buy her some two years later the price had risen to £30,000.

The liner sailings were re-opened by LADY GWENDOLEN departing on 21st November 1918 for Hull and London, being followed on 27th November by LOCHEE (I) for Newcastle. ARBROATH (I) took up the London sailings from July 1919 being in turn relieved by PERTH (V) on 20th September 1919.

PERTH (V) had been released by the Ministry of Shipping during April 1919 from service between Hull and Rotterdam but had as yet to make her maiden voyage for the Company on the route she had been built for. The vessel, with a speed of 12 knots on a consumption of 35 tons of coal per day, had berths for 208 passengers and a certificate to carry 398 persons in addition to a crew of 37 in the summer, reducing to 29 in the winter when passenger traffic was low. The berths were not all in cabins and were segregated as follows:

1st class —	Gentlemen:		Ladies:	
	Cabins	32	Cabins	28
	Smoking Room	10	Music Room	12
	Dining Room	16		
		58		40
2nd Class —	Gentlemen:		Ladies:	
	Poop	12	Poop	12
	Stern Sheets	10	Stern Sheets	10
	Main Deck	26	Main Deck	26
	Dining Saloon	14		
		62		48

The Dining Saloons as a rule were not used to sleep passengers. Additional 2nd class deck accommodation could be provided under the focsle head and on the after-hatch if so required.

Although LADY GWENDOLEN had been sold in June 1919 when more suitable vessels became available, passenger traffic was still very low and could not justify the retention of two passenger steamers, so when an offer of £85,000 was received in April 1920 from British & South American Steam Navigation Co. Ltd. for ARBROATH (I), who proposed using her on Cape Town, Mauritius, Madras, Mombasa sailings, this was accepted.

Additional tonnage was required for the Newcastle and Hull sailings in 1920 and the Company chartered for six-monthly periods the Glasgow owned FELSPAR (799/08) from April, and then from October the Methil owned RAYFORD (471/94) and CORNUBIA (420/90) of London.

In anticipation of the London traffic improving, the Company in 1920 purchased for £10,300 the ex-German steamer ALEXANDRA (1,014/09) with berths for 50 passengers, and she was employed on the route from November 1921 having been renamed ARBROATH (II). She did not remain in the fleet long and was sold the following year to Canadian owners for £25,000, as by this time the new oil-fired steamer LONDON (VI) had been delivered — the first steamer in the fleet to burn oil, and was built to accommodate 30 1st class passengers (reduced to 12 in winter). In later years she also carried 2nd class initially on the tween-decks of numbers 1 and 2 holds. This dormitory accommodation was primitive to say the least, being just tarpaulins laid on the deck and hung up on the centre line to separate male and female passengers, with mattresses placed on the deck, so in rough weather conditions must have been anything but pleasant. Subsequently semi-permanent fittings were installed for use during the summer months so that 2nd class passengers could be carried in a less spartan environment. Under both systems however, the transformation could only take place after cargo working had been completed.

LONDON (VI) off Southend *G. E. Langmuir Collection*

For a few months in 1920 the Company were managers of two ex-German steamers on behalf of The Shipping Controller. They were BABYLON (1,596/96) and ROM (2,080/05) but both were quickly sold to other owners and did not actually trade for the Company.

During 1924, with the passenger traffic showing signs of recovery, the Board considered replacing LONDON (VI) with her limited accommodation for passengers, with a vessel with a greater capacity. With this in mind, the Clyde Shipping Co. Ltd.'s LIZARD (1,176/95) was chartered from June to September at a cost of £890 per month (with the option to purchase for £12,500) but she was not found suitable and matters were left as they were.

The small coaster BROUGHTY (I) had been delivered in October 1921. She had been launched earlier by Larne Shipbuilding Co., in Northern Ireland but they had then gone into liquidation so she had had to be completed by Scott & Sons at Bowling on the Clyde. She cost £39,115. During 1925 this vessel was fitted with tanks so that on her voyages north, she could carry spindle oil for the jute industry from the Thames or linseed oil for the linoleum industry from Hull, whilst on her voyages south she could carry basis material for manufacturing ink. To make this change of cargo possible, steam heater coils were fitted to the tanks and two steam pumps were installed on deck to discharge the liquids. To facilitate the handling of the oil in bulk at Hull, the Company purchased its own tank lighter at a cost of £3,810 and also an oil barge for £425 named ANILINE, then lying derelict at North Queensferry on the Forth. The former after being fitted with twin-screw engines was named KIRKALINE and both were employed sailing between Selby, on the River Ouse, and Hull in connection with the sailings of BROUGHTY (I). Unfortunately during the winter of 1927/28 this service was disrupted as BROUGHTY (I) struck the pier whilst entering Kirkcaldy and subsequently sank. She was later raised and taken to Leith for repairs which cost £2,090.

BOARD OF DIRECTORS 1926
(Standing) Ralph C. Cowper (General Manager), Francis Stevenson, J. C. Buist, Wm. Low, J. A. Law (Secretary)
(Seated) Capt. D. Lumsden, Sir Michael Nairn, Bart., Sir Chas. C. Barrie, KBE, Arthur J. Cox, Thos. H. H. Walker

The centenary of the Company in 1926 came during a period of comparative stability in the coasting liner trades. The fleet had increased from five ships in 1914 to nine some 12 years later, and a network of services was in operation from the Tay to not only London, but also Newcastle, Hull, Southampton and northern France. The majority of the cargoes carried south were locally manufactured goods of various sorts, popular magazines from Thompson the printers, jams made by Keillers, printed stationery and postcards produced by Valentine, and paper from the nearby Guardbridge Paper Works, and these were loaded together with cases of whisky and sacks of seed potatoes brought down the river from Perth by FAIR CITY. During each spring seed potatoes in large quantities were carried to the East Anglian ports of Wisbech, Boston, and King's Lynn.

During June 1927 PERTH (V) was fitted with an experimental radio detection and ranging system (to become known as radar in the later years) to test its use as an aid to coastal navigation but this particular system was not subsequently developed.

The Company took over in 1928 the local sailings between Leith and Kirkcaldy. These sailings carried linoleum products to Leith for export and carried back to Kirkcaldy Danish dairy products landed at Leith (because of the nature of the cargo, the vessel was known locally as "the bacon and egg boat"). Initially chartered tonnage was used, but in March 1930 the lighter W was purchased for £160. However, the lighter was almost immediately sold again when a more suitable vessel, YENDIS, at a purchase price of £1,350, was found at Hull.

A further coastal liner company was acquired in 1929. This was the long established Aberdeen, Newcastle & Hull Steam Co. Ltd. who maintained sailings between these ports, and the company that Ralph C. Cowper had managed prior to joining Dundee, Perth & London Shipping Co. Ltd. in 1917. Aberdeen, Newcastle & Hull Steam Co. Ltd. could trace its origins back to the amalgamation of the Aberdeen & Newcastle Steam Navigation Co., formed in 1844 with the wooden paddle steamer VELOCITY (215/21), and the Aberdeen, Grimsby & Hull Steam Packet Co. founded in 1853, with the iron steamer ABERDEENSHIRE (220/55) — see Appendix J for the vessels owned by these companies. When control passed to Dundee, there were two vessels employed on these sailings, the passenger/cargo steamer HIGHLANDER (1,216/16) and the cargo-only steamer KILDRUMMY (629/24). Initially both ships continued to operate as before but in 1932 KILDRUMMY was switched to a new trade — the carrying of whinstone chips (for road surfaces) from the Tay to the south of England. Many thousands of tons of this stone were loaded at both Newburgh, Fife and at Dundee (taken from Cunmount Quarry near Kingennie, some 7 miles north-east of the city) until war stopped the trade, which was never resumed. KILDRUMMY also in later years relieved on the Southampton route, after she had been transferred in 1937 to the parent company.

Stone cargoes were also carried by another small steamer acquired in 1932. For £2,500 the Company purchased the Dutch-built EVELYN MANOR (396/02) and she was renamed ERROL (I); it had been intended that she be named AIRLIE — unfortunately there was a yacht on the British register of that name, and the owner would not release the name! She was also useful for carrying cargoes of oil cake from Hull to Perth. On 30th July 1935 ERROL (I) was involved in a collision with the steamer CAIRNESK (5,007/26) when $1\frac{1}{2}$ miles S.W. of Inchkeith whilst on passage from Leith to Kirkcaldy and went down close to the island. Leith Salvage & Towage Co. Ltd. were given the task of refloating her and their salvage tug BULLGER (304/07) was sent to the scene with Captain George Bonner, V.C., D.S.C., R.N.R. in charge (he had won his Victoria Cross when serving on the 'Q' Ship DUNRAVEN (3,117/10) in August 1917). He subsequently raised the sunken vessel by attaching two "camels" (they were in fact old submarine hulls with the bow and stern sections removed) by cables to the hull and by using the rise and fall of the tides, gradually moved her into shallow water off Newhaven foreshore, between Leith and Granton. She was moved from there on 17th August into dry dock at Leith but was subsequently declared a constructive total loss and sold to Bo'ness shipbreakers for £560.

ERROL (I) being towed to Leith by the salvage tug BULLGER (1907) after being raised to the surface by using two old submarine hulls as pontoons. *The Scotsman*

The depression of the early 1930s hit both shipowners and shipbuilders, and in an effort to help local industry the Board took the bold decision to order a new cargo steamer, with accommodation for 12 passengers, from the Caledon yard. DUNDEE (VII), the last steam driven vessel to be built for the Company, and costing £69,686, was launched on 28th December 1933. She under-went her trials on 21st February 1934 after which she was brought into service. The earlier vessel of that name had been sold to Glasgow owners the previous summer. In September 1934 ROSYTH (I), which had been purchased after the war for £30,000, was sold to Liverpool owners for just £1,000.

The Thames sailings were now maintained by the new DUNDEE (VII), the war-time built LONDON (VI) and the pre-war PERTH (V), though the latter was normally laid-up during each winter when passenger traffic was light. During the summer seasons of 1932 and 1933 calls were made at Southend Pier, at the mouth of the Thames, on the Wednesday and Saturday sailings, but were discontinued after the two seasons.

PERTH (V) in the Thames *R. A. Snook*

The year 1935 first saw the introduction of motor ships into the fleet and to the Scottish coastal trade. The new ARBROATH (III), built at a cost of £22,500, was launched on 14th August, completed her trials on 20th September and made her maiden voyage the following day. She quickly proved her worth in service and early on was involved in an unusual task, that of laying two telephone cables across the Tay. This called for her first to load the lengths of cable at Woolwich on the Thames and then proceed to Dundee where the actual laying of the cables took two days. ARBROATH (III) was soon joined by her sister ship GLAMIS. Following the arrival of ARBROATH (III) the steamer LOCHEE (I) was sold in May 1936 to Jersey owners for £7,250.

During 1937 various changes in the fleet took place. The 39 year old steamer LOUGA was replaced on the Southampton sailings by the new motor ship LOCHEE (II) on 25th August. Tenders for this vessel had been requested from three yards and all had proved highly competitive with Caledon quoting £58,000, the Forth-based Burntisland Shipbuilding Co. Ltd. £57,675, and the Leith yard of Henry Robb Ltd. £57,250. The Leith yard won the contract and produced a vessel fitted with extensive cargo handling derricks, which although very effective in loading and discharging cargo, restricted visibility from the wheel house which was positioned aft. The trade south to Southampton consisted of manufactured goods as well as whisky for export to North America and elsewhere, whilst for Portsmouth (now a regular port of call) were carried potatoes for the Royal Navy and coal for domestic use. Northwards the cargo was wines from Treport, and as fill-up, bagged cement loaded in the Thames at either Greenhithe or Swanscombe. LOCHEE (II) with her large holds was especially suitable to carry cork from Portugal to either Preston or Kirkcaldy for use in the linoleum industry, and she was switched to this service during the spring and autumn each year until war broke out.

When the new passenger-carrying vessel ABOYNE was introduced by Aberdeen, Newcastle & Hull Steam Co. Ltd. on their sailings to Hull in 1937, the cargo-only steamer KILDRUMMY was transferred to the parent company.

A second-hand motor vessel built at Goole had been bought in 1936 and given the name CLOVA, with further purchases of other Goole-built vessels following in 1939. These were given the names CORTACHY, CROMBIE and ERROL (II) which brought the fleet up to 13.

When the Munich Crisis arose in September 1938 and the outbreak of war seemed imminent, LONDON (VI) was chartered by the Admiralty for a period.

By February 1939 there was concern over the condition of the boilers of the steam lighter KIRKALINE, but rather than replacing them the Board decided to order a new motor lighter, costing £4,630, fitted with portable tanks for the carriage of linseed oil. She was launched the same year and named GALA, joining the two small inland waterway motor barges, GAIRNE and GELDIE, already in service on the Humber.

PASSENGER FARES AND MEALS

Looking back at the various fares charged for a passage between Dundee and London over the years, it appears that the cost of a ticket became relatively cheaper after the introduction of steamers. In 1818 the cost of a cabin ticket was 63/- (20/- = £1.00) and one could travel steerage for just 21/-. By 1836 with paddle steamers on the route the cost of a first cabin ticket was 52/6, second cabin 31/6 and as a deck passenger, just 15/-, all excluding the steward's fee and food. With meals, the prices were 63/-, 40/- and 20/- respectively.

Some 14 years later in 1850 the main cabin fare was 45/- plus a steward's fee of 3/-, whilst the second cabin fare was 28/- plus a steward's fee of 2/-, with all meals included in both classes.

By the 1880s the system of "contracting" meals had been discontinued and instead passengers could either buy what meals they required or pay a fixed sum for all the meals on the voyage. The charges in 1889 show that in the first class cabin, the cost of a berth was now 22/6, breakfast cost 2/6, luncheon 1/-, evening dinner 3/6, tea (plain) 1/6 or tea (with meat) 2/6 or alternatively 10/- for all meals on the voyage — good value when individually the meals on a normal voyage would cost at least 14/6. Of course, if the weather was rough, one might not need the meals! In the second cabin (fare 15/-) the meals were obviously less elaborate as breakfast was only 2/-, mid-day dinner 2/6 with tea (plain) at 1/- and with meat 2/-. The voyage charge in this class was 7/6.

Nearly 50 years later, in 1938, the fares and prices for meals were very similar, with a first class cabin berth costing 42/6, breakfast costing 2/9, luncheon at 3/-, afternoon tea at 1/- and evening dinner costing 4/6. If one travelled second cabin, the price was 27/6 for a berth, with breakfast at 2/-, mid-day dinner at 2/3, high tea at 2/- and supper at 1/9.

With tourists in mind in 1922 the Company were advertising 5-day round-trips to London with a first class cabin fare of 115/-, second cabin at 70/- with all meals included. Various tours were also offered in the summer of 1931 including one from London to Dundee for the sum of 126/-, with accommodation being provided in the Royal British Hotel in Dundee during the two or three days stopover there. In 1938 Dundonians were encouraged to make a trip to see the sights of London for 122/6 (first cabin) with accommodation on board the steamer in London, and free "motor conveyance" to the West End of London each day in port.

Passengers were provided with a brochure giving details of the cost of a voyage and other facilities offered on board the Company's ships — the following pages 37-41 show extracts from the pages of a brochure issued in 1931.

THE PASSENGER SERVICES ARE CONDUCTED BY THE STEAMERS

"PERTH" - - - 2208 TONS GROSS

"LONDON" - - 1491 TONS GROSS

The S.S. "PERTH" is intended to leave LONDON every Wednesday and DUNDEE every Saturday.

The S.S. "LONDON" is intended to leave LONDON every Saturday and DUNDEE every Wednesday.

(Unless prevented by weather, unforeseen circumstances, etc.)
See Conditions of Carriage.

ACCOMMODATION

S.S. "Perth."—The accommodation for First Cabin passengers is situated amidships. There is a large and airy Dining Saloon which is reserved exclusively for its proper use, and is not converted into sleeping accommodation. The Smoke Room and the Music Room are situated on the Promenade Deck. They are well appointed and comfortably furnished. On the Boat Deck are two Private Suites consisting of Stateroom, Sitting Room and Bath Room.

The Second Cabin accommodation is situated aft, and is unrivalled for comfort by any other coasting steamer.

S.S. "London."—The accommodation for First Cabin passengers is situated amidships. The Dining Saloon on this steamer also is reserved entirely for its proper use, and is not converted into sleeping accommodation.

The Second Cabin accommodation is situated forward of amidships.

Both steamers have a number of Two-berth Cabins.

INCLUSIVE TOURS

The Company are continuing their policy of organising Inclusive Tours which provide not only the passenger fares by steamer, but residence at various attractive holiday resorts. The Company is at all times willing to quote terms for Special Parties.

On Holiday Tours the fares quoted cover accommodation in a Four-berth Cabin. There are Two-berth Cabins on each steamer, for which no extra charge is made, and these are allocated strictly according to priority of booking. For the use of a Four-berth Cabin for two passengers an additional charge of 20/- each passenger per single journey is made.

INFORMATION FOR PASSENGERS

Booking.—Passages may be booked at either of the Company's London Offices :

61 MARK LANE, E.C.3.

Telephone : Royal 3166.
Telegrams : "Depeeanel, Fen, London."

or

DUNDEE WHARF, THREE COLT STREET, LIMEHOUSE, E.14.

Telephone : East 0658.

Passages may also be booked at the Offices of Messrs THOS. COOK & SON, LTD., Messrs DEAN & DAWSON, LTD., or at accredited Tourist Agencies in London and Suburbs.

There are Branch Offices of the Company at :

HULL—DUNDEE CHAMBERS.

Telephone : 35807.

SOUTHAMPTON—32 OXFORD STREET.

Telephone : Central 3624.

A Form is enclosed which passengers are requested to use in order that their requirements may be clearly set forth and provided for where possible. If a letter is written the following information is required :—

(*a*) Whether First or Second Cabin.
(*b*) Whether Single or Return.
(*c*) Whether the berth required is for a lady or a gentleman.
(*d*) If for Children, the ages and whether boy or girl.

Return Tickets.—Passengers holding Return Tickets are requested to state as early as possible the date of the Return Journey. Berths can only be reserved subject to the accommodation being available. Return Tickets are valid for six months, but passengers are requested to note that from October to April inclusive, Second Cabin accommodation only is available.

Passengers wishing to book berths for the Return Journey must do so through the Company's Offices, or through a recognised Tourist Agency. *Berths booked through the Pursers or Stewards cannot be guaranteed.*

Payment of Fares.—Berths which have been reserved must be paid for *at least five days before sailing date*, otherwise the Company reserve the right to re-allocate.

Embarkation.—

AT LONDON.—Dundee Wharf, Three Colt Street, Limehouse, E.14.

AT DUNDEE.—Victoria Dock, ten minutes' walk from both L.M.S. and L.N.E. railway stations.

Dundee Wharf, Limehouse, is five minutes' walk from Burdett Road, which is opposite Limehouse Church. The following L.G.O.C. 'Bus Routes pass Burdett Road :—5 A, 15 A, 23, 40 B, 92, 105 A, 106, 122, 123, 222, 223.

For the convenience of passengers the Company run a SPECIAL MOTOR COACH SERVICE during the Summer season which connects with the steamer arrivals and sailings.

A reasonable amount of hand baggage will be conveyed, but the Company will not accept heavy packages, for which special arrangements can be made.

This Motor Coach Service will run as follows :—

FROM CHARING CROSS UNDERGROUND STATION
(Embankment Entrance)

TO DUNDEE WHARF

EVERY WEDNESDAY AND EVERY SATURDAY

One hour and a half before advertised time of sailing.

Charge 1/- per passenger.

Passengers can only be picked up at the starting point.

Passengers who wish to take advantage of this means of conveyance to the steamer must intimate the fact to the Company's Office, 61 MARK LANE, E.C. 3 (Telephone Royal 3166) not later than Tuesday afternoon in the case of the S.S. "Perth's" sailing, or Friday afternoon in the case of the S.S. "London's" sailing.

INFORMATION FOR PASSENGERS—*contd.*

The Motor Coach Service connecting with the arrival of the steamers is as follows :—

FROM DUNDEE WHARF TO THE WEST END

EVERY MONDAY AND EVERY FRIDAY AT 9.15 A.M.

(Or as soon thereafter as the steamer reaches the wharf.)

The Motor Coach will run via Commercial Road, Aldgate, Fenchurch Street, Bank, Holborn, south end of Southampton Row, Oxford Circus, Piccadilly, Trafalgar Square to Charing Cross Underground Station (Embankment Entrance).

Charge, 1/- per passenger (irrespective of distance conveyed).

The Coach will stop at intermediate points (traffic regulations permitting).

Tickets may be obtained from the Purser on board the steamer, and only those passengers who have purchased such Tickets by noon on the day prior to arrival will be guaranteed accommodation. Passengers who have not booked can only be conveyed provided there is room, and they must obtain a Ticket in London from the Passenger Clerk on board the steamer.

Hotels.—The hotels at which passengers reside on the Inclusive Tours are all heavily booked up during the season, and in order that satisfactory reservations may be made, early application is essential.

Sleeping on Board.—When the sailing hour from either end is at 10 a.m. or earlier, it has been arranged for the convenience of passengers that they may sleep on board the previous night without extra charge, but in order to obtain this privilege passengers must give previous intimation of their intention to do so.

Children.—Children under 14 years of age, if accompanied by parents or guardian, are charged half fare on ordinary, non-inclusive, local tickets, excluding victualling. Children, accompanied by parents or guardians, proceeding on Inclusive Tours, specially quoted for.

Passengers' Luggage.—Each passenger is allowed 112 lbs. of personal luggage free, which is carried *entirely at the risk of the passenger.* If the weight exceeds 112 lbs., the Company reserve the right to make a charge. This provision is made in order to avoid the misuse of the privilege whereby 112 lbs. is carried free, but the charge, if made, does not involve the Company in any responsibility for the luggage or the contents. Baggage must comprise only the personal luggage of passengers, and merchandise will not be carried under the designation of passengers' baggage.

Note.—Passengers are strongly recommended to insure their luggage, and arrangements have been made with the Eagle, Star & British Dominions Insurance Co., Ltd., whereby luggage can be insured on the following terms :—

PREMIUMS (inclusive of Stamp Duty)
United Kingdom only (Ireland included)

	Total Sum Insured.			
Period.	£25	£50	£75	£100
Two Weeks - - - - - -	2/-	2/10	4/3	5/8
Four Weeks - - - - - -	2/6	5/-	7/6	10/-

For further particulars see special Leaflet in the Offices of the Company or their Agents.

The Policy covers luggage against Fire, Theft, Loss, Pilferage and Damage whilst in transit by land or sea, and whilst in any Hotel or Premises.

PASSENGER FARES

LONDON TO AND FROM DUNDEE

ADULTS

FIRST CABIN

Bridge and Main Deck

	Exclusive of Victualling	Inclusive of Victualling
Single	42/6	57/6
Return	80/–	110/–

SECOND CABIN

Main Deck

	Exclusive of Victualling	Inclusive of Victualling
Single	27/6	37/6
Return	40/–	57/6

JUVENILES

FIRST CABIN

Bridge and Main Deck

	Exclusive of Victualling	Inclusive of Victualling
Single	21/3	32/6
Return	40/–	57/6

SECOND CABIN

Main Deck

	Exclusive of Victualling	Inclusive of Victualling
Single	13/9	21/–
Return	20/–	35/–

Poop Deck Berths, Second Cabin, S.S. "Perth" only, **2/6** extra, single journey.

Private Cabins—

Berth for 1 passenger in 1 Room (Single Fare)	£4 10 0
Berth for 2 passengers in 1 Room (Single Fare)	£6 0 0

The Return Fare is double the Single Fare. Both fares are exclusive of victualling.

Private Suites.—S.S. "Perth" only. Comprising Sitting Room and Bedroom with Bathroom adjoining.

When occupied by 1 or 2 passengers (Single Fare)	£7 10 0
When occupied by 3 or 4 passengers (Single Fare)	£12 0 0

Exclusive of Victualling.

The Return Fare is double the Single Fare.

When the Suite is occupied by 3 or 4 passengers the Sitting Room is converted into a Stateroom with sleeping accommodation.

DUNDEE and PERTH

OVER one hundred years ago, in 1826, the Dundee, Perth & London Shipping Company was formed by the Dundee and London and Perth and London Shipping Companies combining. There has always been a very close connection between the two cities, and it is for this reason that through fares are in operation between London and Perth. On disembarking at Dundee passengers are conveyed to Perth by Motor Coach, and pass along the beautiful Carse of Gowrie. This is, as it were, the Avenue which leads from the Gateway to all that is most attractive in Scottish scenery.

LONDON TO AND FROM PERTH

ADULTS

FIRST CABIN

Bridge and Main Deck

	Exclusive of Victualling	Inclusive of Victualling
Single	43/9	58/9
Return	82/6	112/6

SECOND CABIN

Main Deck

	Exclusive of Victualling	Inclusive of Victualling
Single	28/9	38/9
Return	42/6	60/–

JUVENILES

FIRST CABIN

Bridge and Main Deck

	Exclusive of Victualling	Inclusive of Victualling
Single	21/11	33/2
Return	41/3	58/9

SECOND CABIN

Main Deck

	Exclusive of Victualling	Inclusive of Victualling
Single	14/5	21/8
Return	21/3	36/3

Poop Deck Berths, Second Cabin, S.S. "Perth" only, 2/6 extra, single journey.

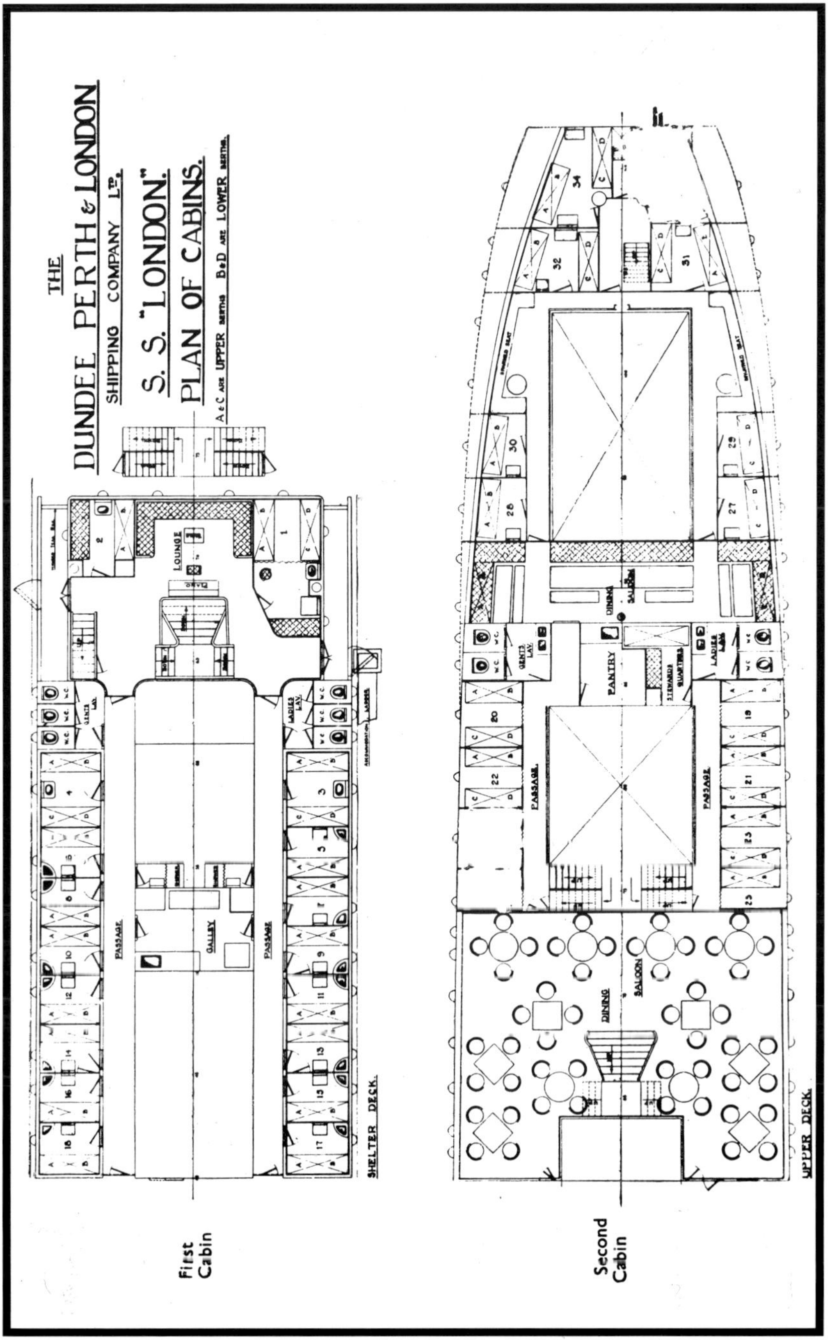
THE
DUNDEE PERTH & LONDON
SHIPPING COMPANY LTD.
S. S. "LONDON."
PLAN OF CABINS.
A & C ARE UPPER BERTHS B & D ARE LOWER BERTHS.
LOUNGE
GENTS LAV.
LADIES LAV.
PASSAGE
GALLEY
SHELTER DECK.
First Cabin
DINING SALOON
PANTRY
STEWARDS QUARTERS
UPPER DECK.
Second Cabin

WAR AGAIN 1939-1945

The outbreak of war in September 1939 brought to an end the London passenger sailings which had been maintained uninterrupted in peace-time since the inception of the Company. It had a safety record unrivalled on the coast — not a passenger lost since the introduction of steamers 105 years before. With the three passenger steamers that did come to grief in that period, HIBERNIA wrecked in January 1876, CAMBRIA sunk after a collision in May 1891, and DUNDEE (III) also sunk after a collision in December 1909, there was no loss of life of either passengers or crew. Although the Company could claim that every passenger arrived safely at their destination, it did in fact lose one of its most experienced masters, Captain James Kidd, in a shipboard accident during rough weather, when he was crushed by shifting baggage stowed on the deck of the paddle steamer PERTH (III).

With five of the Company's vessels requisitioned it was not possible to maintain normal sailings, LONDON (VI) had been taken-up for service on 28th August as an examination vessel, and ERROL (II) and LOCHEE (II) as supply ships, to be followed by GLAMIS on 5th September. ABOYNE, normally operating from Aberdeen to Hull, was hurriedly transferred to Dundee to maintain the London sailings with PERTH (V), now sailing as a cargo-only ship, and DUNDEE (VII). Sailings to Treport in northern France were suspended. After the invasion of Holland in May 1940, the Company was allocated the Dutch steamer ARIADNE (1,170/19), which had escaped captivity, to assist for a time on the London sailings.

LONDON (VI) was renamed HOLDFAST during her service as an examination vessel but she was released back to her owners in August 1940. Subsequently in January 1942 she was once again requisitioned, this time as a pipe-laying vessel. She was commissioned again as H.M.S. HOLDFAST in October 1942, and then carried out trials to prove the feasibility of laying a pipe-line across the Bristol Channel between South Wales and the North Devon coast, before laying the "PLUTO" pipe-line across the English Channel shortly after D-Day in June 1944. This pipe-line subsequently supplied fuel to the Allied forces advancing through Europe. LONDON (VI) was not to return to the Company's service as she was sold in July 1946 for £24,500 to the Ministry of Transport, and renamed EMPIRE TAW, she was used to recover the pipe-line she had laid to France some two years earlier.

EMPIRE TAW *W.S.P.L.*

ERROL (II) was employed carrying supplies to the Royal Navy at Scapa Flow in the Orkney Islands until D-Day in 1944 when she carried supplies to Normandy.

LOCHEE (II) was initially employed in carrying cased petrol to northern France until May 1940 after which she served Gibraltar in the same capacity. On 28th December 1940 sailing from Preston to Gibraltar, she activated a magnetic mine in the Irish Sea and although the engine room was badly damaged and the master, Captain John Murray, blown off the bridge (he survived), she made port and after six months in dock with repairs costing £10,000, she was back in service again in the summer of 1941. She was the first merchant ship to enter Algiers after the Allied North African landings in November 1942, and then followed the British forces along the Italian coast, having the misfortune to run ashore near Naples whilst doing so in February 1944, and was not refloated for some two months. Prior to D-Day she went to Scapa Flow but later like the smaller ERROL (II) was sent to the Normandy beaches — with her large holds and being fitted with twelve derricks she was ideally suited for such a task.

GLAMIS was sent to the other side of Scotland and until June 1942 was employed sailing between north-west English ports and Northern Ireland. She then returned to the east coast and ran from Leith or Methil in the Firth of Forth to Scapa Flow. Between August and December 1943 she returned to the Irish Sea and ran between Liverpool and the Isle of Man. She was derequisitioned for a short time but in preparation for D-Day she was once again requisitioned in April 1944 and subsequently sailed out of the Solent to Normandy. When the Allied forces had advanced further into Europe and the port of Antwerp was re-opened, she moved up to the River Scheldt.

GLAMIS's sister-ship ARBROATH (III) was requisitioned in June 1940 and employed as was ERROL (II) in carrying supplies to the Royal Navy at Scapa Flow. Between July 1942 and November 1943 she was involved in supplying the garrison in Iceland. She joined her sister ship GLAMIS off Normandy and later up the River Scheldt. On one of her return voyages working out of Ostend, she brought back to London a one-man German mini-submarine, the first to be recovered intact. Apparently there had been a battery malfunction which resulted in the crew member being overcome by fumes and it had then drifted ashore.

The only ship to be lost by the Company was GOWRIE (II). She was attacked on 9th January 1940 by two German planes some four miles east of Stonehaven while on passage from Hull to Aberdeen. The first of 31 bombs was dropped at 11.05 a.m. but it was not until 35 minutes later that the 31st bomb exploded close alongside and brought the vessel to a standstill as a result of the starboard boiler bursting. The crew were forced to leave their ship and she sank at 2.00 p.m. The Danish ship ENGLAND (2,767/32) had stood off at a respectful distance during the attack and then picked up the crew and landed them at Methil. ENGLAND herself suffered a similar fate on 3rd February 1941 and went down with all her crew except for the 2nd mate.

The only other loss that the Company suffered was during September 1940 when Dundee Wharf on the Thames was badly damaged in a bomb attack on London and as a result was out of action for some time.

Early in 1940 the Company received an offer from The Carron Co. of Grangemouth of £13,000 for KILDRUMMY — this was rejected. Instead, the vessel was chartered to North of Scotland, Orkney & Shetland Steam Navigation Co. Ltd. of Aberdeen until 1942, after which she took the sailings between Dundee and Hull.

CROMBIE had an uneventful war, the only mishap being at the end of March 1940 when her engine broke down. The master in an attempt to "sail" to

Dundee, rigged a hatch tarpaulin sheet as a sail but a gale got up and the vessel was blown out to sea instead. Fortunately she was picked up by a mine-sweeping trawler and towed in to Dundee on 2nd April.

Even the steam lighter FAIR CITY was requisitioned in October 1940 for service in the Forth. She proved to have insufficient power so was sent back to the Tay after only a short time.

PERTH (V) continued on the London sailings as a cargo-only ship until requisitioned in October 1940 as an accommodation ship at Rosyth Naval Dockyard to house 300 shipyard workers who were completing the new battleship H.M.S. KING GEORGE V, which had been moved for safety from the Tyne. In March 1941 PERTH was taken up for a more worthwhile task, that of rescue ship to ocean convoys. She sailed from Dundee on 6th March 1941 to take up her station on the Clyde. With her passenger cabins and handy size she was well suited to the task and during her very first voyage she was called upon on 11th May to rescue the 60 man crew of SOMERSET (8,790/18) which had been struck by a bomb. Her resources were more severely taxed on 17th November 1942 when she was accompanying convoy ONS 144 to Halifax, Nova Scotia. The convoy was attacked by a U-boat pack and two ships, WIDESTONE (3,192/30) and MOUNT TAURUS (6,696/20) were torpedoed. PERTH stood-by MOUNT TAURUS and picked up 38 of her crew. Early on the 18th the attack recommenced and this time the American fruit carrier PARISMINA (4,732/08) and the ex-French tanker PRESIDENT SERGENT (5,344/23) flying the British flag and under the commmand of Captain Patrick Dove, were torpedoed. PERTH was soon on the scene to pick up the crews. PRESIDENT SERGENT remained afloat the longest and 10 of her ship's company, including the commodore of the convoy and Captain Dove (and his cat!) were taken off by the PERTH's motor boat shortly before the vessel sank. More of the crew were picked up from boats and rafts. The crew of PARISMINA had the toughest time with their ship sinking so quickly that no boats could be launched. The crew of PERTH had to climb down the scrambling nets to drag the exhausted men out of the water. With some 136 survivors on board, PERTH then had to take evasive action from an attack on herself and despite the unsteady conditions created by the changes of helm, the ship's surgeon continued to undertake an operation on a Chinese seaman who had fractured his skull in jumping into a boat. The patient was subsequently landed at Halifax, Nova Scotia well on his way to recovery.

When the tanker EMPIRE SPENSER (8,194/42) was attacked on the night of 7/8th December 1942 in convoy HX217, on passage from Curaçao via New York, to Stanlow, Cheshire, it was only the gallantry of the crew of PERTH that saved 57 of the 58 crew from the sea of flames that engulfed the area around the torpedoed vessel.

In just over four years of service as a rescue ship, PERTH escorted 60 convoys and rescued 455 survivors. She sailed from Halifax N.S. for Greenock on her last escort on 7th May 1945.

ABOYNE, which had been transferred to the London sailings in 1939, was the next ship to be taken up as a convoy rescue ship. She commenced escort duties in July 1943 and her master developed the "Aboyne Method" of transferring injured men by means of a 61-foot derrick rather than by using a boat. By mid-1943, however, the peak of the Battle of the Atlantic had passed so that during 26 convoys escorted she was only called upon to pick up 20 survivors.

A third ship, DUNDEE (VII), was taken up as a convoy rescue vessel in May 1943, having been previously requisitioned in October 1941 to carry supplies to the Iceland garrison. She also escorted 26 convoys in her two years service but in her case she only picked up 11 survivors. She sailed on her final escort from Halifax N.S. on 3rd May 1945.

From March 1941 the Danish owned motor vessel LILLEAA (936/22) was crewed and managed on behalf of the Ministry of War Transport. Starting in June 1941 she was employed carrying coal from Barry, South Wales to various ports on the West coast of Britain, but from December 1942 she was stationed in Scapa Flow, remaining there for the rest of the war except for a short period in March 1943 when she had to be towed to Dundee because of engine problems. She was handed back to the Danish Government in October 1945.

Two other ships were managed on behalf of the Ministry of War Transport, EMPIRE CAPE from July 1944, EMPIRE GARLAND from September 1945, and EMPIRE CONISBOROUGH from October 1945. The former was subsequently bought by the Company for £37,000 in October 1945 and renamed GOWRIE (III).

With the end of the war in Europe in May 1945, those ships that had been on war service began to return to Dundee. The first to do so was ARBROATH (III) on 12th June 1945, to be followed by DUNDEE (VII) on the 14th and PERTH (V) the next day. During July ABOYNE and GLAMIS returned but LOCHEE (II) and ERROL (II) did not arrive back until 1st September and 30th December 1945 respectively.

The war had not been too disastrous for the Company as only one vessel was lost despite the fact that such ships as PERTH (V), DUNDEE (VII), ABOYNE and LOCHEE (II) had been employed in areas of great danger. However, the coastal liner trade was in disarray and it would require a lot of effort to recover trade that during the war years had transferred on to other forms of transport. A proposal in October 1944 that the Company should join with other Scottish coastal liner companies to form London Scottish Lines Ltd. was rejected as it was felt that this would not be in the best interests of the Company.

POST-WAR YEARS

The demobilised fleet returned in 1945 to conditions totally different from those of 1939. There was no immediate possibility of restarting a remunerative passenger service to London as the 30 year old PERTH (V), after her four years' service in the North Atlantic, was rather the worse for wear and DUNDEE (VII) was too big for the volume of cargo likely to be on offer over the immediate post-war period. ABOYNE, with the decision having been made not to resume the Aberdeen and Hull passenger sailings, was available but proved too expensive to operate on the London sailings. Cargo-only sailings between these ports was instead provided by CLOVA.

In the light of these circumstances the Company sold PERTH (V) in April 1946 to the Falkland Islands Co. Ltd., London, who converted her to burn oil fuel and then renamed her LAFONIA. She sailed on 19th October 1946 for Port Stanley from where she traded to Montevideo, Uruguay and once a year made a trip to London carrying the season's wool. However, by 1950 she had insufficient capacity to carry the volume of wool offering, so was cold to Italian owners who renamed her VALFIORITA and operated her between Italy and East Africa and later to the Aegean Sea, before she was broken up in Italy in 1962 after nearly 47 years' service. DUNDEE (VII) was time chartered for a couple of years and employed carrying fruit from the

PERTH (V) as VALIRORITA *A. Duncan*

Mediterranean to the United Kingdom until sold to Liverpool owners in May 1948. ABOYNE was chartered to the Clyde Shipping Co. Ltd. of Glasgow for their coastal liner services in December 1945, and was subsequently bought by them in October 1946. The Aberdeen, Newcastle & Hull Steam Co. Ltd., went into liquidation at the same time as this last sale.

To maintain the Company's other coastal sailings, suitable vessels were purchased. One of the ships that the Company managed on behalf of the Ministry of War Transport, EMPIRE CAPE, was purchased in October 1945 for £37,000 and renamed GOWRIE (III). Another pre-war Goole built coaster named CONIDA was purchased in November 1945. She had been managed by the Company for her owners since January 1940 and was now renamed DRON — she did not stay with the fleet for long, being sold after only four years in service.

The Company had re-entered the towage business in March 1940 when they had bought the firm of V. A. Cappon Tugs Ltd. For £3,000 they acquired the goodwill and trade of this Dundee based firm and for £250 each the services of two rather elderly tugs GAUNTLET (1891) and MENTOR (1883). This firm had been in business since 1913 — for details of their tugs see Appendix K. With a view to improving the efficiency of this service, the Company in January 1946 bought two slightly more modern tugs from the Clyde Shipping Co. Ltd., FLYING SWALLOW (1905) for £8,000 and FLYING CORMORANT (1908) for £10,000. They were renamed BENVIE (though originally the choice had been for BARRY) and BUDDON. The two older tugs were sold and GAUNTLET, towing MENTOR, left the Tay in July 1946 bound for the breakers yard in Belgium. However, with jobs becoming fewer, both BENVIE and BUDDON were laid-up in June 1953 and were themselves then sold to breakers in the Forth. Towage services on the Tay passed now to the Dundee Harbour Trustees.

In March 1940 the Company also purchased for £2,750 the goodwill and trade of the Leith to Newcastle sailings of James Currie & Co. However, their vessel built for that trade, EDINA (489/39), was currently under charter to The North of Scotland & Orkney & Shetland Steam Navigation Co. Ltd. and remained so until March 1946. At that time the Company purchased her for a sum of £52,500.

There was no future for the smallest ships in the fleet, FAIR CITY and ROSYTH (II). The regular sailings between Leith and Kirkcaldy were not resumed and those between Dundee and Perth were withdrawn in July 1946 because of the fierce competition from both road and rail services. FAIR CITY was first laid-up in Dundee and then subsequently sold in June 1947 for service as a sand boat on the Tay. ROSYTH (II) was to remain in service for a further two years but was involved in two costly incidents. In April 1947 she broke adrift from her moorings at the Eastern Wharf, Dundee and struck OLNA FIRTH (509/33) and DRUMLOUGH (311/21) and also the Caledon yard's slipway, resulting in a claim of £4,380 for damages on top of a bill of £1,500 for repairs. In November of the same year she sank at her moorings at Perth and had to be pumped out and raised. She was sold for £500 as a sand boat but her bad luck seems to have stayed with her, as she sank in dock at Dundee in October 1950, had to be abandoned in a gale in January 1952 (but was recovered) and finally foundered in the Tay in February 1956.

LUNAN *G. H. Somner Collection*

The Company took delivery of their first purpose built post-war vessel LUNAN on 2nd October 1946 but in turn sold the 22 year old KILDRUMMY. The latter vessel had been employed since May 1946 in carrying coal from Barry to Dublin or Belfast and now went to a new company, Coquet Shipping Co. Ltd., run in conjunction with Anthony & Bainbridge Ltd., of Newcastle. She was renamed COQUETDALE and was later joined by COQUETSIDE (ex-EMPIRE CONGO) and both steamers were then employed in the coal trade until sold in 1951, COQUETDALE fetching a price of £24,500. Coquet Shipping Co. Ltd. then ordered a motor vessel costing some £90,000 which was named COQUETDYKE. She was sold four years later for £225,000 after which the Company was bought out by the other shareholders.

COQUETDALE *W. H. Brown*

Another small coaster joined the fleet in 1947 when SPRINGHAVEN was purchased for £45,000 and renamed GANNOCHY.

In 1948 various ships were renamed with LOCHEE (II) becoming PERTH (VI), GOWRIE (III) becoming LOCHEE (III) and EDINA becoming GOWRIE (IV).

PERTH (VI) — note the most forward samson posts have been removed *Fotoflite incorporating Skyfotos*

ARBROATH (III) was out of service for some months from May 1949 after being involved in a collision off the Yorkshire coast.

The name LONDON re-appeared in the fleet during 1951 when the seventh vessel of that name was delivered by Burntisland Shipbuilding Co. Ltd. In the same year the faithful old BROUGHTY (I), now 30 years old and the last steam coaster in the fleet, was sold for £6,500.

RETURN TO DEEP-SEA TRADING 1946-1956

After period of 50 years the Company re-entered the deep-sea tramp market again in July 1946 with the purchase for £77,500 of EMPIRE BARD, built by the Caledon yard in 1942. She had been constructed as a Scandinavian-type general purpose vessel capable of carrying long items of cargo or timber. She was given the name ANGUSBURN and employed tramping to the Mediterranean.

ANGUSBURN *G. E. P. Brownell/W.S.P.L.*

Two years later the Company purchased the 20-year old CLUNEPARK from the well-known Glasgow shipping company of J. & J. Denholm Ltd. for the sum of £110,000. She was the largest vessel to be owned by the Company and was given the name ANGUSMUIR.

Another of the same type of vessel as ANGUSBURN (although built by William Gray & Co. Ltd., West Hartlepool) was purchased in December 1951 for £185,000 and given the name of ANGUSBRAE. With this last acquisition the Company's fleet reached its peak of 15 ships.

During 1951/52 the highest freight rates were reached and in this climate it was decided to convert ANGUSBURN to burn oil fuel. This task was carried out on the Tyne in 1951 at a cost of nearly £20,000.

ANGUSBRAE when some 300 miles south of the Lizard, on passage from Melilla in North Africa to Workington in north-west England with a cargo of iron ore, had the misfortune to lose her rudder and stern frame. On 28th December 1951, under the command of Captain George Wood, she was hove-to in a strong westerly gale. During the night a loud crack was heard from the steering flat and on inspection it was found that the quadrant was jammed hard-a-starboard. The quadrant was re-centred but the vessel continued to steer very sluggishly, swinging through an arc of 280° to 315° during the rest of the night. By noon on the 29th the weather having moderated, an endeavour was made to resume course but the vessel refused to answer her helm. Captain Wood realised that something serious was wrong so stopped the ship, put on a life-jacket and despite the fact that a rough sea and heavy swell was running, went over the stern on a rope ladder to try and assess the extent of the damage. With his ship deeply laden it was not possible to ascertain the total extent of the damage but he soon saw the rudder was missing. A call for assistance was sent out and the following morning the powerful Dutch salvage tug ZWARTE ZEE (836/33) arrived on the scene and took ANGUSBRAE in tow. After only some four hours in tow the visibility became poor and a collision took place between the tug and the Danish motor vessel BJORN CLAUSEN (1,589/49), which had attempted to pass between the two vessels not realising that a tow line connected them. ZWARTE ZEE was holed and sent out a message of distress. Under the circumstances, the tow-line had to be slipped but in the process it fouled the screw of the tug. With the tug drifting down on ANGUSBRAE, Captain Wood had to use his engines to prevent contact being made and this he successfully managed. The Danish vessel meantime stood-by both immobilised vessels until arrangements could be made to send assistance out.

The British tug DEXTEROUS (600/42) was diverted to assist ANGUSBRAE. She had been on her way to the American ship FLYING ENTERPRISE (6,711/44) lying some 380 miles west of Land's End which had developed a crack in her hull and was then listing 30° to port. She arrived with ANGUSBRAE on the afternoon of 1st January 1952, and soon had connected 90 fathoms of 10-inch nylon tow-line and got underway for the Bristol Channel. Arriving in Barry Roads on the afternoon of 7th January, harbour tugs took on the task of moving ANGUSBRAE into Cardiff Docks for repairs. Meantime FLYING ENTERPRISE had been taken in tow by the Admiralty tug TURMOIL (1,136/45). On 10th January, when only some 50 miles from Falmouth, she turned turtle but before doing so, allowed the only crew on board, Captain Kurt Carlsen and the tug's mate Kenneth Dancey, to abandon ship (now nearly lying on her side) by walking along the ship's funnel onto the tug's deck. ZWARTE ZEE was "rescued" by the Dutch tug THAMES (602/38).

In early 1954 as post-war built tonnage became more plentiful, and freight rates for the smaller ships became less attractive and profitable, it was decided to dispose of ANGUSBURN and ANGUSMUIR when their current charters terminated.

ANGUSBURN had up till then been continuously employed and in the last year had been seen in many ports in different parts of the world. In February 1953 she had sailed from London to Salt River, an anchorage situated some miles west of Kingston, Jamaica where she loaded sugar and returned to the Thames in May. She then set sail for Rijeka, Yugoslavia and after loading esparto grass at Tripoli, Libya she arrived at Methil, Fife in September. Her next voyage took her from Grangemouth, on the upper reaches of the Forth, to Archangel in northern Russia and back to the Tyne, from where she departed in October for Odense, Denmark and then onwards to Leningrad, returning to Hull in November. She then went back to the Mediterranean again with a voyage from the Tyne to Algiers, Port Said, and Tripoli (Libya) before arriving back in Methil at the end of the year. She made her last voyage for the Company when she sailed from Methil on 30th January 1954 for the Tyne where she loaded for Naples, before once again proceeding to Tripoli (Libya) to load for Methil. She arrived in the Tyne on 21st March 1954 and after discharging her cargo was then sold.

ANGUSMUIR had been employed continuously carrying iron ore from North Africa to Workington and made her last voyage for the Company on 4th March 1954 when she sailed from Workington to Melilla, arriving back at Workington on 28th March when she was handed over to her new owners. Under her new name of AGUILA she continued to carry iron ore to the United Kingdom until January 1957.

With freight rates improving unexpectedly, ANGUSBRAE was retained for a further two years, but when she was due for an expensive survey, it was decided to sell her as a good price could be achieved at that time for second-hand tonnage. She too had been seen in many ports during these last years of service. She had spent the first four months of 1954 trading between Benisaf, Algeria and Port Talbot, South Wales with iron ore before she departed for Digby, Nova Scotia on 12th May, returning to Hull in June. She next sailed from Hull for the Polish port of Gdynia and having returned to Leith, moved to the Tyne from where she sailed on 17th July for Igarka, a river port situated some 400 miles up the River Yenisey. This involved a journey of just over 6,000 miles (the longtitude of Igarka (88°E) is the same as Calcutta) passing the North Cape into the Barents Sea, skirting to the south of Novaya Zemlya into the Kara Sea and then making the long voyage up the river to load timber for Calais at this inland Russian port on behalf of "Sovfracht".

She returned by way of Tromso and Kopervik in Norway to replenish her bunkers — her permanent bunker space amounted to 223 tons but provision had been made for reserve bunkers of 361 tons to be carried in No 2 hold. With consumption of about 21 tons per day at 9½ knots, this gave her a range of just about one month's steaming. Having discharged her cargo at Calais, she sailed for Kopervik and Bergen and then once again passed the North Cape, this time entering the White Sea to tie-up at Archangel (longtitude 40°E, the same as Jedda in the Red Sea). Whilst in port at Archangel, the crew played football against a Russian factory team, but were beaten 3-1. The crew had used copies of The Reader's Digest magazine (banned in Russia) as shinguards and these were discarded afterwards on the field — fortunately there were no repercussions!

She loaded timber for Bristol and after a call at Bergen to top-up her bunkers, arrived in the Avon during mid-October. She then sailed from there to the Mediterranean and made two voyages between North Africa and Grangemouth with esparto grass, before arriving at Leith on 15th March 1955 for dry-docking. She sailed from Leith on 3rd April 1955 for service in North American waters and arrived back at Hull on 2nd February 1956 from Newfoundland and was then paid-off. Sold to Dutch owners, she was renamed HISPANIA and sailed from Hull on 16th February for Rotterdam where she was converted to burn oil fuel.

WESTWARD HO! 1951-1966

With the constant need to find employment for the coastal ships during the summer months, Mr. John R. Cowper who had taken over from his father as General Manager of the Company in 1947, travelled to Canada in October 1950 to explore the possibility of vessels being chartered to operate from the Canadian eastern seaboard to ports such as Hamilton, Detroit and Cleveland on the Great Lakes. At this time the St. Lawrence Seaway was still under construction and only ocean-going vessels under 260 feet in length and 45 feet beam could pass through the 21 locks between Montreal and Lake Ontario. He was successful in arranging a three year contract between April and November each year with the Newfoundland-Great Lakes Steamship Co., initially for two vessels, to carry general cargo from Hamilton and Toronto to St. John's, Newfoundland, returning with tramp bulk cargoes. PERTH (VI) sailed from Southampton on 12th April 1951 for Montreal and was followed by LUNAN. The next year LONDON (VII) joined the other two in Canadian waters, LUNAN being fixed to carry 800 tons of structural steel to Detroit on her outward trip. The end of the 1952 season was rather marred by PERTH striking Renewse Rock near Cape Race in fog and having to return to St. John's with damage to her double bottom and screw.

The appearance in the St. Lawrence and the Great Lakes of red-funnelled Dundee ships was a welcome sight to exiled Scots. However, on one occasion there was great indignation among the Caledonian community in Detroit about an apparent slight to LUNAN. It was the custom of the Detroit Port Commission to present a shield to the first ocean-going ship to dock after the opening of the season. In 1953 LUNAN arrived at the port before all her rivals but the shield was presented to a German ship of the Hamburg-Chicago Line. The organisers had overlooked LUNAN as they studied the movements of potential winners up the St. Lawrence to Lake Ontario, and refused to change their plans to welcome the German ship, referring to LUNAN as "a confounded tramp" despite the fact that she was operating for a Canadian liner company. The St. Andrews Society of Detroit even passed a resolution deploring the injustice to LUNAN. However, justice reigned in the end, as in 1956 LUNAN, although a comparative late starter across the Atlantic but with no intermediate ports of call in the Great Lakes, arrived at Detroit first, other ships having been delayed by ice and then having to make intermediate calls prior to docking at Detroit.

With a greater demand for tonnage on the Great Lakes in 1953, the Company offered the charterers the use of ARBROATH (III) as a fourth vessel. The proposal was turned down on the grounds that the vessel was too small. Meantime however the Company had ordered a new ship costing £360,000 to be named DUNDEE (VIII) from Burntisland Shipbuilding Co. Ltd. She was built specifically for the Great Lakes trade, designed with a vertical bow and being one foot six inches in length below the maximum that could pass through the locks above Montreal. She was provided with 40,000 cubic feet of refrigerated space to carry frozen fish fillets from Newfoundland to the Great Lakes ports.

DUNDEE (VIII) sailed from Burntisland on 22nd April 1954 for Manchester where, under charter to Manchester Liners Ltd., she loaded for Montreal and Toronto. LUNAN and PERTH (VI) followed westwards soon afterwards. LONDON (VII) did not cross the Atlantic this year, and neither would have LUNAN, which was now too small for the trade, but no other vessel was available. Because of the agitation about the operation of non-Canadian vessels in Canadian coastal waters, the Company formed a Canadian subsidiary, Dundee, Perth & London Shipping Company (Canada) Ltd., and ultimately this new company took over the goodwill and assets of the

DUNDEE (VIII) entering Burin Harbour, Newfoundland *George Wilson*

Newfoundland-Great Lakes Steamship Co. After her first season in Canada DUNDEE (VIII) returned to Burntisland between January and March 1955 for certain modifications to be made.

LONDON (VII) was sent across the Atlantic again in 1957 to open a new service between Montreal and Botwood, Newfoundland. The first voyage of this new service had an unfortunate start as ice conditions were the worst for 50 years and the voyage to Botwood, which should have taken four days, took no less than 16.

Towards the end of the 1958 season LUNAN struck a rock in Murray Bay in the St. Lawrence and received severe bottom damage, with a fire subsequently breaking out in the engine room which gutted the accommodation. She was towed to Lauzon near Quebec and laid-up for the winter. She was sold in February 1959 for £65,000 in her damaged condition with the estimated cost of repairs being 194,000 Canadian dollars. To replace her the Company purchased from Currie Line Ltd., Leith, their steamer HIGHLAND (1,876/44) and, renamed GOWRIE (V), she sailed from Leith on 10th April, 1959 for Montreal.

The opening of the St. Lawrence Seaway on 25th April 1959, gave large ocean-going vessels access to the Great Lakes and also reduced the number of locks to be passed through from 21 to seven over the 110 mile stretch between Montreal and Prescott, Ontario.

When it was announced that the Royal Yacht BRITANNIA with the Queen and Duke of Edinburgh on board would officially open the St. Lawrence Seaway in June 1959, the Company was honoured to be approached to make available the expertise of Captain George Wood, master of DUNDEE (VIII), who was regarded as one of the most experienced masters using the canal system into the Great Lakes. Strange as it may seem, the Company had actually been longer in the Great Lakes trade than any other United Kingdom line, having entered it in 1951 some three years earlier than Manchester Liners.

The navigating officer of BRITANNIA, Commander Peter Berger, Royal Navy, accompanied by Lieutenant-Commander King, Royal Canadian Navy, took passage on DUNDEE to familiarise themselves with the procedures in transitting the locks. One of their concerns was that damage to the paintwork of BRITANNIA might be caused when passing through certain "tight" locks. Captain Wood suggested fitting rubber belting some two and a half feet below the waterline so that it could not be seen but yet prevent the yacht's side rubbing along the lock wall. This was in fact carried out and worked most effectively. DUNDEE and BRITANNIA actually passed each other on the day, BRITANNIA going eastbound whilst DUNDEE was going northbound.

Trading conditions were became increasingly more difficult resulting in a rate cutting war, and as a result arrangements were made with The Clarke Steamship Co. Ltd. of Quebec to run joint sailings between Lake Ontario and Newfoundland. At times the Company's vessels were chartered to other Canadian owners outside the St. Lawrence area. Dundee registered vessels were now to be seen in small Labrador ports and little LONDON (VII), which had been built for the Dundee-London trade, penetrated to Baker Lake (64.20 N, 95.30 W), a tiny ''Mountie'' station at the head of an inlet off Hudson Bay, on 2nd August 1961. Unfortunately near Chesterfield Inlet towards her journey's end, she struck an unchartered rock and suffered severe bottom damage, which resulted in the fuel becoming contaminated. Fortunately there was a deep tank amidships from which fuel could be pumped so she was able to complete her voyage before, loaded with empty oil drums, making her way back south for repairs. She arrived at Montreal on 27th August and subsequently docked at Quebec for repairs. This was to be her last season in Canadian waters for the Company, and she arrived back at Manchester on 11th November 1961.

Trading conditions in Canada became even more difficult in 1962 mainly due to dock labour problems at the ports, and although GOWRIE (V) and PERTH (VI) were found employment, it was to be their last season. GOWRIE (V) was sold to Greek owners in May 1963, whilst PERTH (VI), having arrived back at Preston on 23rd December 1962 from Halifax, Nova Scotia, resumed coastal tramping for a while.

Between 1964 and 1966 DUNDEE (VIII) continued to operate in Canadian waters alone but, because of the continuing dock labour troubles that still beset Canadian ports, had to be switched to trading between New York and the West Indies for much of the time. She sailed from the United Kingdom in March 1966 for her last season, returning to the Tyne for lay-up during the following December. In January 1967 she was sold for £100,000 to Israeli interests and sailed from the Tyne on 27th January 1967 via Flushing for Haifa, now renamed DORON.

During the 12 seasons DUNDEE (VIII) had seen service in Canadian waters, she had for seven seasons been under the command of Captain George Wood, who had previously gained experience of the Great Lakes in 1952 on LUNAN and in 1953 on PERTH (VI). Although specifically constructed to carry frozen fish westwards and consumer goods eastwards to Newfoundland, she visited many other ports and carried many other sorts of cargo. On one occasion she was sent to Goose Bay, Labrador, a trip of some 70 miles up Hamilton Inlet, to load surplus army equipment, and had to carry two Eskimo pilots, neither of whom spoke more than a few words of English.

DUNDEE made several voyages into the Pacific, the only Company vessel ever to do so. Chartered to Namenic Line, controlled by President Somoza of Nicaragua, she loaded a cargo of foodstuffs, clothing, machinery and general cargo at various United States eastern seaboard ports, and sailed from New York on 10th December 1959 bound initially for Cristobal at the Atlantic end of the Panama Canal, a voyage of just over a week. It was customary to discharge and load for intermediate points at each port of call, but with only three of these ports having wharves, the goods for the other ports had to be discharged/loaded overside into/out of barges when anchored offshore. Calls were made at Panama and Balboa in the Canal Zone, Puntarenas in Costa Rica, San Juan del Sur, Puerto Somoza and Corinto in Nicaragua, La Union, Imapala, La Libertad, and Acajutla in El Salvador, and San Jose and Champerico in Guatemala. Northbound cargoes for the United States were coffee, sugar, fruit, other edible commodities and frozen meat — the latter from Puerto Somoza. There was a long term contract between the United States Government and President Somoza to ship these commodities in order to secure dollars for the Nicaraguan Government. After her return to New York in mid-January 1960, she loaded again for Central America early February and completed her charter during March. On one of the trips DUNDEE carried as passengers President Somoza's brother, a general in the Nicaraguan army, together with his wife, six children and two nannies to Panama where he was to attend a United States army training course. She did not return to New York in March 1960 but instead proceeded to Belize and Kingston, Jamaica where she loaded sugar for Liverpool. After discharging there she proceeded to the Tyne for her annual docking, arriving on 16th June 1960.

On another occasion having sailed from the Tyne on 20th March 1964 for Canada under the command of Captain Fryett, she was switched to New York and on 3rd May she made her way south with calls at Barbados, Port of Spain, Belem (some 75 miles up the River Para), Portel (a river port 200 miles west of Belem), and finally at Fortaleza on the northern coast of Brazil, before returning to New York on 3rd July 1964. At the end of that season DUNDEE once more sailed for the south leaving New York on 1st December. This time she called at Barbados and Grenada before putting into Belem. She then sailed 1,000 miles up the mighty River Amazon to Manaus, arriving there on 28th December. New Year was spent in port (a unique opportunity for the crew to celebrate Hogmanay in the Southern Hemisphere). She sailed down river again on 4th January 1965 and reached New York on 11th March.

Officially all navigation on the St. Lawrence Seaway finished on 7th December each year, and if any ship was caught in the Lakes after the freeze-up the resultant stay-over could be expensive. All water in the systems had to be drained off, exposed deck machinery protected from the elements and a skeleton crew kept on board. The cost of these precautions and the subsequent dry-docking in the following Spring could cost the owners about £10,000 so the Company made sure their ships were well clear of the Lakes before cold weather approached. DUNDEE therefore found herself in the "closed" season employed carrying such commodities as sugar to Rotterdam and tobacco to Bristol from the West Indies, fruit from Patras, Greece to the United Kingdom and on one occasion esparto grass from North Africa to her home port. Her arrival at Dundee on 2nd February 1957 was only the second time she had called there — the first had been a brief call in April 1954 on her maiden voyage to Manchester from Burntisland.

Whilst the Company's flag is no longer seen in Canadian waters, two of the vessels — LUNAN and LONDON (VII) — remained in these waters for some years. The former was sold in a damaged condition to Quebec owners in February 1959 and the latter in September 1964 to Newfoundland owners.

FLEET VALUATION

As previously mentioned, the number of vessels (excluding river and small craft) owned by the Company rose in December 1951 to 15 cargo vessels and two tugs. The total value of the hulls and machinery for marine insurance purposes amounted to £1,060,500 as at 31st March 1952. A breakdown of the value of each ship in the fleet is given below:

Name	Gross tons/ Year built	Year Acqd	Purchase Price	Insurance: Value	Cost per day
ANGUSBRAE	2905/43	1951	£185,000	£160,000	£13.18. 6d
ANGUSBURN	2851/42	1946	£ 77,500	£160,000	£15.17. 3d
ANGUSMUIR	3535/28	1948	£110,000	£ 88,000	£11. 3.11d
ARBROATH (III)	553/35	1935	£ 22,000	£ 36,000	£ 5. 8. 1d
CLOVA	310/35	1936	£ 10,500	£ 16,000	£ 2. 8. 4d
CORTACHY	271/34	1939	£ 11,500	£ 16,000	£ 2.13. 2d
CROMBIE	239/34	1939	£ 11,500	£ 16,000	£ 2.13. 2d
ERROL (II)	311/36	1939	£ 10,000	£ 16,000	£ 2. 5. 6d
GANNOCHY	485/37	1947	£ 45,000	£ 36,000	£ 4.11. 3d
GLAMIS	555/36	1936	£ 23,980	£ 36,000	£ 5. 2. 3d
GOWRIE (IV)	489/39	1946	£ 52,500	£ 30,000	£ 4. 5. 3d
LOCHEE (III)	872/41	1945	£ 37,000	£ 72,000	£ 9.15. 1d
LONDON (VII)	706/51	1951	£135,000	£144,000	£10.13. 2d
LUNAN	1018/46	1946	£ 96,000	£120,000	£10. 2. 2d
PERTH (VI)	994/37	1937	£ 57,250	£100,000	£12.11. 7d
BENVIE	185/05	1946	£ 8,000	£ 6,500	£ -.11. 9d
BUDDON	203/08	1946	£ 10,000	£ 8,000	£ -.14. 5d

When vessels were subsequently sold they usually fetched a good price which compared favourably with their insurance value and in most cases their original cost. This was especially so in the case of the three ANGUS tramp steamers. The wartime built ANGUSBURN which was bought from the Ministry of Transport when under the Company's management for a bargain price of £77,500 (market value then £245,000) and later converted to burn oil fuel at a cost of a further £20,000, was sold in 1954 after eight years service for £90,000. However, it transpired that only some 11 months later she was sold to Finnish owners for the huge sum of £130,000. ANGUSMUIR when 26 years old and bought some six years before for £110,000 fetched £56,000, whilst ANGUSBRAE, still coal-burning, and now 13 years old and bought for £185,000 some five years earlier sold for £122,000 in 1956. This figure was some £32,000 more than her oil-burning sister ship ANGUSBURN sold for some two years earlier.

Even the value of the smaller motor vessels held up well, with CLOVA when 17 years old and bought for £10,500 in 1936, fetching £14,000 in 1954, and GOWRIE (IV) when 19 years old and bought at the high post-war price of £52,500 going for £22,500 after 12 years service.

LOOKING SOUTH

In July 1954 the Company acquired a minority interest in the small London based firm of Lockett Wilson Ltd.

John Wilson, a deck officer who had lost an arm when his ship was torpedoed in a Malta convoy during World War II, first entered the business of shipowning/shipbroking in June 1949, when he and a James R. Massey of London, both described as contractors, purchased a motor barge, previously used on inland waterways, and renamed her WILMAS (the first three letters of their names).

John Wilson bought-out his partner's interest during the following October and employed her sailing to Ostend, Dunkirk and Paris. Subsequently in April 1951 he sold the vessel to French owners. The capital released then allowed him to purchase an interest in the motor vessel PARKSTONE (200/29), currently owned by I. P. Langford (Shipping) Ltd. of Gloucester. From January 1950 32 shares in this vessel had been held by a Peter Lockett, and it was 16 of these shares that John Wilson acquired in May 1951. This was to be the start of a long business association between these two men.

Peter Lockett had served in the Royal Air Force during World War II as a pilot, was shot-down, and then imprisoned in the notorious prisoner-of-war camp at Colditz, from which he attempted to escape. After the war he had married a French girl and set up home in Paris. His first venture into shipping, of which he knew little, was about 1950 when he discovered there was a chronic shortage of barrels in which to import wine from Algeria, so he came up with the idea that wine could just as easily be transported in tankers. He purchased what he considered was a suitable vessel for this purpose, only to find that he could not get a certificate of seaworthiness for her. At that moment he fortunately met John Wilson, who was now also married to a French lady, Adrienne, his second wife, and through his contacts soon found "un pigeon" to buy the unsuitable vessel. John Wilson having got Peter Lockett out of his predicament, the latter was happy to be guided by his more experienced colleague in the future.

John Wilson, residing in France, had noticed that PARKSTONE had been trading to Rouen and Paris since May 1950. His acquisition of shares in this vessel in May 1951 was the opening he had been looking for and with the intention of expanding this trade the partners formed Lockett Wilson Ltd. soon afterwards. Few people think of Paris as a seaport, but the port of Paris, Gennevilliers, which is close to the centre of the French capital, was equipped with modern plant for the efficient handling of general cargo.

Meantime John Wilson continued to work on the principle of "buying and selling" vessels, buying as cheaply as possible and then selling when the opportunity arose but in between times employing such vessels wherever he could. He acquired the old steamer DUNAVON (235/08) in June 1951 and subsequently had her refitted with a diesel engine. MORION (401/45) was purchased in August 1951 but in October of the same year both she and PARKSTONE were sold to other owners although the partners continued to hold mortgages on both vessels for some time afterwards.

Early in 1952 two further ships were purchased, PURBECK (199/36), one time "running partner" of PARKSTONE out of Poole, and the West Country owned ROSELYNE (313/43). Sailings up the Seine were now run on a regular basis from Dundee Wharf on the Thames, the first contact between the Company and the partners, but by no means the last. ROSELYNE was sold in 1953 which then allowed the partners to acquire for £17,500 the Company's CORTACHY which they renamed CONCORDE (I).

The fact that Lockett Wilson Ltd. were not only using Dundee Wharf but were also in the market to buy ships was not lost on the Company, who saw the possibilities of finding employment for their vessels, now that the traditional coasting trades in which they had been so long involved, were being slowly replaced by road and rail transport. In July 1954 the decision was made to take a minority interest in Lockett Wilson Ltd., with the capital invested being represented by the transfer of CLOVA (1935) (soon renamed CLICHY) and CROMBIE (1934) to the new firm of Lockett Wilson Line Ltd. In December 1955 the Company acquired the controlling interest which allowed the original partners to concentrate their efforts in another venture — more of this later.

CLOVA *G. E. P. Brownell/W.S.P.L.*

Soon Lockett Wilson Line were not only operating sailings from London to Paris, but also from Goole and Hull to Paris and Brussels. Although there were now four vessels in the fleet, three of which were originally employed on the Dundee trades, frequently this number had to be supplemented by chartered tonnage. However, by 1957 these services were not proving quite so profitable because of the adverse effect of the devaluation of the French franc as well as restrictions on imports into France. The fleet was reduced to three in 1959 on the sale of PURBECK.

Better times returned which prompted the decision to have a purpose built vessel constructed by the associated Brazen Island Shipyard Ltd. at Polruan. VENDOME, as the new vessel was named, made her first voyage on 12th October 1960 by which time CROMBIE had been sold to foreign owners. In 1961 CLICHY ex-CLOVA was sold to the associated Channel Shipping Ltd (which see in the next section), leaving CONCORDE (I) ex-CORTACHY (sold later that year) and VENDOME (supplemented by chartered tonnage) to maintain sailings to Paris, Rouen and Treport from Goole and Ipswich, with those to Brussels being taken over by Brussels Steam Ship Co. Ltd., in which the company had recently acquired an interest.

VENDOME was joined on the services at the end of 1962 by VAUBAN, also built at Polruan, and both traded successfully for some years. Consideration was given to constructing yet a third vessel by the same yard but this idea was shelved in the light of forecasted trading conditions.

By 1965 the rising costs of stevedoring, the appearance of foreign competition, and the introduction of "roll-on roll-off" as well as containerised services resulted in inroads being made into the profitability of conventional sea transport. In 1968 the decision was made to dispose of the two relatively modern vessels and Lockett Wilson Line Ltd. finally ceased trading in 1972.

CHANNEL ISLAND CONNECTIONS

During December 1961 the Board authorised the acquisition of a 49% holding in Channel Shipping Ltd. of Jersey. This was achieved by the transfer of BROUGHTY (II), now displaced from the London sailings. Initially chartered to Channel Shipping Ltd. to maintain sailings from Liverpool, she arrived at Jersey for the first time on 10th December 1961. She was to continue on these sailings until 27th June 1963.

Channel Shipping Ltd. came into being in December 1955, and was formed by John Wilson and Peter Lockett in much the same manner as they had founded Lockett Wilson Ltd. some years earlier. In the case of the latter firm they had purchased CORTACHY from the Company and this time it was ERROL (II) with the intention that she should be employed on charter to the associated Lockett Wilson Line Ltd. on the River Seine sailings or carrying china clay from Cornwall to France. She was renamed GROUVILLE (I). This name, to be followed by others, were those of the railway stations on the former Jersey Eastern Railway which used to run from St Helier to Gorey, opened in 1873 and closed in 1929.

Late in 1956 Channel Shipping Ltd. bought two small tankers, SHELL DRIVER (349/28) and BEN HENSHAW (377/33). They were sent to Brazen Island Shipyard Ltd. at Polruan (an associated firm in the group) and after being converted to dry cargo vessels, they entered the china clay trade as GOREY (I) and GRANTEZ (the latter being a district in the parish of St Ouen, Jersey in which John Wilson now lived). However, GRANTEZ was sold later the same year when a sale opportunity arose.

No further change took place in the fleet until November 1959 when the Dutch owned FRIEDA (485/51) was purchased and renamed FAUVIC. She was taken up on charter by Cunard Steam-ship Co. Ltd. to maintain their sailings between Liverpool, Channel Islands and Havre, with her funnel painted in her charterer's colours. To finance this expansion, Peter Lockett's brother Charles, also an ex-Royal Air Force pilot, imprisoned after landing behind enemy lines, joined the partnership, holding a mortgage of £26,500 on the vessel, with Peter Lockett holding one for £11,500.

A year later the London registered AISNE (215/38) was purchased from William H. Müller & Co. a competitor on the Seine sailings, and renamed CLARY. She was however, sold in the following year and in her place came CLICHY (310/35) ex-CLOVA from the fleet of Lockett Wilson Line Ltd., with

CLICHY *A. Duncan*

this time John Wilson's wife Adrienne holding a mortgage on her for £11,000. The firm also bought the Norfolk owned LOWESTOFT TRADER (311/34) which was renamed PONTAC, but she was sold within six months.

With changes in management came changes in trade too. In March 1962 Channel Shipping Ltd. in association with English China Clays Ltd. formed Western Shipping Ltd. specifically to carry china clay. FAUVIC was sold for £42,500 to the new company and was renamed MELEDOR and she was joined in this new venture by the Dutch built LIJNBAANSGRACHT (494/52) which was renamed TREVISCOE, both vessels being managed by Channel Shipping Ltd.

The Company became further involved with Channel Shipping Ltd. when LONDON (VII) was chartered to supplement the sailings of BROUGHTY (II) on the Liverpool service between 6th May 1962 and 20th November 1962.

When Cunard Steam-ship Co. Ltd. decided in January 1963 to discontinue sailings from Liverpool the decision was made that Channel Shipping Ltd. should continue them. However, when a good price was offered for BROUGHTY (II) for conversion to a liquified gas carrier, this was accepted so from June 1963 chartered tonnage was used to maintain the sailings until 1967, when the goodwill of that trade was sold to Manchester Shipping Ltd. (part of the Watts, Watts group). The port of Runcorn near Manchester had been used since 1965 as a substitute for Liverpool because of labour problems met with at the latter port.

ERROL (III) *Fotolite incorporating Skyfotos*

With the long term china clay charters now running out, GOREY (I) was sold in July 1963, and the other two vessels in the fleet, GROUVILLE (I) ex-ERROL (II) and CLICHY ex-CLOVA were now employed in supplementing Lockett Wilson Line Ltd. vessels on the Paris sailings. They were joined in 1963 by the Dutch built MARNE (427/49), renamed GOREY (II), and ROTTUM (452/57). The first pair of ships were sold in 1964 to other Jersey owners but were then taken up on charter for a while to support the Paris sailings.

Two more ships were purchased late in 1964, the Swedish built LADY ANSTRUTHER (499/46), renamed ERROL (III), for £21,000 and the Dutch built (and the third vessel to be bought from William H. Müller & Co.) ESCAUT (384/47), renamed GROUVILLE (II). However, ERROL (III) was sold for £35,000, a handsome profit in four months, whilst the other three in the fleet, GOREY (II), ROTTUM (later renamed CONCORDE (II)) and GROUVILLE (II) were chartered to Paris Maritime Service (in which John Wilson had a 50% holding in conjunction with SOMARCO of Paris) and employed on the River Seine services of Lockett Wilson Line Ltd.

ERROL (III) leaving Jersey *Dave Hocquard*

Charles Lockett was killed on 26th August 1966 at Alderney when attempting to land his aircraft on the island, and his holding in Channel Shipping Ltd. passed to his widow Evelyn.

With "roll-on roll-off" and containerisation services now offering shippers a more convenient method of transporting goods, the profitability and the days of conventional Lockett Wilson Line Ltd. sailings to Paris were obviously numbered, so the decision was made that Channel Shipping Ltd. should go into voluntary liquidation. In January 1968 the interest in Western Shipping Ltd., now reduced to one ship after the loss of MELEDOR in April 1965, was sold. GROUVILLE (II) was sold in September 1968 to Maltese owners, and the sale of GOREY (II) followed a month later. CONCORDE (II) was at the same time transferred to J. G. Renouf & Co. Ltd. (a subsidiary of Channel Shipping Ltd.) until a buyer could be found and she was eventually sold to London owners in November 1970.

SHIPBUILDING AND REPAIRING

In January 1957 the Company took a controlling interest in the Brazen Island Shipyard Ltd. of Polruan Bay, Fowey, which had been formed by John Wilson of the associated company Channel Shipping Ltd. A lease was taken from Fowey Harbour Commissioners for a sum of £1,600 per year on two slipways, suitable for vessels up to 500 tons deadweight and equipped to deal with repair and survey work as well as the building of small craft. Polruan is situated opposite Fowey, a small port located on the south coast of Cornwall, and famous for the shipment of china clay all over the world.

The yard undertook the conversion to dry cargo vessels of Channel Shipping Ltd.'s newly acquired tankers SHELL DRIVER and BEN HENSHAW, and some survey work afloat on deepsea vessels laid-up at Fowey, as well as carrying out voyage repairs to Channel Shipping Ltd. vessels calling at Fowey.

The yard received its first shipbuilding order in June 1957 for a motor hopper barge for service with Fowey Harbour Commissioners. LANTIC BAY (147/58) was launched on 14th July 1958. The second vessel to be laid-down was for Lockett Wilson Line Ltd. Launched on 6th July 1960, VENDOME was delivered to her owners on 12th October 1960 for employment on Paris sailings from London and Hull, though on occasions she served on the Dundee — London service. The third vessel to be built at the yard was Lockett Wilson Line Ltd.'s VAUBAN which was launched on 9th November 1962, with the prospect of yet a third vessel for the same owners being contemplated. However, with signs that trading conditions on the River Seine sailings were changing, this third vessel was never laid-down.

The decision was made in the autumn of 1963 to close down the yard because of a lack of work generally and the fact that shipbuilding/ship-repairing did not fit into Dundee, Perth & London Shipping Co. Ltd.'s corporate policy. The capital outlay on the yard was fully repaid and in addition the associated Lockett Wilson Line Ltd. now owned two modern and economical coasters.

VAUBAN

THE END OF COASTAL SAILINGS

Against a background of increasing difficulties in the coastal home trades, the opportunity to participate in ventures outside the Company's traditional trades, as described earlier, was one way of keeping vessels gainfully employed. With the liner trades being seasonal, the carriage of coal from the north-east to ports in the south of England had been up to now a steady source of revenue, but there had been a dramatic reduction in the tonnage that the Company's vessels had carried from 24,000 tons in the winter of 1951/52 to just 3,000 tons a year later. This was caused by the gas and electricity industries carrying coal in their own ships.

After the sale/transfer of three ships in 1953/54 to Lockett Wilson Line Ltd., it still left six vessels (and also LONDON (VII) when not in service in Canadian waters) to be found employment on either coastal liner trades or on coastal tramping. This number was reduced by one in December 1955 when ERROL (II) was sold to Channel Shipping Ltd. With the up-turn in trade to London it also became necessary to replace the 18 year old GLAMIS, now no longer capable of maintaining a voyage between Dundee and London "within three tides" (essential if the vessel was not to arrive when it was low water at the destination) and for the first and only time in the history of the Company, an order was placed in July 1954 with a Dutch shipbuilder for a motor vessel costing £114,163, this price being a substantial saving compared with one built in the United Kingdom. BROUGHTY (II) came into service in June 1955 and with LONDON (VII) provided a twice-weekly service to London with goods reaching there in 34 hours. The Saturday sailings, arriving London on Monday mornings, were popular and enabled the coastal liner trade to equal rail and road in speed of service.

The problem of maintaining the shorter distance trades became more critical and when a heavy loss of cargo from Hull occurred due to a change in the distribution of cattle feed stuffs, the Aberdeen to Newcastle and Hull sailings (in operation since 1866) had to be discontinued in October 1955. For many years the Company had employed seven ships with a total carrying capacity of 9,000 tons on the liner services to London and Hull, but this capacity was now reduced to 2,300 tons and only three vessels were employed. The Newcastle and Hull sailings from Dundee and Kirkcaldy were also under threat and those from Dundee were suspended in May 1957. The Kirkcaldy connection was maintained until November 1957 with chartered tonnage but it too was then suspended, leaving only liner services to London and occasionally to Southampton.

GOWRIE (IV), which had been employed tramping, sailed from Dundee for the last time on 1st October 1957 prior to being sold. From Dundee she went to the Tyne, Helsinki, Mantyluoto (Finland), Copenhagen, Tayport (a small port opposite Dundee in Fife), Southampton, Dunkirk, and Honfleur before arriving at Liverpool on 9th November 1957. Whilst in drydock for a survey prior to handover to her new owners, it was noticed that there was some bottom damage, presumably received when she ran ashore in Sweden during Sepember 1955, and it was estimated that it would cost about £35,000 to repair. However, she passed the survey and was given a certificate of seaworthiness so the sale was completed and she sailed on 5th February 1958 from Liverpool bound for the Caribbean. Although she had proved a reliable vessel in the past, after various engine problems she eventually arrived at Kingston, Jamaica in tow on 25th April 1958 and finally foundered in 1964.

The year 1958 did not start well for the Company. GANNOCHY while on passage from North Wales to Liverpool with a cargo of stone foundered in the Mersey Channel on 25th February. She sprang a leak and after developing a list of 47° sank in just 27 minutes. Because the wreck was causing an obstruction in the channel, it had to be removed, the alternatives being to raise it at a cost of £21,000 or blow it up at a cost of about £3,000. The second alternative was used!

GANNOCHY *L. van Ginderen*

BROUGHTY (II) was involved in a collision in the Thames on 23rd December 1958 and had to be hurriedly beached after her side had been penetrated at the rear of No. 2 hold. She was subsequently refloated with the aid of two tugs, the cost of the towage and repairs coming to £5,310.

Delivery was taken on 27th May 1958 of the coastal tanker KINGENNIE, the first such vessel in the fleet. She was fixed on a five year charter to British Petroleum Tankers Ltd. — she was to be the last ship ordered by the Company and was in fact never to visit her home port. The nearest she got was to Grangemouth in August 1958, the rest of her time being spent much further south.

Whereas the group surplus on trading in the year to April 1959 was £73,150, by April 1960 this had turned into a deficit of £65,419, the first loss in the Company's history. There was, however, a modest recovery in April 1961 when a surplus of £28,876 was achieved, partly by the sale of GLAMIS in January 1961.

Important changes were taking place within the Company. The most radical was the termination of the liner service between Dundee and London, which had been run since the formation of the Company in 1826. The "London boat" BROUGHTY (II) sailed for the last time on 18th November 1961 and from 21st November a train service was substituted. The train ran thrice weekly at a cost to the Company of £525 for 25 wagons. The only coastal liner service remaining was the occasional service to Southampton with potatoes. The displaced BROUGHTY (II) was initially chartered to the associated company Channel Shipping Ltd. — described in an earlier section — and subsequently in April 1962 was sold to that firm.

Two further sales took place in 1962, that of GALA in August and ARBROATH (III) in November. GALA, which had had her tanks removed in 1940 so that she could be used as a dry cargo vessel, never had them re-installed as the tanks (in store) had been destroyed in an air raid on Hull.

Also in 1962 the Company acquired a 50% interest in the Brussels Steamship Co. Ltd. of London, in association with George Gibson & Co. Ltd. of Leith. This company had operated a steamer service from the Humber and Thames to Brussels since 1873 — for details of their ships see Appendix P. With this purchase came two steamers CITY OF BRUSSELS (691/47) and CITY OF LONDON (668/27). Both were old and inefficient so were sold quite quickly and Lockett Wilson Line Ltd. vessels and chartered tonnage were used to maintain the sailings. The Company's interest in the Brussels Steamship Co. Ltd. was sold to George Gibson & Co. Ltd. in 1967.

The coastal fleet was reduced to four vessels by the beginning of 1963, LOCHEE (III) , LONDON (VII), PERTH (VI) and the tanker KINGENNIE. LOCHEE (III) was until May 1963 regularly employed carrying cement from the Thames to Scottish ports, but on Scotland's own cement works being opened in April at Dunbar, some 30 miles east of Edinburgh, the traffic was very much reduced. During 1964 she was chartered to William Robertson Shipowners Ltd. of Glasgow. LOCHEE (III) called at Dundee in August 1965 and was to be the last Company ship to do so.

LONDON (VII) was used on occasions to supplement BROUGHTY (II) on her sailings between Liverpool and the Channel Islands but otherwise undertook any coastal tramping that was available. She was joined in such work by PERTH (V) which had not returned to Canadian waters after the 1962 season. However, in May 1963 PERTH (V) was sold. She had made no call at her home port between 1949 and February 1963 (except for a period of lying-up between January and March 1959). Her last voyage in the red funnel colours of the Company terminated at Newport, Mon. on 6th May 1963 on her arrival from Dunkirk. The sale of LONDON (VII) followed in September 1964 to Canadian owners, while in August 1966 LOCHEE (III) was sold to Greek owners and she sailed from Runcorn on 10th August as AGHIOS SPYRIDON for Castellammare di Stabia via Plymouth and Great Yarmouth.

The year 1967 was to be the end of the line in many ways — Mr John R. Cowper resigned in January as General Manager because of ill-health and his place was taken by Mr James M. Chalmers, who had been the Company Secretary since 1962. On 3rd March KINGENNIE tied-up in the Tyne after a voyage from Swansea via Dunkirk and Ghent, and the Company flag was run down for the last time. She was sold for £125,000 (she had cost £120,000 to build some nine years earlier) and with DUNDEE (VIII) having been already sold in January, was unique in that she was the last ship to be built and also the last ship to be owned by the Company. To operate a single ship under present day trading conditions was just not practical so there was little choice in the matter. However, she continued to be managed by the Company on behalf of her new owners until sold by them to Greek interests in 1972. The shipowning era of just over 140 years was at an end.

CAPTAIN ALEXANDER (SANDY) CAMPBELL, M.B.E.

The master to command the last ship owned by the Company, the coastal tanker KINGENNIE, was Captain Alexander Campbell, M.B.E., who served the Company through war and peace for 46 years.

Born in Glasgow on 24th April 1902 at Cathcart Street (now Weir Street), his parents were James Campbell (born 1870) from Lochgilphead, Argyllshire, a master in the home trade, whilst his mother, Flora, came from Castletown, Caithness. He went to Scotland Street School in 1907 and studied there until he was 14 years old. On leaving school in 1916, having previously crewed yachts on the Clyde in his holidays, he signed-on at Glasgow on 13th July 1916 as a seaman at 15/- per week on the small Glasgow coaster LOCH NELL (123/77) owned by John G. Stewart, and commanded by his father. His first voyage was from Glasgow to Ayr and Girvan. LOCH NELL, a real work-horse of the Clyde, carried coal from Ayr to Campbeltown and to such Irish ports as Belfast and Donaghadee, granite chippings and kerb stones from Furnace on Loch Fyne, Argyllshire to Glasgow, and during the latter part of World War I, loaded mines and detonators at Ardrossan for transfer to a United States minelayer lying in Lamlash Bay, Isle of Arran. When coal and chippings were loaded, the crew of three were responsible for trimming the cargo into the nooks and crannies of the vessel's single hold, and for this heavy and dirty work they received the handsome sum of ½d per ton *between them!*

When LOCH NELL was sold in March 1919, he transferred to another ship of the same owners, LOCH LEVEN (305/10), commanded by Captain L. W. Alexander. This somewhat larger vessel traded from Ayrshire ports to Liverpool, Manchester and Garston on the Upper Mersey with coal southwards, returning north in ballast. He remained with her until she in turn was sold in January 1920 and John G. Stewart went out of business.

He next joined the new steamer FORT LAVERNOCK (435/20), owned by Fort Shipping Co. Ltd. of Cardiff, in February 1920 and remained with her until the following November, when he transferred to another of the same company's steamers, ROSSMORE (627/07). Both these vessels traded out of South Wales ports to the near Continent, again carrying coal outwards and returning in ballast. He stayed with ROSSMORE for a few months before coming ashore.

By 1920 Sandy Campbell was on pay of £2.10/- per week, out of which he had to buy his own food (mostly tinned), and provide himself with utensils in which to cook it. He also had to find his own bedding for his bunk in the sparse, usually unheated forecastle, and this consisted of a "donkey's breakfast" — a jute sacking cover filled with straw, which he could acquire from a ship's chandler for the sum of one shilling (1/-). A pillow cost 2d more.

With jobs difficult to find in the post-war period, he took whatever he could find. He made a single voyage to Huelva, southern Spain, to load iron ore on the Ardrossan registered steamer BARON KELVIN (1865/07).

During the summer of 1921 he joined his father, now a fish buyer, on the fish carrier NIGHTINGALE (97/99) of Glasgow. It involved Sandy rowing his father round fishing boats working in the Clyde or Lochgilphead area and this proved a hard job, mostly working at night and resulting in little sleep. His father would board each fishing boat and make a deal to buy their catch, and later the boats would come alongside NIGHTINGALE to transfer the fish to her. NIGHTINGALE would then set off early in the morning to steam to the nearest market to sell the fish at the best price possible, leaving the fishing boats to continue their work uninterrupted.

Sandy Campbell came to the Company on 18th October 1921 when he joined BROUGHTY (I), then fitting out at Bowling on the River Clyde, as a seaman. He was to stay with her until April 1923, when he came ashore

Captain Alexander (Sandy) Campbell MBE

at Dundee to study for his mate's (Home Trade) certificate. He passed that on 23rd June 1924 and became mate of GOWRIE (II) in December the same year. In February 1925 he transferred to LOCHEE (I) as relief 1st mate for a fortnight, and then joined the Glasgow-owned steamer CONISTON (468/21) as mate, this vessel having been chartered by the Company to cope with the potato trade to the south. After a spell of six weeks on her he then joined the passenger steamer PERTH (V) as relief 2nd mate for a week before transferring to LOUGA as 2nd mate, remaining with her until August 1926. For a period between May and July 1926 he served as relief mate on LOCHEE (I) and GOWRIE (II).

In August 1926 he joined BROUGHTY (I), this time as mate instead of seaman as nearly six years ago, and stayed with her until November 1926, when he transferred to LOCHEE (I) as 1st mate. He remained with her until April 1927 when he then became mate of GOWRIE (II) for nearly eight months. He served as relief 2nd mate on the passenger steamer LONDON (VI) for about six weeks before joining the small cargo steamer ROSYTH (I) as mate in January 1928. Because of the master's sudden illness during June 1928, Sandy became temporary master of the vessel for two months during which time he obtained his Tay Pilot's Licence. He came ashore on 16th January 1929 to sit the examination for the master (Home Trade) certificate and this he obtained on 27th June 1929.

ROSYTH (I) *G. E. Langmuir Collection*

After a short spell on PERTH (V) as 2nd mate, he transferred to LONDON (VI) in a similar capacity and was to stay with this ship for six and a half years. When he married on 7th December 1932 he was then serving as mate.

His first appointment as master came in the autumn of 1935 when he stood by the new motor vessel ARBROATH (III) then nearing completion at the local Caledon yard. He remained with her for nearly two years before taking command of the new and larger motor vessel LOCHEE (II) in August 1937 when she was delivered by her builders, Henry Robb Ltd. of Leith. This new ship was usually employed on the Dundee/Leith to Southampton sailings. On occasions during the spring and autumn of each year when she was despatched to Portugal to load cork, Sandy Campbell would come ashore as this destination was outside the limits of his certificate, and his place would be taken by his 1st mate, John Murray, who held a master's deep-sea certificate.

Sandy Campbell left LOCHEE (II) on 27th April 1939 some months prior to hostilities breaking out, and was to only sail on her again twice despite the fact that the vessel (renamed in 1948 PERTH (VI)) remained in the fleet until 1963. When LOCHEE (II) was not available for the Southampton sailings, the steamer KILDRUMMY was substituted and it was to this vessel that he was transferred in April 1939. After the outbreak of war, he became master in quick succession of ARBROATH (III), ABOYNE, CONIDA and again ARBROATH (III) before taking command of CLOVA in May 1940. He remained on her until July 1942 except for short spells on KILDRUMMY and ABOYNE during the early part of 1942.

The steamer DUNDEE (VII) was his next command. He took her over in the Thames during July 1942 and he remained with her until May 1943 when the vessel was taken up as a convoy rescue ship. He then went once more to ABOYNE but she in turn was also taken up as a rescue ship in July 1943.

For the rest of the war Captain Campbell commanded KILDRUMMY employed sailing between Dundee and Hull. On 10th July 1944 he was awarded the MBE (Member of the Order of the British Empire) in recognition of his services. As a master with long experience in the coasting trade, his knowledge was invaluable to convoy commodores who frequently chose his ship as their headquarters.

He continued in command of KILDRUMMY after the war had ended and only left her when she was transferred to the Coquet Shipping Co. Ltd. in the autumn of 1946. He then took command at Cardiff of the managed vessel EMPIRE CAPE prior to her acquisition by the Company and being renamed GOWRIE (III). A quick succession as relief master of LOCHEE (II) and again GOWRIE (III) took place before he returned to ABOYNE. He delivered the latter vessel to Belfast on 25th September 1946 prior to her sale to the Clyde Shipping Co. Ltd. of Glasgow.

He then went to Aberdeen to stand by the new motor vessel LUNAN and sailed her out of that port on 22nd October 1946. He remained with her as master until December 1950 when it was then known that she would be going to Canada early in 1951, so transferred to GOWRIE (IV) then lying at Leith. On delivery in March 1951 of the new LONDON (VII) by Burntisland Shipyard he moved to her and for the next 13 years he spent a considerable amount of time in command of this vessel when she was employed on the Thames service.

During the times that LONDON (VII) was employed in Canadian waters he transferred to GLAMIS, as well as carrying out reliefs on LUNAN during a few weeks in 1956 and 1957. From July 1957 he took command of BROUGHTY (II) for three months subsequently being her relief master for a few weeks each year during 1959, 1960 and 1961. He returned in January 1959 as relief master of PERTH (VI) — ex-LOCHEE (II) — for a short period.

In May 1960 he sailed DUNDEE (VIII) from Liverpool to South Shields during her short stay in this country between Canadian seasons. He subsequently "collected" her at Avonmouth in August 1963 and took her round to Hull, and in May 1965 from South Shields for "delivery" to Liverpool prior to her setting out to cross the Atlantic once again.

From June 1960 Sandy Campbell's permanent commands were either LOCHEE (III) or LONDON (VII) when employed on the Thames sailings, as GLAMIS had been earmarked for sale. In turn he was to deliver LONDON (VII) to Grangemouth on 5th September 1964 prior to her sale to Canadian owners, and then LOCHEE (III) to Runcorn on 29th July 1966 on her sale to Greek owners. For a period from March 1965 the vessel had been employed between Manchester/Liverpool and Northern Ireland.

While waiting for another command, Captain Campbell undertook a holiday relief on Channel Shipping Co. Ltd.'s GROUVILLE (II) during September 1966. In November of the same year he took command of the coastal tanker KINGENNIE at the Isle of Grain on the River Medway. He was to remain with her until he came ashore on 6th February 1967 shortly before the ownership of the vessel changed hands.

Although Sandy Campbell was now 65, his sea time was not yet over. KINGENNIE, still managed and crewed by the Company, required a master for a short period so he rejoined her on 25th July 1967 and made voyages from the Isle of Grain to Copenhagen, Gothenburg, Ghent, Dunkirk and Swansea. After his discharge on 2nd September 1967 he remained ashore during 1968 but when the crewing department found themselves having to find a master at short notice to replace one that had suddenly taken ill, he was rushed out to Paris to sail Channel Shipping Co. Ltd.'s CONCORDE (II) from the Seine to Ipswich.

Sandy Campbell was "pressed into service" again in 1969 when a suitably qualified 2nd mate could not be found for KINGENNIE. He joined this ship again on 10th August at the Isle of Grain and after two voyages, one to Ghent and the other to Swansea and Leixoes, northern Portugal, he finally signed off at the Isle of Grain on 26th August 1969.

M.T.V. "KINGENNIE"—1,369 TONS DEADWEIGHT

KINGENNIE

During his 53 years at sea, Captain Sandy Campbell MBE had spent some eight years as a seaman, nearly 10 years as a mate, and the rest of his service as a master of 18 different ships ranging in tonnage from 409 to 1,781 tons gross. He continued to reside in Dundee until his death in July 1993, aged 91.

EPILOGUE

Although the Company sold KINGENNIE in March 1967 and were then no longer shipowners, they still had an interest in Lockett Wilson Line, and through them Channel Shipping, and their five ships, but when these ships could no longer compete with groupage services using roll-on roll-off ferries and containers, they were sold in 1968.

Dundee Wharf on the Thames, the site of which had been purchased by the Company in 1897 at a cost of £186,028, was sold for over £278,000 in October 1969. The wharf had been damaged in an air raid in September 1940 and in the early 1950s had been extensively rebuilt and extended so that by 1958 it was considered one of the most modern wharves on the Thames. From 1952 the wharf had been the terminal of the Lockett Wilson Line's Paris service and had been kept busy until 1961 when the Dundee sailings were suspended. Subsequently in 1964 Lockett Wilson Line moved their terminal to Ipswich, but this was in some degree offset by the Brussels Steamship Co.'s sailings which moved to the wharf when the Company acquired an interest in that firm. By 1966 however, the operation of the wharf was unrewarding and a loss was made on its operation in 1967. The wharf was closed down on 31st December 1968.

Dundee Wharf, Limehouse, London

The Company still had some connections with the sea as the result of various acquisitions over the years. In 1955 they had acquired a firm of ship chandlers, Andrew Gray Ltd., with premises quite close to their head office, and the agency side of this business was strengthened some years later by the purchase of two other long established agencies, Leslie Shipping Co. and P. S. Nicoll & Co. Ltd. The former firm was at one time the owner of a fleet of tramp steamers but had latterly confined its activities to agency work, stevedoring and warehousing. Leslie Shipping Co. had some years earlier taken over the agency of another once active shipowning firm, Andrew Leitch & Co., managers of the Dundee Loch Line Steam Shipping Co., who had been one of the original tenants of the Company's head office building.

A substantial interest had been held since 1966 in Dundee Stevedores & Porters Ltd. and later the Company bought the entire share capital. It also acquired James Allison & Sons (Sailmakers) Ltd., a firm that had once owned the iron barques COUNTESS OF DERBY (775/77) and a COUNTESS OF ROTHES (769/76) until sold in 1895/96 as well as making sails, and this firm was now amalgamated with Andrew Gray Ltd. to form Allison-Gray Ltd., dealing in a comprehensive range of shipping and oil rig supplies.

A London bid for the control of the Company was accepted by the Board and the majority of the shareholders in July 1972, and the subsequent activities of the group in an ever-widening field of road haulage and warehousing are no part of this history. To preserve the Company's traditional name however, P. S. Nicoll & Co. Ltd., was renamed Dundee, Perth & London Shipping Co. Ltd., becoming responsible for the Company's activities based on Dundee.

For many years the North Sea oil industry made its presence felt on Dundee and it revolutionised the business of the port with it becoming a base for supply vessels at Queen Elizabeth Wharf which British Petroleum took on a 21 year lease. The Company became more deeply involved in North Sea operations in 1973 when an agreement was reached with Thiess-Petrosea International to operate a supply base from the western section of Eastern Wharf. This 600-foot wharf with its broad apron construction by the Dundee Harbour Trust, was re-opened as Princess Alexandra Wharf in May 1974, and became one of the most efficient bases on the east coast of Scotland.

BOARD OF DIRECTORS 1976
(Standing) A. W. Beasley, A. Wallace, C. D. Lepper (Secretary), S. Aitken
(Seated) J. M. Chalmers (Managing Director), K. M. D. Mills (Chairman), H. B. Pirie

The dependence of the Company from the coastal liner trades to North Sea oil and transport and industrial activities was achieved by the mid-70s and many years of co-operation with British Petroleum were enjoyed. However, British Petroleum's access to the British supply base at Peterhead meant that their activities were severely rationalised and the Company's off-harbour storage space was sold for redevelopment in September 1992. Meantime, Princess Alexandra Wharf was handed back to the Dundee Harbour Authority.

Around this time serious development of Dundee's historic and natural geographic links with Scandinavia and the Baltic began to take place with the obvious emphasis on forest products. Over recent years the Company has acted as agents for both shipping and cargo interests for ever increasing tonnages of newsprint and chemical pulps.

The Company eventually became part of the Coalite Group, which itself was taken over by the Chesterfield-based fuel distribution group Anglo United plc in 1989. In April 1993, however, the Company returned to local ownership after more than 20 years, when Cortachy Holdings Ltd., owned by the current chairman and managing director, a team of father and son, James M. Chalmers and Alasdair D. Chalmers, together with the Bank of Scotland, acquired the Company and so once again became part of the local business community. The Dundee, Perth & London Shipping Company Ltd. and its subsidiaries has now interests in property, freight forwarding, ships' agency, travel agencies, industrial supplies and personnel.

Dundee, having celebrated its 800th anniversary in 1991, flourished over a century ago with the development of the jute industry and there was a time when ships queued in the estuary for a berth at which to unload jute from the Indian sub-continent. Jute, a significant import and is still spun, woven and made into sacks, carpet backing and twine, and has to battle not only against cheap foreign products but also against the new fibre polypropylene. The emphasis of traffic has moved from the old impounded docks (some of which were filled-in to make way for the Tay Road Bridge opened on 18th August 1966), to riverside wharves and the port has spent considerable sums over the years in upgrading these and its other infrastructure such as sheds and cranage. In addition to forest products and jute, Dundee handles significant quantities of crude oil and oil products and agricultural bulks.

The ships of the Dundee, Perth & London Shipping Company Ltd. no longer sail for the Thames and the Humber from their traditional berths in Victoria Dock close to the Company offices, but the Company is still very much to the fore. With a proven record of adaptability, and its strong links with the sea through its ships' agency business, it looks forward with optimism to completing its double century in the year 2026.

For many decades, Dundee, Perth & London ships, with their familiar red and black funnels and Tayside nomenclature were very much part of the Dundee scene, so much so in fact, that there was a local saying that "the three best known men in Dundee were the Lord Provost, the Chief Constable and the Skipper o' the PERTH".

Victoria Dock, Dundee about 1891 — in the foreground, the iron sailing ship MIDDLESEX (1884) under survey, and in the background, CAMBRIA, with the lighter CAROLINE alongside, and LONDON (IV) *G.E. Langmuir Collection*

FLEET LISTS
Notes

1. The notation (I), (II) etc. after a ship's name indicates the first, second etc. ship of that name in the combined fleets.
2. The dates following the name are those of entry and leaving the particular fleet.
3. All sailing vessels were constructed of wood, except CLEOPATRA (Appendix A, No. 40) which was built of iron.
4. All powered vessels were constructed of steel and screw propelled unless otherwise stated.
5. Official Number for vessels is shown after the letters ''O.N.''.
6. Tonnages for sailing vessels are ''registered'', with those of powered vessels being gross — ''g'', and net — ''n''.
7. Dimensions for all vessels are registered length x beam x depth to the nearest foot for sailing vessels, and in feet and tenths of a foot for powered vessels.
8. Details of ships' engines show (for steamers) whether compound, or triple expansion (if appropriate), and (for motor vessels) the number of stroke cycles of the single acting engine.
9. Horse power is shown for steamers as ''hp'' — registered or nominal, or for motor vessels as ''bhp'' — brake.
10. The date of building shown is that recorded on the vessel's registration document.
11. the fact that a powered vessel changed and did not change its name on transfer of ownership is shown. However, with sailing vessels this entry has been omitted as none of them changed name.
12. The ships' histories are correct as at March 1995.

APPENDIX A — DUNDEE, PERTH & LONDON SHIPPING CO. — SAILING VESSELS

1. BRIDPORT PACKET (1826-1827) Smack.
117 reg. 66 x 21 x 11 feet.
1793: Built at Bridport for John Richardson & Co., Perth. *10.1806:* Taken over by Dundee & Perth Shipping Co. *7.1826:* Taken over by the Company (value £1,168) *9.1827:* Sold to Thomas Keith, Dundee. *4.1828:* Sold to Thomas Malcolm, Dundee. *4.1837:* Sold to D. Smith & others, Montrose. *25.8.1837:* Foundered off the island of Bornholm, Baltic Sea after springing a leak while on passage from Portrush, Ireland to Memel, Prussia

2. NEWCASTLE & BERWICK PACKET (1826-1831) Sloop.
54 reg. 50 x 18 x 9 feet.
1798: Built at Berwick-on-Tweed for Berwick Shipping Co., Berwick-on-Tweed. *1805:* Sold to Dundee Shipping Co., Dundee. *10.1806:* Taken over by Dundee & Perth Shipping Co. *7.1826:* Taken over by the Company (value £587). *6.1831:* Sold to David Watson, Dundee. *3.1839:* Sold to David Gibb, Dundee. *1.1843:* Sank near Aberdeen.

3. OSNABURGH (1826-1827) Smack.
104 reg. 62 x 21 x 11 feet.
6.1800: Built at Bridport for John Richardson & Co., Perth. *10.1806:* Taken over by Dundee & Perth Shipping Co. *7.1826:* Taken over by the Company (value £2,199). *7.1827:* Sold to Martin Bryde & Thomas Gray, Montrose. *10.1839:* Sold to E. Snook, London. *5.1841:* Dismasted and driven ashore at North Sunderland, Northumborland, where she became a total loss.

4. LORD KINNAIRD (1826-1829) Smack.
121 reg. 66 x 22 x 11 feet.
12.1802: Built at Bridport for John Richardson & Co., Perth. *10.1806:* Taken over by Dundee & Perth Shipping Co. *1.1819:* Sold to Dundee & Perth Union Co., Dundee. *1824:* Re-purchased by Dundee & Perth Shipping Co., Dundee. *7.1826:* Taken over by the Company (value £1,351). *8.1829:* Sold to Scott & Duell, Montrose. *4.1832:* Sold to J. E. Blewitt, Plymouth. *8.1835:* Stranded at entrance to Arbroath and later broken up.

5. TAY (I) (1826-1830) Sloop.
55 reg. 45 x 16 x 7 feet.
1.1807: Built at Dundee for Dundee & Perth Shipping Co. *7.1826:* Taken over by the Company (value £321). *9.1830:* Sold to James Beatton, Dundee. *3.1831:* Sold to William Scott, Dundee. *1.1839:* Sold to J. Greig, Dundee. *7.1841:* Sold to J. Hunter (of Dysart), Kirkcaldy and later to Thomas Graham (her master). *9.1845:* Sold to Thomas Graham & William Spain, Sunderland. *3.1847:* Sold to J. Weatherburn, Newcastle. *5.1848:* Transferred to Mrs. M. A. Weatherburn. *31.1.1849:* Foundered off St. Abbs Head, Berwickshire.

6. DEFIANCE (1826-1827) Smack.
93 reg. 59 x 20 x 10 feet.
1807: Built at Bridport for Tay Shipping Co., Dundee. *1808:* Sold to Dundee & Perth Shipping Co. *7.1826:* Taken over by the Company (value £1,821). *9.1827:* Sold to Arbroath & London Shipping Co., London. *5.1841:* Sold to D. Allan & W. F. Black, London. *20.9.1843:* Wrecked near Arbroath while bound inward from London.

7. UNION (1826-1834) Smack.
113 reg. 65 x 21 x 11 feet.
11.1807: Built at Bridport for Tay Shipping Co., Dundee. *1808:* Sold to Dundee & Perth Shipping Co. *7.1826:* Taken over by the Company (value £1,446). *9.1834:* Sold to W. & E. Kendall, Gloucester and re-rigged as a schooner. *10.1836:* Sold to P. W. Lamb & R. Hurry (of Waterford), Cork. *17.10.1840:* Wrecked near Amlwch while on passage from Ireland to Liverpool.

The London Boat 1826

8. PERTH (I) (1826-1830) Sloop.
43 reg. 44 x 16 x 7 feet.
6.1809: Built at Dundee for Dundee & Perth Shipping Co. *7.1826:* Taken over by the Company (value £312). *6.1830:* Sold to William Chapman (of Broughty Ferry), Dundee. *5.1838:* Sold to William Kerr, Dundee. *2.1839:* Repurchased by William Chapman, Dundee. *1.1840:* Sold to James Thomson & others, Dundee. *11.1842:* Sold to Mrs. E. Borrie, Dundee. *12.1842:* Sold to G. Scrymegour, Dundee. *6.1843:* Sold to T. Moncur & T. Adam, Dundee. *10.1846:* Transferred to ownership of T. Moncur, T. Adam, and John Kinnear, Dundee. *9.1848:* Sold to John Collins, Dundee. *3.1849:* Sold to William Flarty, Sunderland. *10.1850:* Sold to D. Croy, Dingwall. *7.1869:* No longer afloat and records closed.

9. MARY (I) (1826-1834) Sloop.
O.N. 10219. 56 reg. 52 x 16 x 9 feet.
9.1811: Built at Dundee for Dundee & Perth Shipping Co. *7.1826:* Taken over by the Company (value £684). *9.1834:* Sold to J. M. Vintner, Dundee. *2.1842:* Sold to Charles Fleming, Dundee. *4.1843:* Transferred to Dundee & Hull Shipping Co., Dundee. *4.1844:* Sold to John Farrow, Dundee. *8.1853:* Sold to J. Simpson & D. Pipe, Arbroath. *6.1854:* Transferred to J. Simpson & A. Gavine Thomson, Arbroath. *16.12.1867:* Struck Boulmer Steel Rock and abandoned off Dunstanburgh Castle, Northumberland.

10. ANNA (1826-1838) Sloop.
86 reg. 56 x 17 x 10 feet.
4.1813: Built at Dundee for Dundee & Perth Shipping Co. *7.1826:* Taken over by the Company (value £837). *2.1838:* Sold to James Webster, Dundee. *23.7.1843:* Wrecked near Berwick-on-Tweed.

11. OLIVE (1826-1834) Smack.
O.N. 22272. 90 reg. 64 x 18 x 12 feet.
10.1814: Built at Berwick-on-Tweed for Commercial Shipping Co., Berwick-on-Tweed. *12.1822:* Sold to Dundee & Perth Union Shipping Co. *7.1826:* Taken over by the Company (value £1,766). *5.1834:* Sold to D. Myles, Dundee, and re-rigged as a schooner. *11.1834:* Sold to William Bennett, Dundee. *9.1844:* Repurchased by D. Myles, Dundee. *1.1849:* Sold to J. Howard, Dundee. *4.1851:* Sold to C. Low & J. Deuchars, Dundee. *10.1.1864:* Wrecked on Fowler Rock off Dundee and declared a constructive total loss.

12. COURIER (1826-1849) Smack.
O.N. 3578. 141 reg. 70 x 22 x 12 feet.
1816: Built at Newcastle-upon-Tyne for Leith, Hamburgh & Rotterdam Shipping Co., Leith. *1.1823:* Sold to Dundee & Perth Union Shipping Co. *7.1826:* Taken over by the Company (value £2,224). *5.1849:* Sold to James A. Dickson, Arbroath. *1.1854:* Sold to David Salmond, Arbroath. *1.1855:* Sold to James Reid, Arbroath. *13.10.1858:* Wrecked on Newcombe Sands, Lowestoft.

13. ELBE (1826-1849) Smack.
O.N. 12003. 121 reg. 68 x 19 x 11 feet.
1816: Built at Newcastle-upon-Tyne for Leith, Hamburgh & Rotterdam Shipping Co., Leith. *3.1823:* Sold to Dundee & Perth Union Shipping Co. *7.1826:* Taken over by the Company (value £2,183). *1836:* Re-rigged as a schooner. *8.1849:* Sold to Thomas Sproat, Kirkcudbright. *1851:* Re-rigged as a brigantine. *4.1853:* Sold to Samuel Wilson, Dumfries. *7.12.1866:* Lost on voyage from Maryport to Barlochan, near Dalbeathie, Kirkcudbright.

14. GLASGOW (1826-1837) Smack.
O.N. 1352. 107 reg. 68 x 20 x 11 feet.
1816: Built at Newcastle-upon-Tyne for Leith, Hamburgh & Rotterdam Shipping Co., Leith. *2.1825:* Sold to Dundee & Perth Union Shipping Co. *7.1826:* Taken over by the Company (value £2,472). *8.1837:* Sold to Samuel Wilson, Kirkcudbright. *1865:* Lengthened to 98 feet, tonnages now 157g, 132n. *4.1891:* Sold to William Walker junior, Dumfries. *1893:* Sold to Mary Halliday, Dumfries. *1.1897:* Sold to Donald MacGregor, Inverness. *4.1901:* Sold to J. MacDonald (K. Grant, manager), Inverness and reduced to a lighter.

15. PERTH (II) (1826-1837) Smack.
O.N. 6857. 132 reg. 69 x 22 x 12 feet.
11.1816: Built at Blyth for Dundee & Perth Shipping Co., *7.1826:* Taken over by the Company (value £2,344). *3.1837:* Sold to George Cameron, Dundee. *12.1846:* Sold to William Davidson & David Luckie, Dundee. *11.1848:* Owner became David Luckie. *8.1854:* Sold to John Leslie, Aberdeen. *1.11.1861:* Foundered between Newcastle and Aberdeen with a cargo of coal — all six crew lost.

16. DUNDEE (I) (1826-1834) Smack.
151 reg. 73 x 22 x 12 feet.
12.1818: Built by John Calman, Dundee for Dundee & Perth Shipping Co. *7.1826:* Taken over by the Company (value £2,845). *8.1834:* Sold to John Calman, Dundee. *1836:* Lost off Holland.

17. MERSEY (I) (1826-1830) Sloop.
O.N. 17998. 73 reg. 55 x 18 x 10 feet.
1.1819: Built by A. B. Gowan, Berwick-on-Tweed for Dundee & Perth Union Shipping Co. *7.1826:* Taken over by the Company (value £791). *9.1830:* Sold to D. Sutherland, Montrose. *5.1852:* Sold to A. Mitchell, Aberdeen. *5.1853:* Sold to D. Sutherland senior & junior, Montrose. *6.1854:* Sold to David Low, Montrose. *18.8.1856:* Sank off Filey, Yorkshire.

18. FISHERS (1826-1847) Sloop.
31 reg. 42 x 14 x 7 feet.
10.1820: Built by James Smart, Dundee for Dundee & Perth Shipping Co. *7.1826:* Taken over by the Company (value £416). *11.1847:* Sold to Peter Henderson, Dundee. *6.1849:* Stranded but salvaged by John Calman, Dundee. *2.1850:* Sold to David Walker, Dundee. *4.1.1854:* Wrecked in the Firth of Tay.

19. FRIENDS (1826-1832) Sloop.
O.N. 18026. 38 reg. 43 x 15 x 7 feet.
1821: Built at Leith for Bo'ness owners. *6.1823:* Purchased by Dundee & Perth Union Shipping Co. *7.1826:* Taken over by the Company (value £274). *4.1832:* Sold to F. Greig & R. Kilgour, Kirkcaldy. *10.1836:* Owner became R. Kilgour. *3.1838:* Sold to P. D. Swan, Kirkcaldy. *6.1842:* Sold to George Fowler (of Pittenweem), Kirkcaldy. *3.1861:* Sold to Angus Murray, Wick. *3.8.1867:* Lost off Holborn Head, Thurso, Caithness.

20. FORFARSHIRE (1826-1832) Smack.
145 reg. 77 x 22 x 12 feet.
5.1823: Built by John Calman, Dundee for Dundee & Perth Union Shipping Co. *7.1826:* Taken over by the :company (value £3,090). *4.10.1832:* Lost off St. Abbs Head, Berwickshire.

21. JANE (1826-1848) Sloop.
69 reg. 55 x 17 x 10 feet.
4.1823: Built by James Brown, Perth for Dundee & Perth Shipping Co. *7.1826:* Taken over by the Company (value £1,199). *11.1848:* Sold to Alexander Noble, Fraserburgh. *30.3.1850:* Lost with all hands in a gale off Newcastle-upon-Tyne while on passage from Perth to London.

22. LONDON (I) (1826-1847) Smack.
O.N. 26638. 115 reg. 69 x 20 x 11 feet.
1824: Built by Richard Russell & Son, Lyme for Dundee & Perth Shipping Co. *7.1826:* Taken over by the Company (value £3,859). *9.1847:* Sold to Robert Tosh, Dundee and re-rigged as a schooner. *1851:* Registered at London. *1861:* Re-registered at Dundee. *5.2.1862:* Ran ashore on Beacon Rock off Dundee, while on passage from London and became a total loss.

23. LIVERPOOL (1826-1827) Sloop.
O.N. 26703. 99 reg. 61 x 19 x 11 feet.
1.1826: Built by Thomas Wilkie, Newburgh for Dundee & Perth Shipping Co. *7.1826:* Taken over by the Company (value £1,391). *5.12.1826:* Driven ashore at Great Ormes Head, North Wales but refloated and drydocked at Liverpool. *1.1827:* Condemned and sold by public auction for £200. *10.1827:* Sold to P. Horn & P. Hayes, Wexford and re-rigged as a brig. *1.1838:* Sold to R. Phelan, Waterford. *12.1848:* Transferred to Mrs. M. Phelan, Waterford. *12.1850:* Sold to Thomas Powre, Waterford. *1858:* Lost.

24. SOVEREIGN (1828-1853) Smack.
O.N. 7212. 159 reg. 76 x 22 x 13 feet.
7.1828: Built by John Calman, Dundee for the Company. *1836:* Re-rigged as a schooner. *5.1853:* Sold to G. W. Brewer, Dundee. *2.1854:* Sold to David Mackenzie, Arbroath. *4.1863:* Sold to D. G. Pinkney, Sunderland. *6.1864:* Sold to S. G. Halls, Colchester. *1875:* Sold to W. J. Garling, Colchester. *1880:* Sold to H. Vane, Colchester. *30.10.1882:* Wrecked on Newcombe Sands, Lowestoft while on passage from Seaham to Portsmouth with a cargo of coal.

25. ROSE (II) (1828-1849) Sloop.
O.N. 15096. 88 reg. 59 x 19 x 10 feet.
11.1828: Built by John Calman, Dundee for the Company. *10.1849:* Sold to Robert Rollo & John White, Dundee. *4.1855:* Sold to William Colchester (of Ipswich) & John Watts (of Harwich). *1857:* Lengthened to 79 feet, and re-rigged as schooner, tonnage now 106. *3.1864:* Sold to J. Whitmore & J. Watts, Harwich. *3.1868:* Sold to William Flick, Ipswich. *30.3.1901:* Wrecked off Felixstowe, Suffolk, while on passage from Ipswich to Guernsey with a cargo of stone.

26. DAME (1829-1836) Sloop.
63 reg. 55 x 18 x 10 feet.
1807: Built at Dundee for Dundee owners. *1824:* Owned by George Clark, Dundee. *5.1829:* Purchased by the Company. *5.1836:* Sold to John Kennedy, Dundee. *3.10.1842:* Sank off Dunkirk while on passage from Dundee to Dunkirk, Northern France.

27. GIPSY (1829-1848) Sloop.
65 reg. 54 x 17 x 9 feet.
1805: Built at Dundee for Dundee owners. *9.1824:* Owned by George Clark, Dundee. *5.1829:* Purchased by the Company. *12.1848:* Sold to J. Guthrie & R. Melville, Arbroath. *7.1851:* Sold to William Wilkie, Arbroath. *9.1851:* Sold to James Cables, Arbroath. *10.1854:* Driven ashore near Redcar, Yorkshire and became a total loss.

28. TID (1829-1836) Schooner.
80 reg. 59 x 18 x 11 feet.
8.1800: Built by John Calman, Dundee for Dundee owners. *9.1824:* Owned by George Clark, Dundee. *5.1829:* Purchased by the Company. *10.1835:* Ran ashore on Elbe Sands, River Tay but refloated. *9.1836:* Sold to Thomas Adamson, Dundee. *3.1839:* Sold to Nicoll Webster, Sime & Coul, Dundee. *12.1847:* Missing while on passage from Stettin.

29. FORTH (1830-1849) Sloop.
72 reg. 54 x 17 x 10 feet.
6.1830: Built by John Calman for the Company. *5.1849:* Sold to James Crichton, Dundee. *5.1851:* Sold to Thomas Wren & Sons, Stockton. *1855:* Lost.

30. SWAN (1830-1868) Sloop.
O.N.7175. 62 reg. 55 x 14 x 8 feet.
6.1830: Built by David Calman, Dundee for the Company. *7.1868:* Sold to Andrew Law, Dundee. *23.7.1868:* Wrecked in the Pentland Firth while on passage from Peterhead to Easdale, Argyllshire, in ballast.

31. TAY (III) (1830-1868) Sloop.
O.N. 7173. 60 reg. 58 x 16 x 8 feet.
12.1830: Built by David Calman, Dundee for the Company. *8.1868:* Sold to Robert A. Mudie, Dundee. *1870:* Broken up.

32. STAR (1831-1849) Sloop.
O.N. 10428. 64 reg. 53 x 16 x 10 feet.
7.1831: Built by James Horsburgh, William Roger & John Smith, Dundee for the Company. *6.1849:* Sold to John Allan & James Moir, Banff. *5.1856:* Sold to L. Woodford, Sunderland. *27.1.1867:* Lost near Cromarty.

33. LARK (1831-1868) Schooner.
O.N. 7174. 47 reg. 54 x 14 x 8 feet.
12.1831: Built by James Horsburgh & Joseph Garland, Dundee for the Company. *7.1868:* Sold to William Edwards, Newburgh. *7.1873:* Sold to William Gunn, Granton. *12.1881:* Broken up.

34. CLYDE (1834-1849) Sloop.
O.N. 801. 74 reg. 58 x 19 x 10 feet.
7.1834: Built by Garland & Horsburgh, Dundee for the Company. *5.1849:* Sold to James Brown & George Robertson, Montrose, and re-rigged as a schooner. *3.11.1861:* Ran ashore near Gravelines, Northern France and became a total loss.

35. MERSEY (II) (1834-1849) Sloop.
O.N. 10205. 79 reg. 56 x 17 x 10 feet.
7.1834: Built by Garland & Horsburgh, Dundee for the Company. *6.1849:* Sold to Peter Mill, Arbroath, and re-rigged as a schooner. *12.1863:* Sold to Joseph Salmond, Arbroath. *9.9.1886:* Wrecked 2 miles from Golspie, Sutherland while on passage from Nairn to Littleferry, Sutherland in ballast.

36. MARY (II) (1835-1849) Sloop.
O.N. 7209. 75 reg. 57 x 17 x 10 feet.
2.1835: Built by John Calman, Dundee for the Company. *7.1849:* Sold to John Johnston & Neil Ross, Dundee, and re-rigged as a schooner. *5.1865:* John Johnston became sole owner. *18.2.1867:* Lost off Coquet Island, Northumberland.

37. ROE (1835-1849) Sloop.
O.N. 7179. 62 reg. 52 x 16 x 10 feet.
12.1835: Built by A. & R. Brown, Dundee for the Company. *4.1849:* Sold to Peter Ritchie, Dundee. *1855:* Re-rigged as a schooner. *9.12.1861:* Wrecked at Whitby, Yorkshire.

38. DART (1836-1849) Sloop.
64 reg. 54 x 16 x 10 feet.
7.1836: Built by A. & R. Brown, Dundee for the Company. *5.1849:* Sold to George Bruce, Arbroath. *1853:* Re-rigged as a schooner. *1853:* Wrecked at St. Abbs Head, Berwickshire.

39. SWIFT (1838-1849) Sloop.
O.N. 21711. 75 reg. 56 x 17 x 10 feet.
10.1838: Built by Dundee Shipbuilding Co. (Robert Young & Henry Chapman), Dundee for the Company. *7.1849:* Sold to Peter Gibson, Port William, Wigtownshire. *5.1854:* Passed to Mary Gibson. *10.1855:* Passed to son Robert Gibson on her decease. *2.1856:* Sold to James & John Lightbody, Glasgow. *1872:* Re-rigged as a schooner. *22.4.1880:* Stranded at Port Charlotte, Islay but refloated. *5.1880:* Sold to J. Morrow, Glasgow. *10.1884:* Sold to John McGibbon (of Port Ellen), Glasgow. *5.1886:* Broken up at Irvine, Ayrshire.

40. CLEOPATRA (1847-1863) Schooner.
O.N. 7170. 200 reg. 117 x 23 x 13 feet.
6.1847: Built by Alexander Denny, Dumbarton (Yard No. 4) for the Company. *2.1863:* Sold to G. Duncan & Co., London, and re-rigged as a schooner. *1874:* Sold to T. D. Boyd (of Amoy, China). *2.1875:* Sold to A. J. Johnson, Melbourne. *1877:* Sold to William Sinnott, Melbourne. *1882:* Sold to William H. Smith & Sons Ltd., Melbourne and later to J. Hockin, Melbourne. *1887:* Reduced to a lighter. *1894:* Sold to J. Madden, Melbourne. *1918:* Dropped from Register — presumed dismantled.

41. ZENOBIA (1847-1861) Schooner.
O.N. 7123. 190 reg. 107 x 24 x 13 feet.
8.1847: Built by John Brown & Co., Dundee for the Company. *9.1861:* Sold to A. Hunter, London. *2.1867:* Sold to J. May & W. Tanner, Newhaven, Sussex. *11.1875:* William Tanner became managing owner. *12.1880:* Condemned and broken up.

42. VICTORIA (1849-1863) Schooner.
O.N. 7206. 194 reg. 102 x 22 x 14 feet.
10.1849: Built by John Brown, Dundee for the Company. *1.1863:* Sold to B. B. Mason, Hull. *19.3.1872:* Foundered off the North Foreland, Straits of Dover.

43. SOLICITOR (1852-1856) Schooner.
O.N. 425. 146 reg. 90 x 21 x 12 feet.
1849: Built by Calman & Martin, Dundee for C. R. Calman, London. *12.1852:* Purchased by the Company. *12.1856:* Sold to Ellerby & Co., Hull. *6.1859:* Lost.

44. GEORGE DUNCAN (1853-1860) Schooner.
O.N. 7110. 158 reg. 92 x 20 x 12 feet.
9.1847: Built by David Calman, Dundee for Dundee & Hull Shipping Co. *9.1853:* Purchased by the Company. *23.1.1860:* Sank near Shipwash Sands, Norfolk while on passage from Dundee to London.

45. FALCON (1854-1863) Schooner.
O.N. 7107. 122 reg. 93 x 20 x 12 feet.
3.1854: Built by Tay Shipbuilding Co., Dundee for the Company. *4.1863:* Sold to G. H. Hamby, Ipswich. *1882:* Sold to S. Cawthorn, Ipswich. *6.1888:* Broken up.

46. QUEEN (I) (1857-1861) Schooner.
O.N. 7114. 115 reg. 73 x 18 x 12 feet.
5.1842: Built by Menzies & Co., Leith for Dundee & Hull Shipping Co. *2.1857:* Taken over by the Company. *8.2.1861:* Wrecked in a gale on Whitby Sands, Yorkshire.

APPENDIX B — DUNDEE, PERTH & LONDON SHIPPING CO. (1826-1914), DUNDEE, PERTH & LONDON SHIPPING CO. LTD. (1914-1967) — STEAMERS AND MOTOR VESSELS

1. SIR WILLIAM WALLACE (1830-1851) Wood — Paddle tug.
70 g, 43 n. 75.6 x 16.7 x 7.6 feet.
Engines (2), 34 hp.
12.1830: Built by Thomas Adamson, Dundee. *1842:* Reduced to a lighter. *1851:* Broken up.

2. DUNDEE (II) (1834-1864) Wood — Paddle.
O.N. 7154. 638g, 399n. 167.6 x 28.5 x 18.3 feet.
Engine by Robert Napier, Port Glasgow, 300hp
2.1834: Built by John Wood, Port Glasgow. *11.1864:* Sold to French owner for service in the cattle trade between Genoa and Alexandria and renamed NETTUNO — no further record.

PERTH (III) off Dundee

3. PERTH (III) (1834-1861) Wood — Paddle.
O.N. 7127. 635g, 399n. 167.6 x 28.2 x 18.3 feet.
Engine by Robert Napier, Port Glasgow, 300hp
4.1834: Built by John Wood, Port Glasgow. *7.1861:* Sold to General Steam Navigation Co., London, name unchanged. *8.11.1864:* Destroyed by fire in the Royal Dockyard at Deptford when in use as a hulk.

4. LONDON (II) (1837-1853) Wood — Paddle.
O.N. 32519. 687g, 406n. 167.0 x 26.7 x 18.0 feet.
Engine by Robert Napier, Port Glasgow.
7.1837: Built by John Wood, Port Glasgow. *5.1853:* Sold to E. Baxter & Son, G. Armitstead and others, Dundee, name unchanged. *6.1853:* Sold to Sydney & Melbourne Steam Packet Co., Sydney, New South Wales. name unchanged. *7.1856:* Sold to Australasian Steam Navigation Co. (R. M. Robey and E. M. Sayers, managers), Sydney, N.S.W., named unchanged. *1861:* Sold to Harkort & Co., Hong Kong, name unchanged. *6.1863:* Broken up.

5. MARS (1848-1851) Iron.
89 g, 62n. 81.8 x 19.2 x 8.7 feet.
Engine by Caird & Co., Glasgow, 20hp
6.1848: Built by Alexander Denny, Dumbarton (Yard No. 8). *3.5.1851:* Sank after striking a rock 1 mile east of Crail, Fife while on passage from Grangemouth to Dundee.

6. NEPTUNE (1848-1854) Iron.
O.N. 40922. 89g, 62n. 82.8 x 19.2 x 8.8 feet.
Engine by Caird & Co., Glasgow, 20hp
6.1848: Built by Alexander Denny, Dumbarton (Yard No. 7). *10.1851:* Lengthened to 90.8 feet, tonnages now 111g, 84n. *5.1854:* Sold to G. L. Alison, Dundee, engine removed and reduced to a schooner, name unchanged. *11.1857:* Sold to Mauritius owners, name unchanged. *9.1862:* Drops out of the Register — last reported sailing out of Mauritius.

7. HERCULES (I) (1849-1853) Wood — Paddle tug.
O.N. 41471. 97g, 36n. 83.7 x 17.0 x 9.6 feet.
Beam engine, James Steel, Dundee, 62hp
6.1849: Built by Calman & Martin, Dundee. *2.1853:* Sold to John Oswald, Melbourne, name unchanged, and rebuilt. *4.1853:* Sailed from Dundee with engine unshipped for passage to Australia. *2.1854:* Owners now Alexander Dove & John Oswald, Melbourne. *11.1883:* Sold to James Deane, Melbourne, name unchanged, and rebuilt. *10.1885:* Sold to Melbourne Coal, Shipping & Engineering Co. Ltd., Melbourne, name unchanged. *4.1886:* Name of owners became Melbourne Steamship Co. Ltd. *2.1925:* Sold to William M. McBain & George Barnes, Melbourne, and reduced to a lighter. *7.1930:* Broken up.

8. HERCULES (II) (1853-1865) Wood — Paddle tug.
O.N. 7143. 62g, 41n. 80.5 x 17.1 x 8.4 feet.
Engine 30hp
7.1853: Built by J. Downey, North Shields, *5.1865:* Sold to James Easson, Perth, name unchanged. *5.1866:* Sold to David Edwards (owner and master), Dundee, name unchanged. *7.1867:* Sold to William Turnbull, North Shields, name unchanged. *2.1871:* Sold to Anthony Strong, North Shields, name unchanged. *10.1873:* Reverted to ownership of William Turnbull. *7.1880:* Sold to John Simpson & Robert Hedley, South Shields, name unchanged. *11.1882:* Broken up.

LONDON (III) as MARIA ANTOINETTA *From a painting in the Naval Musuem, Dubrovnik*

9. LONDON (III) (1854-1854) Iron.
512g, 333n. 184.0 x 26.2 x 15.0 feet.
2-cyl., by builders, 120hp
5.1854: Built by R. Napier & Sons, Govan, Glasgow. *8.1854:* Sold to H. J. Barker & B. W. Ford (of Constantinople), London, name unchanged. *9.1856:* Sold to H. Oppenheim, Constantinople, Turkey and renamed MARIA ANTONIETTA. *1901:* Believed broken up.

HULL *G. E. Langmuir Collection*

10. LONDON (IV)/HULL (1856-1909) Iron.
O.N. 15088. 622g, 423n. 209.9 x 28.2 x 15.9 feet.
2-cyl., by builders, 140hp
4.1856: Built by Gourlay Bros. & Co., Dundee (Yard No. 3). *18.11.1865:* Sank after collision with the steamer HARVEST QUEEN (562/60) in the River Tay off Monifieth. *22.12.1866:* Salvaged by Henry Gourlay and repaired. *1872:* Lengthened to 243.9 feet, and tonnages now 763g, 495n; new engine fitted, compound, 2-cyl., by builders, 140 hp. *1892:* Renamed HULL. *20.1.1897:* Beached near Pile Light off Tayport, Fife after a collision with the steamer ALICE TAYLOR (714/91) of Dundee. *28.10.1909:* Sailed from Dundee for breaking up at Bridgeness near Bo'ness, West Lothian, by Forth Shipbreaking Co.

11. QUEEN (II) (1857-1876) Iron.
O.N. 7109. 294g, 181n. 159.9 x 22.1 x 13.1 feet.
2-cyl., by builders, 100hp
8.1854: Built by R. Napier & Sons, Port Glasgow (Yard No. 62) for Dundee & Hull Shipping Co., Dundee. *2.1857:* Taken over by the Company. *6.1876:* Sold to W. B. Thompson, Dundee, name unchanged, and fitted with new engine, compound, 2-cyl., by builders, 58hp. *1.1882:* Sold to W. McIlwraith, Glasgow, name unchanged. *11.1885:* Sold to W. H. Sollas, London, name unchanged. *4.1888:* Sold to Cia. Hispano-Argelina, Almeria, Spain and renamed ESPERANZA. *1896:* Sold to A. Ruiz, Almeria, name unchanged. *18.1.1908:* Sank after collision outside Bilbao, Spain, while outbound in ballast for San Esteban, northern Spain.

12. HAMBURG (1857-1863) Iron.
O.N. 19287. 385g, 284n. 180.5 x 25.2 x 13.6 feet.
2-cyl., by builders, 90hp
7.1857: Built by Gourlay Bros. & Co., Dundee (Yard No. 5). *1.1863:* Sold to General Steam Navigation Co., London, name unchanged. *6.11.1886:* Sold to James Livingston for £300 and broken up.

13. SAMSON (1857-1869) Iron – Paddle tug.
O.N. 19290. 82g, 36n. 81.8 x 18.3 x 9.5 feet.
Lever engine, 2-cyl., by builders, 40hp
10.1857: Completed by T. D. Marshall, South Shields, *10.1869:* Sold to Alexander Edwards (of Newburgh), Dundee, name unchanged. *9.1870:* Sold to James Currie (of Leith), London, name unchanged. *10.1870:* Sold to The Governor & Co. of the Copper Miners in England (James Shaw, manager), London, name unchanged. *6.1884:* Sold to William A. Osborn & Humphrey Wallis, Bristol, name unchanged. *6.1885:* Sold to George Nurse & William Galbraith, Bristol, altered to screw propulsion, fitted with 1-cyl. engine of 9hp made by G. K. Stothert & Co., Bristol. Renamed CLIFTON. *6.1903:* Reverted to the ownership of William A. Osborn & Humphrey Wallis, name unchanged and lengthened to 103.2 feet, tonnages now 102g 77n. *9.1921:* Owners became Osborn & Wallis Ltd. *7.1930:* Broken up by John Cashmore Ltd. at Newport, Mon.

14. EAGLE (1858-1871) Iron.
O.N. 20366. 318g, 215n. 164.3 x 22.8 x 12.6 feet.
2-cyl., by builders, 85hp.
2.1858: Built by Gourlay Bros. & Co., Dundee (Yard No. 6). *8.1871:* Sold to Peter Barr & Archibald Fawcett, Leith and later to J. N. Moore, Swansea, name unchanged. *29.7.1879:* Sank about 25 miles NNE of Bishops Rock while on passage from Swansea to Dublin with a cargo of coal.

15. SCOTIA (I) (1861-1862) Iron.
O.N. 29459. 655g, 482n. 211.3 x 28.2 x 16.5 feet.
2-cyl., by builders, 140hp.
9.1861: Built by Gourlay Bros. & Co., Dundee (Yard No. 11). *6.1862:* Sold to Peirano, Danovaro & Co., Genoa and renamed ADRIATICO. *1876:* Lengthened to 236.8 feet, tonnages now 1,154g, 742n. *1878:* Sold to Rubattino & co., Genoa, name unchanged. *1881:* Transferred to Navigazione Generale Italiana, Genoa. *1884:* New engine fitted, compound, 2-cyl. by Peirano, Danovaro & Co., Genoa, 143 hp. *1894:* Fitted with new engine, compound, 2-cyl., by Odero & Co., Genoa, 112hp. *1914:* Sold to G. Pittaluga, Genoa, name unchanged. *1926:* Broken up.

16. SCOTIA (II) (1862-1870) Iron.
O.N. 45194. 658g, 191n. 211.4 x 28.8 x 16.5 feet.
2-cyl., by builders, 155hp.
10.1862: Built by Gourlay Bros. & Co., Dundee (Yard No. 14). *9.1869:* Lengthened by builders to 251.4 feet, tonnages now 802g, 535n; new engine fitted, compound, 2-cyl, 155hp. *3.8.1870:* Run down in fog by s.s. MAGNA CHARTA (964/65) off Gotland, Sweden while on passage from Newcastle to Cronstadt with a cargo of coal.

17. ANGLIA (1863-1883) Iron.
O.N. 45816. 664g, 452n. 213.4 x 28.0 x 16.3 feet.
2-cyl., by builders, 155hp.
9.1863: Built by Gourlay Bros. & Co., Dundee (Yard No. 18). *19.12.1867:* In collision with the brigantine GEORGE (149/65) near Newarp Light Vessel, the sailing vessel sinking with the loss of six lives. *1871:* Lengthened by builders to 253.4 feet, tonnages now 827g, 520n; new engine fitted, compound, 2-cyl., 155hp. *19.11.1875:* Struck a rock while steaming through inside passage to Farne Islands when bound for London. *7.1883:* Sold to George Gibson & Co., Leith, name unchanged. *1898:* Fitted with new compound 2-cyl. engine, 179 hp, by J & J Thomson, Glasgow, tonnages now 908g, 453n. *18.2.1903:* Sank after collision with the Danish s.s. OLGA (777/75) in the North Sea while on passage from Rotterdam to Leith with general cargo.

18. HIBERNIA (1865-1876) Iron.
O.N. 52561. 658g, 454n. 217.8 x 27.9 x 16.1 feet.
2-cyl., by builders, 180hp.
1.1865: Built by Gourlay Bros. & Co., Dundee (Yard No. 22). *1872:* Lengthened by builders to 259.4 feet, tonnages now 850g, 512n; fitted with new engine, compound, 2-cyl., by builders, 200hp. *23.10.1873:* In collision with the sailing barque BRITISH BANNER (387/55) of Newcastle off Shipwash Sands, Norfolk – latter sank with the loss of six crew. *30.1.1876:* Stranded on the Farne Islands, Northumberland, while on passage from London to Dundee with a general cargo. Refloated but grounded again on Holy Island Harbour Bar. *5.2.1876:* Broke in two and abandoned. *6.1876:* Wreck sold to a Mr. Barclay of Dunbar for £385 plus £30 for her cargo of jute.

19. ATLAS (1865-1873) Iron-Paddle tug.
O.N. 45829. 96g, 45n. 84.8 x 18.6 x 9.6 feet.
Side-Lever (2), by builders, 50hp.
2.1865: Built by Gourlay Bros. & Co., Dundee (Yard No 23). *3.1873:* Sold to David Edwards & Robert Anderson, Dundee, name unchanged. *12.1873:* Sold to W. & J. Watkins, London, name unchanged. *2.1874:* Renamed TITAN. *10.1888:* Sold to Robert White, Hartlepool, name unchanged. *5.1890:* Sold to J. Batey & Son , Newcastle, name unchanged. *6.1920:* Owners became Lawson-Batey Tugs Ltd., Newcastle. *4.1937:* Broken up at Dunston by Clayton & Davie Ltd.

20. GALLIA (1865-1868) Iron.
O.N. 52568. 441g, 355n. 190.5 x 24.1 x 13.7 feet.
2-cyl., by builders, 90hp.
8.1865: Built by Gourlay Bros. & Co., Dundee (Yard No. 26) as a speculation and launched without a name, being subsequently bought by the company and named GALLIA. *1.8.1868:* Sold to H. C. Moss, London and renamed VICTORIA. *15.9.1868:* Arrived at Ferrol, Spain from Shields for delivery to foreign owners — no further record.

21. CAMBRIA (1868-1891) Iron.
O.N. 60784. 729g, 456n. 216.0 x 28.2 x 16.1 feet.
2-cyl., by builders, 180hp.
5.1868: Built by Gourlay Bros. & Co., Dundee (Yard No. 35). *1873:* Lengthened by W. B. Thompson, Dundee to 266.0 feet tonnages now 944g, 599n. *1874:* New engine fitted by W. B. Thompson, Dundee, 2-cyl., 230hp. *3.1879:* Damaged in collision with the s.s. SPERO (871/78) of Newcastle off Scarborough and beached in River Tyne. *1888:* New engine fitted, triple, 3-cyl., by builders, 260hp. *14.5.1891:* Beached on Cross Sands after collision with the s.s. KILLINGWORTH (527/55) 5 miles from Great Yarmouth, Norfolk while on passage from London to Grangemouth on charter to The Carron Co. — 24 passengers and 26 crew taken off by lifeboat. Subsequently became a total loss.

22. SCOTIA (III) (1875-1880) Iron.
O.N. 73387. 453g, 288n. 179.5 x 24.1 x 14.3 feet.
Compound, 2-cyl., by builders, 98hp.
5.1875: Built by W. B. Thompson, Dundee (Yard No. 7). *8.1880:* Sold to Cie. Anon. des Paquetbots du Finistère, Havre, France and renamed FINISTÈRE. *1912:* Sold to Charles Schiaffino, A. Jouvet & Cie., Algiers, name unchanged. *1920:* Owners' title now Schiaffino & Cie. *1925:* Sold to N. M. Gavalas, Piraeus, Greece and renamed CALLIOPI. *5.9.1927:* Ran ashore near Volo (now Volos), Greece but later refloated. *1930:* Broken up.

BRITANNIA in Victoria Dock, Dundee *Dundee District Libraries*

23. BRITANNIA (1877-1889) Iron.
O.N. 75202. 938g, 499n. 254.8 x 29.5 x 16.7 feet.
Compound, 2-cyl., by builders, 250hp.
3.1877: Built by Gourlay Bros. & Co., Dundee (Yard No. 79). *3.1885:* In collision with the Broughty Ferry fishing boat GOOD INTENT in the River Tay, the latter sinking. *3.1887:* In collision with the sailing ship DARLING DOWNS (1,715/52) off Newcastle, the latter sinking. *2.1889:* Sold to George Gibson & Co., Leith, name unchanged. *1893:* New engine fitted, triple, 3-cyl. by S. & H. Morton & Co., Leith, 210hp. *5.6.1904:* Sank after collision with the Norwegian s.s. FLUGT (776/71) south of Flamborough Head, Yorkshire while on passage from Leith to Dunkirk via the Tyne and Middlesbrough with a general cargo.

24. NORTH SEA (1881-1896) Iron.
O.N. 82741. 1,117g, 725n. 230.0 x 30.9 x 15.9 feet.
Compound, 2-cyl., by Pearce Bros., Dundee, 120hp.
4.1881: Built by Alexander Stephen & Sons, Dundee (Yard No. 75). *2.1888:* Sank in shallow water after a collision in the River Tyne, and later refloated. *2.1896:* Sold to North Sea Steam Ship Co. Ltd., (J. P. Bruce, manager), Dundee, name unchanged. *8.5.1896:* Ran ashore on Stroma Island, Pentland Firth in fog while on passage from Glasgow to Copenhagen with a cargo of coal, and later broke up.

25. WHITE SEA (1881-1896) Iron.
O.N. 82743. 1,119g, 725n. 230.3 x 30.7 x 15.9 feet.
Compound, 2-cyl., by Pearce Bros., Dundee, 120hp.
5.1881: Built by Alexander Stephen & Sons, Dundee (Yard No. 76). *1.1896:* Sold to Palgrave, Murphy & Co., Dublin and renamed CITY OF COLOGNE. *7.1917:* Sold to Transport & Trading Co. Ltd. (of London), Dublin, name unchanged. *11.1921:* Sold to C. Petzalis and El. Dounias, Spetsai, Greece and renamed ANDREAS on previous owners going into liquidation. *1926:* C. Petzalis became sole owner. *1927:* Sold to Apostopoulo Freres, Cavalla, Greece and renamed STATHIS A. *11.1933:* Arrived at Savona, Italy for breaking up.

26. DUNDEE (III) (1883-1885)
O.N. 86373. 1,565g, 783n. 270 x 32.7 x 17.7 feet.
Compound, 2-cyl., by builders, 350hp.
5.1883: Built by Gourlay Bros. & Co., Dundee (Yard No. 117). *4.1885:* Sold to the Italian Government and renamed VOLTA. No longer listed after 1920.

DUNDEE (IV) at Dundee *G. E. Langmuir Collection*

27. DUNDEE (IV) (1885-1909)
O.N. 89097. 1,305g, 687n. 270.0 x 34.1 x 15.7 feet.
Triple, 3-cyl., by builders, 300hp.
11.1885: Built by Gourlay Bros. & Co., Dundee (Yard No. 128). *2.1893:* Lost propeller when off the Yorkshire coast and towed to Dundee. *1.1909:* In collision with the brig GOOD HOPE off Caister, Norfolk, the latter sinking with loss of four lives. *3.12.1909:* In collision with the s.s THAMES (1,372/87) of Grangemouth while on passage from Dundee to London and run ashore above Chatham & Dover Railway Pier, River Medway, Kent with engine room flooded. Later slipped off into deep water and capsized. *10.5.1910:* Raised and beached but declared a constructive total loss. *31.8.1910:* Left the River Medway in tow for Felixstowe, Suffolk to be broken up.

28. RED SEA (1889-1892)
O.N. 96403. 1,930g, 1,251n. 275.0 x 37.2 x 15.8 feet.
Triple, 3-cyl., by builders, 180hp.
7.1889: Built by W. B. Thompson & Co. Ltd., Dundee (Yard No. 90). *9.1892:* Sold to Booth Steam Ship Co. Ltd., Liverpool and renamed HILARY. *1.1905:* Sold to Rhederei Hilary G.m.b.H. (Sander, Wieler & Co., managers), Danzig, name unchanged. *1908:* Now registered at Cologne. *1911:* Sold to H. Fukagawa, Tarumi, Japan and renamed MISUMI MARU. *1916:* Sold to Towa Kisen K.K., Kobe and renamed TORYU MARU. *1923:* Sold to Hashimoto Seitaro, Shigaken, name unchanged. *1925:* Sold to Koike Goshi Kaisha, Tarumi, name unchanged. *1926:* Sold to Koryu Shokai Goshi Kensha, Kobe, name unchanged. *1928:* Sold to Yamamoto Shoten Goshi Kaisha, Kobe, name unchanged. *2.5.1945:* Torpedoed and sunk by the United States submarine RATON west of Chemulpo, Korea.

RED SEA as HILARY *G. E. Langmuir Collection*

29. CAROLINE (1890-1904) Wood.
O.N. 84681. 121g, 71n. 93.0 x 23.6 x 9.6 feet.
Compound, 2-cyl., by Whyte & Cooper, Dundee, 15hp.
Built in Sweden as a sailing vessel. *3.1888:* Acquired by W. Malcolm, Bo'ness, name unchanged. *9.1889:* Purchased by Robert Gunn & William Kidd, Dundee, name unchanged and converted into a steamer. *6.1890:* Purchased by the Company, name unchanged. *8.1904:* Broken up.

30. PERTH (IV)/ARBROATH (I) (1890-1920)
O.N. 96411. 1,729g, 956n. 280.0 x 36.6 x 16.9 feet.
Triple, 3-cyl., by builders, 450hp.
7.1890: Built by W. B. Thompson & Co. Ltd., Dundee (Yard No. 95). *2.1915:* Renamed ARBROATH. *12.1917:* Requisitioned by the Admiralty as a transport for service in the Mediterranean. *3.1918:* Transferred for service between Southampton and Havre. *7.1919:* Returned to owners. *4.1920:* Sold to British & South American Steam Navigation Co. Ltd. (R. P. Houston & Co., managers), Liverpool and renamed HELLOPES. *4.1927:* Sold to Devlet Denizyollare Isletmesi, Istanbul, Turkey and renamed KONYA. *1938:* Name of owners became Denizbank unum Müdürlügü. *7.1939:* Name of owners became Devlet Denizyoolari Ilsetmesi unum Müdürlügü. *5.1944:* Name of owners became Devlet Denizyolari ve Limanlari Isletmesei unum Müdürlügü. *3.1952:* Name of owners became Denizalib Bankasi T. A. O. *6.1955:* Name of owners became Deniz Nakliyati T. A. S. *12.1955:* Laid-up at Istanbul. *3.1959:* Reported broken up at Halic by Hurdacilik Turk Anonim Ortakligi.

PERTH (IV) in Victoria Dock, Dundee *Dundee District Libraries*

31. LONDON (V) (1892-1918)
O.N. 99213. 1,706g, 858n. 280.0 x 36.6 x 16.9 feet.
Triple, 3-cyl., by builders, 425 hp.
5.1892: Built by Gourlay Bros. & Co., Dundee (Yard No. 153). *4.1901:* Fire broke out in a hold while on passage to London with a general cargo and 13 passengers, which crew fought for 11 hours whilst the vessel put back to Dundee. *14.2.1913:* In collision with the sailing vessel EDINBURGH (1,473/85) while on passage from Dundee to London, when 2 miles west of Haisborough Light Vessel, Norfolk, with the latter sinking with the loss of 31 lives. *23.6.1918:* Torpedoed and sunk 4 miles E. by S. of Whitby by U 88 while on passage from Methil to London with a cargo of coal and general.

LONDON (V) in Thames *G. H. Somner Collection*

32. CARBON/FAIR CITY (1904-1947)
O.N. 118739. 131g, 75n. 90.0 x 20.0 x 8.3 feet.
Compound, 2-cyl., by Cooper & Greig, Dundee, 15hp.
4.1904: Built by Dundee Shipbuilders' Co. Ltd., Dundee (Yard No. 145). *1920:* Engine built in 1899 fitted, compound, 2-cyl, by Lobnitz & Co., Renfrew, 18hp, and renamed FAIR CITY. *8.1940:* Requisitioned by the Admiralty for service in the Firth of Forth. *10.1940:* Found to have insufficient power so returned to owners. *7.1946.* Laid-up at Dundee. *6.1947:* Sold to Tay Sand Co. Ltd., Dundee and renamed TAYFIRTH. *3.1954:* Broken up by James A. White, St. Davids-on-Forth, Fife.

FAIR CITY at Dundee *G. E. Langmuir Collection*

33. GOWRIE (I) (1909-1917)
O.N. 123330. 1,031g, 441n. 240.1 x 32.2 x 16.6 feet.
Triple, 3-cyl., by builders, 216hp.
8.1909: Built by Caledon Shipbuilding & Engineering Co. Ltd., Dundee (Yard No. 210). *10.10.1917:* Torpedoed and sunk by U 53 when 14 miles NE of Cherbourg while on passage to that port from Newhaven with a general cargo and mails.

GOWRIE (I) *G. E. Langmuir Collection*

34. DUNDEE (V) (1911-1917)
O.N. 123338. 2,187g, 987n. 290.1 x 41.2 x 18.6 feet.
Triple, 3-cyl., by builders, 452hp.
11.1911: Built by Caledon Shipbuilding & Engineering Co. Ltd., Dundee (Yard No. 221). *10.1915:* Commissioned as an Armed Boarding Steamer and attached to 10th Cruiser Squadron. *16.3.1917:* In company with H.M.S. ACHILLES was in action with the German raider LEOPARD. *3.9.1917:* Torpedoed and sunk by UC 19 at the entrance to the English Channel, eight lost.

35. PERTH (V) (1915-1946)
O.N. 123346. 2,208g, 1,110n. 280.2 x 40.2 x 19.8 feet.
Triple, 3-cyl., by builders, 345hp.
7.1915: Built by Caledon Shipbuilding & Engineering Co. Ltd., Dundee (Yard No. 240). *27.8.1915:* Commissioned as an Armed Boarding Steamer and based in the Red Sea at Perim. *1.10.1918:* When acting as sole convoy escort on a voyage from Gibraltar to the English Channel, took part in a five hour gun battle with a U-boat. *4.1919:* Returned to owner. *9.1919:* Resumed commercial sailings. *14.10.1940:* Requisitioned as an accommodation ship at Rosyth. *3.1941:* Taken over for service as a convoy rescue ship. *6.1945:* Returned to owners. *4.1946:* Sold to Falkland Islands Co. Ltd., London, fitted to burn oil fuel, and renamed LAFONIA. *1.1950:* Sold at London to Lloyd Mediterraneo S.p.A., Rome, Italy and renamed VALFIORITA. *1961* Sold to Carlo Ghetti Lolli & Co., S.p.A., Rome, name unchanged. *8.11.1962:* Dismantling commenced at Nogaro by Armando Berretta.

PERTH (V) *G. H. Somner Collection*

36. TAY & TYNE (1917-1917)
O.N. 123329. 556g, 237n. 180.1 x 26.1 x 12.4 feet.
Triple, 3-cyl., by Cooper & Greig, Dundee, 97hp.
1.1909: Built by Dundee Shipbuilding Co. Ltd., Dundee (Yard No. 204) for Dundee & Newcastle Steamship Co. Ltd., Dundee. *3.1917:* Taken over by the Company. *6.1917:* Requisitioned by the Admiralty. *9.1917:* Sold to the Admiralty for service as a 'Q' ship. *1920:* Converted to storeship and renamed INDUSTRY. *31.10.1924:* Sold to Möre Fylkes Ruteselskap, Mölde, Norway and renamed MÖREJARL I, later MÖREJARL and registered at Christiansund. *1950:* Owners restyled Möre og Ramsdal Fylkesbatar. *1951:* Sold to Ceuleman & Sons, Antwerp for scrapping. *1.1952:* Demolition commenced.

TAY & TYNE *G. E. Langmuir Collection/Ambrose Greenway Collection*

37. LOCHEE (I) (1918-1936)
O.N. 123347. 1,064g, 543n. 212.2 x 33.9 x 13.3 feet.
Triple, 3-cyl., by Richardsons, Westgarth & Co. Ltd., Sunderland, 176hp.
2.1918: Built by Charles Hill & Sons, Bristol (Yard No. 126). *12.2.1927:* Ran ashore on Inchkeith, Firth of Forth and refloated badly damaged. *5.1936:* Sold to Onesimus Dorey & Sons Ltd., Guernsey and renamed PORTELET. *2.2.1940:* Sank after striking a mine when 3 miles SW by W of Smith's Knoll Light Vessel, while on passage from Ipswich to Sunderland in ballast — two of 11 crew lost.

LOCHEE (I) *G. H. Somner Collection*

38. LADY GWENDOLEN (1918-1919)
O.N. 132505. 2,163g, 133n. 300.2 x 39.7 x 17.5 feet.
Triple, 3-cyl., by builders, 362hp.
9.1911: Built by Clyde Shipbuilding & Engineering Co. Ltd., Port Glasgow (Yard No. 294) for British & Irish Steam Packet Co. Ltd., Dublin. *5.1916:* Requisitioned for Russian Government service for use of the Governor of Archangel. *13.2.1918:* Arrived at London from Archangel and returned to her owners. *7.1918:* Purchased by the Company, name unchanged. *6.1919:* Sold to New York, Newfoundland & Halifax Steam Ship Co. Ltd., (C. T. Bowring & Co. Ltd., managers), Liverpool and renamed ROSALIND. *9.1921:* Registered at St John's, Newfoundland. *9.1923:* Re-registered at Liverpool. *2.1929:* Sold to Bermuda & West Indies Steam Ship Co. Ltd., Hamilton, Bermuda, name unchanged. *3.1936:* Sold to "Zetska Plovidba" A. D., Kotor, Yugoslavia and renamed LOVCEN. *1940:* Sold to Cia. Centro Americana de Navegacion Ltda, Panama, name unchanged. *1941:* Sold to United States Government and renamed COLUMBIA and later BRIGADIER GENERAL HARRY E RETHERS. *1946:* Sold to Chan Kin Cheong, Canton, China and renamed WAH CHUNG. *1950:* Sold to Grande Shipping Corporation S.A., Panama and renamed TERESA. *1952:* Reported broken up in China.

LADY GWENDOLEN *D. Donnan*

39. NORTH INCH (1919-1921)
O.N. 119163. 100g, 30n. 66.5 x 18.3 x 8.8 feet.
Compound, 2-cyl., by Denny & Co., Dumbarton, 7hp.
9.1904: Built by William Denny & Bros, Dumbarton (Yard No. 735) for Andrew MacG. Leslie, Glasgow as GARMOYLE. *11.1908:* Sold to A.F. Henry & MacGregor Ltd., Leith, name unchanged. *4.1919:* Purchased by the Company and renamed NORTH INCH. *7.1921:* Sold to Colin & Colin S. McPhail, Glasgow and renamed STRONSHIRA. *1.1933:* Sold to Shira Steam Ship Co. Ltd., Glasgow, name unchanged. *4.1946:* Sold to Arran Sea Transport & Supply Co. Ltd., Brodick, name unchanged. *10.1946:* Renamed ARRAN ROSE. *21.2.1948:* Ran ashore in Carnlough Harbour, Northern Ireland, but later refloated and towed to Belfast. *5.1949:* Towed to Ardrossan, Ayrshire for repairs. *12.1953:* Sold to James A. White, North Queensferry, Fife, name unchanged. *1960:* Broken up at St Davids-on-Forth.

40. DUNDEE (VI) (1919-1933)
O.N. 123348. 1,381g, 562n. 270.6 x 38.1 x 16.2 feet.
Triple, 3 cyl., by builders, 196hp.
6.1919: Built by Caledon Shipbuilding & Engineering Co. Ltd., Dundee (Yard No. 268), having been laid down as WAR WENSUM for The Shipping Controller, London. *8.1933:* Sold to Mossgiel Steam Ship Co. Ltd., (John Bruce & Co., managers), Glasgow and renamed ALCORA. *30.10.1940:* Wrecked 2 miles north of Rattray Head, Aberdeenshire, one of six ships in a convoy to meet a similar fate, while on passage from Seville to River Tees with a cargo of pyrites, cork and general cargo.

DUNDEE (VI) at Kirkcaldy 19.7.1931 *E. J. Wylie*

GOWRIE (II) *G. E. Langmuir Collection*

41. GOWRIE (II) (1919-1940)
O.N. 129243. 689g, 285n. 178.0 x 30.0 x 12.3 feet.
Triple, 3-cyl., by Charles D. Holmes & Co. Ltd., Hull, 93hp.
9.1909: Built by Cochrane & Sons Ltd., Selby (Yard No. 450) for George R. Haller Ltd., Hull as HALLER. *7.1919:* Purchased by the Company and renamed GOWRIE. *9.1.1940:* Sunk in air attack when 4 miles east of Stonehaven, while on passage from Hull to Aberdeen with a general cargo.

42. LOUGA (1919-1937)
O.N. 90918. 945g, 394n. 213.0 x 32.1 x 12.3 feet.
Triple, 3-cyl., by builders, 188hp.
4.1898: Built by Ramage & Ferguson Ltd., Leith (Yard No. 155) for Thomas Cowan, Grangemouth. *3.1899:* Transferred to Rasona Steam Ship Co. Ltd. (Thomas Cowan, manager). *11.1919:* Purchased by the Company, name unchanged. *8.4.1922:* Fire broke out in the engine room, and vessel towed into Blyth, Northumberland. *23.12.1935:* Broke her shaft after leaving Southampton and towed back into port. *9.1937:* Sold to Sandelis Akcine Bendrove, Klaipeda, Lithuania and renamed NIDA. *15.11.1939:* Wrecked on Oland Island, Baltic Sea while on passage from the Tyne to Hernosand, Sweden with a cargo of coke.

LOUGA *Laurence Dunn/G. E. Langmuir Collection*

43. ROSYTH (I) (1919-1934)
O.N. 118734. 409g, 158n. 175.0 x 25.1 x 11.7 feet.
Triple, 3-cyl., by Cooper & Greig, Dundee, 132hp.
12.1903: Built by Dundee Shipbuilders' Co. Ltd., Dundee (Yard No. 143) for their own account. *12.1903:* Sold to Kirkcaldy Steamship Co. Ltd., Kirkcaldy, name unchanged. *31.10.1915:* Stranded at Whitburn, south of the River Tyne. *7.11.1915:* Refloated and towed to Sunderland for repairs. *11.1917:* Sold to Wear Steam Shipping Co. (1917) Ltd., Sunderland, name unchanged. *12.1919:* Purchased by the Company, name unchanged. *9.1934:* Sold to William J. Ireland, Liverpool and renamed QUICKTHORN. *11.1937:* Transferred to Ribble Shipping Co. Ltd. (William J. Ireland, manager), Liverpool. *6.1940:* Sold to G. W. Grace & Co., London, name unchanged. *15.1.1942:* Foundered in heavy weather off Skokholm Island, Pembrokeshire while on passage from Newport, Monmouthshire to Londonderry, Northern Ireland with a cargo of coal.

ROSYTH (II) *G. E. P. Brownell/W.S.P.L.*

44. ARBROATH (II) (1920-1922)
O.N. 144625. 1,014 g, 520 n. 214.6 x 32.1 x 13.7 feet.
Triple, 3-cyl., by builders, 182hp.
1909: Built by Act. Ges. "Neptun", Rostock (Yard No. 288) for Riga-Lübecker Dampfschiffahrts Ges., Lübeck, Germany as ALEXANDRA. *7.1920:* Seized and passed to The Shipping Controller, London. *11.1920:* Purchased by the Company and renamed ARBROATH. *5.1922:* Sold to South Shipping Co. Ltd., Quebec and renamed GASPESIA. *1.1928:* Sold to Clarke Steamship Co. Ltd., Quebec, name unchanged. *3.1946:* Renamed NORTH VOYAGEUR. *8.1950:* Sold to Cia. de Navegacion Mundial S.A., Honduras, name unchanged. *22.10.1950:* Foundered SE of Cape Race, Newfoundland while on passage from Philadelphia, U.S.A. to St John's, Newfoundland with a cargo of anthracite.

45. LONDON (VI) (1921-1942)
O.N. 144702. 1,491g, 794n. 250.5 x 35.3 x 16.8 feet.
Triple, 3-cyl., by builders, 175hp.
1921: Built by Hawthorns & Co. Ltd., Leith (Yard No. 183). *22.3.1923:* Fire broke out in the bunkers and the vessel put into River Tees. *29.8.1937:* Sank in collision off Humber Light Vessel with the steamer RAYFORD (471/94) of Methil, but refloated and repaired. *9.1938:* On charter to the Admiralty during the Munich crisis period. *28.8.1939:* Requisitioned by the Admiralty as an Examination Vessel. *10.1939:* Renamed HOLDFAST. *8.1940:* Returned to owners. *1.1942:* Requisitioned by the Admiralty for conversion to a pipe laying vessel to lay the PLUTO pipe line across the English Channel on D-Day. *10.1942:* Commissioned as H.M.S. HOLDFAST. *7.1946:* Sold to the Ministry of Transport, London and renamed EMPIRE TAW for the recovery of the PLUTO pipe line. *9.1952:* Sold to James Scott & Co. (Cork) Ltd., Cork, for use as a hulk and towed to Passage West, Cork. *1953:* Broken up.

LONDON (VI) *F. A. Plant*

46. BROUGHTY (I) (1921-1951)
O.N. 144705. 504g, 200n. 166.1 x 25.3 x 9.6 feet.
Triple, 3-cyl., by William Beardmore & Co. Ltd., Glasgow, 84hp.
10.1921: Completed by Scott & Sons, Bowling, having been launched by Larne Shipbuilding Co., Larne (Yard No. 80) which had now gone into liquidation. *3.11.1921:* Stranded on her maiden voyage on Abertay Sands while inbound from Hull. *23.11.1927:* Sank at Kirkcaldy, Fife after striking the pier, subsequently being refloated and taken to Leith for repairs. *5.1951:* Sold to J. & A. Gardner & Co. Ltd., Glasgow and renamed ST. RONAIG. *14.12.1955:* Ran ashore at Torr Head, Co. Antrim while on passage from Garston to Westport, Co. Mayo with coal and salt. Abandoned as a total loss and sold for demolition.

BROUGHTY (I) *W. H. Brown*

47. KIRKALINE (1924-1941) Twin-screw lighter.
O.N. 139901. 152g, 103n. 125.8 x 16.4 x 7.3 feet.
Fitted 1925. Two compound, 2-cyl., by F. T. Harker & Co., Stockton.
1918: Built by James R. Piper, Greenwich, London as dumb barge A.C.1282 for the War Department. *1923:* Now owned by Smith's Dock Co. Ltd., Middlesbrough. *12.1924:* Purchased by the Company. *1925:* Fitted with twin screw engines and renamed KIRKALINE for service at Hull. *1.1941:* Sold to Frederick Oldridge, of Bilton, Yorkshire, name unchanged. *2.1942:* Sold to Flixborough Shipping Co. Ltd., of Scunthorpe, name unchanged. *1.1943:* Sold to Lincoln & Hull Water Transport Co. Ltd., Hull, name unchanged, afterwards having her engines removed. *1966:* Sold to D. Cook Ltd., New Holland Shipyard, Barrow-upon-Humber for demolition but sank in shallow water there and abandoned.

48. ANILINE (1924-1942) Lighter.
O.N. 148251. 49g, 33n. 65.8 x 16.3 x 6.6 feet.
Compound, 2-cyl. by Fisher & Co., Paisley, 7hp.
10.1889: Built by J. & J. Hay, Kirkintilloch (last launch from the yard 28.9.1889) for James Ross & Co. (of Falkirk) to carry tar in bulk. *12.1924:* Purchased by the Company, name unchanged. *11.1942:* Sold to Aldridges' Wharf Ltd. (Frederick Aldridge, manager), Hull, name unchanged. *5.1949:* Sold to William Stamp Ltd. of Hull, name unchanged. *6.1958:* Now fitted with an oil engine — conversion prior to this date. *1.1965:* Sold to Bulk Carriers Ltd., Hull, name unchanged. *3.1969:* Sold to C.D.N. Marine Services (Immingham) Ltd., Hull, name unchanged. *1978:* Believed broken up at Hayle, Cornwall.

ANILINE *G. E. Langmuir Collection*

49. W (1930-1930) Lighter.
O.N. 993223. 73 g, 44n. 65.8 x 17.6 x 8.0 feet.
Compound, 2-cyl., by builders, 11hp.
9.1891: Built by John Cran & Co., Leith (Yard No. 28) for James Currie, Leith. *2.1899:* Transferred to Leith, Hull & Hamburg Steam Packet Co. Ltd. (James Currie, manager), Leith, name unchanged. *2.1915:* Sold to Smith & Watt Ltd. (of Dunfermline), name unchanged. *10.1920:* Owners went into liquidation and vessel acquired by North Eastern Shipping Co. Ltd., Leith, name unchanged. *2.1922:* Owners went into liquidation and vessel acquired by Charles Wood, Leith, name unchanged. *3.1930:* Purchased by the Company, but immediately sold to James A. White (of North Queensferry), name unchanged. *1.1938:* Broken up.

50. YENDIS/ROSYTH (II) (1930-1949)
O.N. 132265. 132g, 65n. 99.8 x 18.3 x 7.6 feet.
Compound, 2-cyl., by Cooper & Greig, Dundee, 25hp.
9.1911: Built by J. Scarr & Son, Howden for Leetham & Sons Ltd., Hull as YENDIS. *10.1928:* Sold to Spillers Ltd., Hull, name unchanged. *3.1930:* Purchased by the Company, name unchanged. *8.1935:* Renamed ROSYTH. *4.1947:* Broke moorings whilst lying at Eastern Wharf, Dundee and collided with the steamers OLNA FIRTH (509/33), DRUMLOUGH (311/21) and the Caledon Shipbuilding yard's slipway. *11.1947:* Sank at Perth but later raised. *4.1949:* Sold to George T. MacLennan, Dundee for service as a sand boat and renamed DAVID P. *4.10.1950:* Foundered in Camperdown Dock, Dundee but later raised. *15.1.1952:* Abandoned off Newport, Fife in a gale and drifted down river but later reboarded and towed to Dundee. *8.2.1956:* Foundered near Middle Bank, River Tay. *1957:* Wreck dispersed.

ROSYTH (II) entering Leith *G. E. Langmuir Collection*

51. ERROL (I) (1932-1935)
O.N. 145442. 396g, 226n. 140.0 x 24.6 x 11.5 feet.
Triple, 3-cyl., by Machinefabriek "Overrijn", Leiden, 31hp.
1920: Built by Gebr. Müller, Foxhol for unknown owners as B.W. 1. *12.1920:* Sold to Manor Steam Ship Co. Ltd. (George M. Wheater, manager), Newcastle and renamed EVELYN MANOR. *1.1923:* Sold to John M. Allison, Dundee, name unchanged. *10.1932:* Purchased by the Company and renamed ERROL. *30.7.1935:* In collision with the s.s. CAIRNESK (5,007/26) 1½ miles SW of Inchkeith while on passage from Leith to Kirkcaldy in ballast, and sank off Leith. *17.8.1935:* Raised and beached near Leith where she was examined and being beyond economical repair was towed to Bo'ness, West Lothian for breaking up.

52. DUNDEE (VII) (1934-1948)
O.N. 144713. 1,541g, 625n. 283.8 x 42.3 x 15.8 feet.
Triple, 3-cyl., by Alexander Stephen & Sons Ltd., Glasgow, 361hp.
2.1934: Built by Caledon Shipbuilding & Engineering Co. Ltd., Dundee (Yard No. 345). *5.1943:* Requisitioned for service as a convoy rescue ship. *6.1945:* Returned to owners. *5.1948:* Sold to British & Continental Steam Ship Co. Ltd., Liverpool and renamed DOTTEREL. *4.1950:* Converted to burn oil fuel. *28.8.1961:* Arrived at Bilbao, Spain for breaking up by A. F. Ondas.

DUNDEE (VII) at Limehouse 1934 *G. H. Somner Collection*

53. ARBROATH (III) (1935-1962)
O.N. 144715. 553g, 289n. 167.9 x 30.1 x 11.8 feet.
Oil engine, 4-cyl., 2S.C.S.A., by British Auxiliaries Ltd., Glasgow, 500bhp.
9.1935: Built by Caledon Shipbuilding & Engineering Co. Ltd., Dundee (Yard No. 347). *12.5.1949:* Abandoned off Whitby, Yorkshire after collision with the Finnish s.s. AINA MARIA NURMINEN (4,227/12) but reboarded after 30 minutes when the bulkheads seemed to be holding and beached at Whitby. *1.6.1949:* Refloated and towed to Dundee for repairs. *11.1962:* Sold to James Tyrrell (of Arklow), Dublin and renamed VALZELL. *9.1972:* Broken up by Haulbowline Industries Ltd., Cork.

ARBROATH (III) *W. H. Brown*

GLAMIS *G. E. P. Brownell*

54. GLAMIS (1936-1961)
O.N. 144717. 555g, 280n. 167.9 x 30.1 x 11.8 feet.
Oil engine, 4-cyl., 2S.C.S.A., by British Auxiliaries Ltd., Glasgow, 500bhp.
10.1936: Built by Caledon Shipbuilding & Engineering Co. Ltd., Dundee (Yard No. 359). *1.1961:* Sold to Fotis C. Georgopoulos & others, Piraeus, Greece and renamed ROMYLIA. *1963:* Sold to Stavros Kypraios & Partners, Piraeus, Greece and renamed AGIOS SPYRIDONAS. *1966:* Sold to E. Chaviaras & K. Diamantopoulos, Piraeus, Greece, name unchanged. *1968:* Sold to Prodromos Varvakis & Co., Piraeus, Greece name unchanged. *1975:* Sold to Libra Ltd., Thessaloniki, Greece and renamed ZYGOS 1. *1976:* Sold to Cypraea Stolida Shipping Co. Ltd., Limassol, Cyprus and renamed STOLIDA. *1980:* Sold to Union Progress Shipping Ltd., Nicosia, Cyprus and renamed ROLA. Believed to be still in service.

CLOVA *Fotoflite incorporating Skyfotos*

55. CLOVA (1936-1954)
O.N. 164495. 310g, 157n. 140.4 x 24.6 x 7.8 feet.
Oil engine, 6-cyl., 4S.C.S.A., by Humboldt-Deutzmotoren A.G., Köln-Deutz, 350bhp.
6.1935: Built by Goole Shipbuilding & Repairing Co. Ltd., Goole (Yard No. 310) for T. E. Evans & Co. Ltd., London as ANDONI. *10.1936:* Purchased by the Company and renamed CLOVA. *7.1954:* Sold to Lockett Wilson Line Ltd., London and renamed CLICHY. *3.1961:* Sold to Channel Shipping Ltd., Jersey, name unchanged. *5.1964:* Sold to Berwyn Coasters Ltd., Jersey and renamed BERWYN ACCORD. *8.1966:* Sold to Sea & Continental Waterways Transport Ltd., London and renamed SEA UNION. *10.1967:* Fitted with new engine, 8-cyl., 4S.C.S.A., by Rolls-Royce Ltd., Shrewsbury, 340bhp. *1968:* Sold to Reederei R. Rohwedder, Hamburg, Germany and renamed OREHOVED. *1972:* Sold to Peter J. Slater, Gravesend and later resold to Eurohaven Shipping Co. Ltd., Gravesend and renamed TRADE MARINER. *6.1973:* Sold to Norline Ltd., Maldon and renamed GLEN NOR. *4.1974:* Sold to Grenada Shipping Co. (of Piraeus), Panama and renamed TRADE MARINER. *1983:* Renamed MICHAEL A. *1988:* Sold to Kenneth Adams, Kingstown, St Vincent, name unchanged. *1993:* Deleted from ''Lloyd's Register'' as her continued existence was in doubt.

KILLDRUMMY at Hull *G. H. Somner Collection*

56. KILDRUMMY (1937-1946)
O.N. 144825. 629g, 271n. 175.9 x 27.3 x 11.3 feet.
Triple, 3-cyl., by builders, 84hp.
12.1924: Built by Hall, Russell & Co. Ltd., Aberdeen (Yard No. 687) for Aberdeen, Newcastle & Hull Shipping Co. Ltd., Aberdeen. *10.1929:* Controlling interest passed to the Company. *6.1937:* Transferred to the Company. *11.1946:* Transferred to Coquet Shipping Co. Ltd. (Anthony & Bainbridge Ltd., managers), Newcastle and renamed COQUETDALE. *10.1951:* Sold to Deeside Shipping Co. Ltd. (T. Rose & Co., managers), Sunderland and renamed DEEDALE. *20.7.1959:* Arrived Delfzijl for breaking up by Scheepswerf Bodewes Gruno, Foxhol, *8.9.1959:* Demolition began.

57. LOCHEE (II)/PERTH (VI) (1937-1963)
O.N. 144719. 994g, 535n. 227.0 x 36.2 x 12.0 feet.
Oil engine, 8-cyl., 2S.C.S.A., by British Auxiliaries Ltd., Glasgow, 1000bhp.
8.1937: Built by Henry Robb Ltd., Leith (Yard No. 240). *28.12.1940:* Mined in the River Mersey while on passage from Preston to Gibraltar but towed into port for repairs. *26.2.1944:* Ran ashore east of Naples, Italy, while on passage there from North African ports. *8.4.1944:* Refloated and drydocked at Naples. *6.1944:* Returned to service. *12.1945:* Returned to owners. *1948:* Renamed PERTH. *1953:* Shelter deck closed, tonnages now 1,321g, 769n. *5.1963:* Sold to N. & K. Marcantonalis, Piraeus, Greece and renamed MANTHOS. *1971:* Sold to Ioannis Konstantineas, Piraeus, Greece and renamed VASILIOS. *1978:* Renamed GEORGIOS. *22.9.1979:* Stranded 200 miles south of Suez after engine breakdown while on passage from Volos, Greece to Jizan, Saudi Arabia. *24.9.1979:* Arrived at Suez in tow of Dutch tug ENGELAND (229/68) making water and laid up. *1.10.1979:* Sank at Suez.

LOCHEE (II) sailing out of Leith 1937 *G. H. Somner Collection*

58. ERROL (II) (1939-1955)
O.N. 164716. 311g, 164n. 135.0 x 24.6 x 7.7 feet.
Oil engine, 6-cyl., 4S.C.S.A., by Humboldt-Deutzmotoren A.G., Köln-Deutz, 350bhp.
9.1936: Built by Goole Shipbuilding & Repairing Co. Ltd., Goole (Yard No. 317) for H. Harrison (Shipping) Ltd., London as KESTOR. *1.1938:* New engine fitted, same as original. *2.1939:* Purchased by the Company and renamed ERROL. *12.1955:* Sold to Channel Shipping Ltd., Jersey, name unchanged. *1.1958:* Renamed GROUVILLE. *9.1964:* Sold to Berwyn Coasters Ltd., Jersey and renamed BERWYN BARON. *8.1966:* Sold to George V. Blake, Jersey and renamed FREDERICK HUGHES. *1971:* Fitted with new engine, 8-cyl., 4S.C.S.A., by English Electric Diesels Ltd., Glasgow, 320bhp. *11.1971:* Sold to Cranfield Bros. Ltd., Jersey, name unchanged. *9.1972:* Sold to Mardorf, Peach & Co. Ltd., Jersey, name unchanged. *10.1975:* Sold to A. J. & Annette Pratt, Jersey, name unchanged. *9.1977:* Sold to T. & G. Shipping Ltd., Jersey, name unchanged. *13.4.1979:* Struck Great Yarmouth pier when entering from Rotterdam and declared a total constructive loss. *6.1979:* Sold to Conrad E. Reynolds (of St. Johns, Antigua), Jersey, name unchanged. *1983:* Renamed MISS ANTIGUA. *12.1987:* Port of registry now St. Johns, Antigua & Barbuda. *6.1991:* Laid up at Antigua and later reported to be non-sea going.

ERROL (II) *W.S.P.L.*

59. CORTACHY (1939-1953)
O.N. 163540. 271g, 142n. 130.2 x 24.6 x 7.5 feet.
Oil engine, 6-cyl., 4S.C.S.A., by Humboldt-Deutzmotoren A.G., Köln-Deutz, 350bhp.
11.1934: Built by Goole Shipbuilding & Repairing Co. Ltd., Goole (Yard No. 303) for David Williamson Ltd., London as ARRIVAIN. *9.1939:* Purchased by the Company and renamed CORTACHY. *9.1942:* New engine fitted, 6-cyl., 2S.C.S.A., by Crossley Bros. Ltd, Manchester, 330bhp. *2.1953:* Sold to Lockett Wilson Ltd., Jersey, name unchanged. *7.1954:* Transferred to Lockett Wilson Line Ltd. *1955:* Renamed CONCORDE. *9.1961:* Sold to Beccles Abattoir Ltd., London, name unchanged. *1.1963:* Sold to O. J. Metaxas, Athens, Greece and renamed GERASIMOS A. *1965:* Sold to Evangelos Hadjigeorgiou & Andreas Taliadouros, Piraeus, Greece and renamed METAMORFOSIS. *1976:* Sold to Konstantinos Koulpaxiotis, Piraeus, Greece, name unchanged. *1987:* Deleted from Lloyds Register: "Reported broken up".

CORTACHY *Dave Hocquard*

60. CROMBIE (1939-1954)
O.N. 163528. 239g, 118n. 117.5 x 24.6 x 7.5 feet.
Oil engine, 4-cyl., 4S.C.S.A., by Motorenfabrik Deutz A.G., Köln-Deutz, 250bhp.
10.1934: Built by Goole Shipbuilding & Repairing Co. Ltd., Goole (Yard No. 304) for David Wiliamson Ltd., London as AFFARIC. *10.1939:* Purchased by the Company and renamed CROMBIE. *9.1940:* Fitted with new engine, 6-cyl., 2S.C.S.A., by Crossley Bros. Ltd., Manchester, 330bhp. *7.1954:* Sold to Lockett Wilson Line Ltd, Jersey, name unchanged. *5.1960:* Sold to Partrederi Scantic, Borga, Finland and renamed SCANTIC. *1960:* Sold to Chr. Petersen, Rønne, Bornholm, Denmark, name unchanged. *1962:* Sold to Partrederi Scantic (Albin Gustafsson, manager), Borga, Finland, name unchanged. *1972:* Sold to Tage Gustafsson, Borga, name unchanged. *1978:* Sold to Harry Nyholm, Porvoo, Finland, name unchanged. *1986:* Sold to Widestam Alfons Rafael, Perna, Finland, name unchanged. *12.1986:* Arrived at Naantali, Finland for breaking up by Nater Ltd. O/Y.

CROMBIE *G. E. P. Brownell/W.S.P.L.*

61. GALA (1939-1962).
O.N. 166208. 86g, 67n. 81.1 x 17.6 x 7.3 feet.
Oil engine, 2S.C.S.A., 4-cyl, by Crossley Bros Ltd., Manchester, 100bhp.
10.1939: Built by Henry Scarr Ltd., Hessle as a tanker (portable tanks) and employed at Hull. *1940:* Tanks removed tonnages now 99g, 64n. *8.1962:* Sold to Ellerman's Wilson Line Ltd., Hull, name unchanged. *7.1968:* Sold to James Gillyon (of Beverley, Yorks.), name unchanged. *1974:* Refitted with two oil engines, 4S.C.S.A., each 6-cyl., by Perkins Engines Ltd., Peterborough, 350bhp. *7.1978:* Sold to Samuel Abel (of Wells, Norfolk), name unchanged. *10.1980:* Sold to Sea Aggregates Ltd (of Wells), name unchanged. *10.1982:* Sold to Cape Andreas Shipping Co. Ltd., Limassol, Cyprus, name unchanged. Converted at King's Lynn to a bunkering barge and fitted with five tanks. The expected business did not materialise and in *1985* sold for breaking up at Hull.

62. GOWRIE (III)/LOCHEE (III) (1945-1966)
O.N. 168681. 872g, 458n. 203.0 x 33.2 x 11.7 feet.
Oil engine, 5-cyl., 2S.C.S.A., by British Auxiliaries Ltd., Glasgow, 800bhp.
7.1941: Built by Scott & Sons, Bowling (Yard No. 359) for the Ministry of War Transport as EMPIRE CAPE and managed by William Robertson, Glasgow. *1943:* Management transferred to Tyne-Tees Steam Shipping Co. Ltd., Newcastle. *7.1944:* Management taken over by the Company. *10.1945:* Purchased by the Company and renamed GOWRIE. *1948:* Renamed LOCHEE. *8.1966:* Sold to D. & S. Zoulis Bros. & D. Vlachos, Piraeus, Greece and renamed AGHIOS SPYRIDON. *1968:* Sold to S. C. Vazeos & Co., Piraeus, name unchanged. *1970:* Sold to Abdul Razzak Sattout, Tripoli, Lebanon and renamed ANWAR. *1980:* Owners now Ets. Abdul-Razzak Sattout subsequently Entreprises Abdul-Razzak Sattout. Still in service.

LOCHEE (III) *John G. Callis*

63. DRON (1945-1950)
O.N. 164614. 413 g, 218n. 156.1 x 26.4 x 7.9 feet.
Oil engine, 6-cyl., 4S.C.S.A., by Humboldt-Deutzmotoren A.G., Köln-Deutz, 350bhp.
4.1936: Built by Goole Shipbuilding & Repairing Co. Ltd., Goole (Yard No. 311) for S. G. Jenkins (B. J. Howlett & Co. Ltd., managers) London as CONIDA. *1.1940:* Sold to Steamship Den of Airlie Co. Ltd., (Dundee, Perth & London Shipping Co. Ltd., managers), Dundee, name unchanged. *11.1945:* Purchased by the Company and renamed DRON. *1.1950:* Sold to J. Wharton (Shipping) Ltd., Goole and renamed JACKONIA. *1.1963:* Sold to Transmarine International Ltd., Dublin and renamed IVERAGH. *1966:* Sold to P. J. Tyrell, Dublin, name unchanged. *20.3.1969:* Arrived at Dublin for breaking up by Hammond Lane Foundry Ltd.

DRON as JACKONIA *G. E. P. Brownell/W.S.P.L.*

BENVIE *E. J. Wylie*

64. BENVIE (1946-1953) Tug.
O.N. 121254. 185g, 1n. 107.1 x 23.1 x 9.1 feet.
Compound, 2-cyl., by builders, 99hp.
1905: Built by Ferguson Bros., Port Glasgow (Yard No. 165) for Clyde Shipping Co. Ltd., Glasgow as FLYING SWALLOW. *1.1946:* Purchased by the Company and renamed BENVIE. *26.6.1953:* Arrived at Charlestown, Fife for breaking up by Shipbreaking Industries Ltd. *10.8.1953:* Demolition commenced.

65. BUDDON (1946-1953) Tug.
O.N. 128246. 203g, 2n. 115.1 x 23.6 x 10.3 feet.
Compound, 2-cyl., by builders, 99hp.
1908: Built by Ferguson Bros., Port Glasgow (Yard No. 183) for Clyde Shipping Co. Ltd., Glasgow as FLYING CORMORANT. *1.1946:* Purchased by the Company and renamed BUDDON. *26.6.1953:* Arrived at Charlestown, Fife for breaking up by Shipbreaking Industries Ltd. *10.8.1953:* Demolition commenced.

BUDDON

G.E.P. Brownell Collection/W.S.P.L.

GOWRIE (IV) *G. F. Whitenay*

66. EDINA/GOWRIE (IV) (1946-1958)
O.N. 167022. 489g, 231n. 162.7 x 27.2 x 8.3 feet.
Oil engine, 6-cyl, 2S.C.S.A., by British Auxiliaries Ltd., Glasgow.
11.1939: Built by Henry Robb Ltd., Leith (Yard No. 293) for Leith, Hull & Hamburg Steam Packet Co. Ltd. (James Currie & Co., managers), Leith as EDINA. *7.1940:* Owner's title now Currie Line Ltd., Leith. *3.1946.* Purchased by the Company, name unchanged. *1948:* Renamed GOWRIE. *10.9.1955:* Ran ashore near Joaaloten Light, Sweden while on passage from Xxpila to Fraserburgh, but subsequently refloated. *1.1958:* Sold to William H. McTaggart, Grand Cayman and renamed FORDMAC. *3.1959:* Sold to Fordmac Shipping Co. Ltd., Cayman Islands, name unchanged. *1961:* Sold to N. G. Kirkconnel, Cayman Islands and renamed KIRK MAID. *7.9.1964:* Sank 4 miles off Kingston, Jamaica when inbound from the Dominician Republic with a cargo of timber.

67. ANGUSBURN (1946-1954)
O.N. 166213. 2,851g, 1,693n. 315.5 x 46.6 x 23.0 feet.
Triple, 3-cyl., by North-Eastern Marine Engineering Co. Ltd., Newcastle, 1200ihp.
3.1942: Built by Caledon Shipbuilding & Engineering Co. Ltd., Dundee (Yard No. 396) for the Ministry of War Transport as EMPIRE BARD, and managed by Dover Navigation Co. Ltd., London. *7.1946:* Purchased by the Company and renamed ANGUSBURN. *1951:* Converted to burn oil fuel. *3.1954:* Sold to Brebner Shipping Co. Ltd., London and renamed BRETTENHAMN. *2.1955:* Sold to Rederi A/B Hildegaard, Mariehamn, Finland, name unchanged. *24.4.1971:* Arrived at Carthagena, Spain for breaking up by Francisco Jimenez Ballester. *6.1971:* Demolition commenced.

ANGUSBAIRN approaching New York

68. LUNAN (1946-1959)
O.N. 166222. 1,018g, 552n. 216.0 x 34.0 x 12.2 feet.
Oil engine, 7-cyl., 2S.C.S.A., by British Polar Engines Ltd., Glasgow, 1000bhp.
10.1946: Built by Hall, Russell & Co. Ltd., Aberdeen (Yard No. 795). *13.11.1958:* Struck a rock in the St. Lawrence when bound for Toronto, receiving severe bottom damage. Fire then broke out in the engine room, gutting all the accommodation. Towed to Lauzon, near Quebec and laid-up for the winter. *2.1959:* Sold to Orleans Navigation Inc., Quebec in her damaged condition, repaired and renamed MARIDAN C. *1978:* Sold to Banville Navigation S.A., Panama and renamed J. B. BANVILLE. *1978:* Sold to Humberto Suarez Valdez, Panama and renamed SCORPION I. *1979:* Sold to Velsen Line S.A. (Denizana Shipping Unlimited Inc., managers), Panama, name unchanged. *1993:* Deleted from ''Lloyd's Register'' as her continued existance was in doubt.

GANNOCHY *Fotolite Incorporating Skyfotos*

69. GANNOCHY (1947-1958)
O.N. 164317. 485g, 257n. 163.8 x 26.4 x 10.0 feet.
Oil engine, 8-cyl., 4S.C.S.A., by Humboldt-Deutzmotoren A.G., Köln-Deutz.
3.1937: Built by N.V. Industrieele Maat. ''De Noord'', Alblasserdam (Yard No. 564) for Coast Lines Ltd., Liverpool as HAMPSHIRE COAST. *9.1946:* Sold to Springfjord Shipping Co. Ltd. (Springwell Shipping Co. Ltd., managers), London and renamed SPRINGHAVEN. *12.1947:* Purchased by the Company and renamed GANNOCHY. *1952:* Fitted with an 8-cyl., 4S.C.S.A. oil engine made in 1948 by Port & Dunwoody Ltd., London. *25.2.1958:* Foundered in the Mersey Channel while on passage from Penmaenmawr, Wales to Liverpool with a cargo of stone.

ANGUSMUIR *G. H. Somner Collection*

70. ANGUSMUIR (1948-1954)
O.N. 160318. 3,535g, 2,134n. 350.0 x 49.0 x 23.7 feet.
Triple, 3-cyl., by D. Rowan & Co. Ltd., Glasgow, 339hp.
4.1928: Built by Lithgows Ltd., Port Glasgow (Yard No. 809) for Denholm Line Steamers Ltd. (J. & J. Denholm Ltd., managers), Greenock as CLUNEPARK. *7.1948:* Purchased by the Company and renamed ANGUSMUIR. *3.1954:* Sold to Cia. de Navegacion Aguila Ltda., Puerto Limon, Costa Rica (later Panama) and renamed AGUILA. *6.10.1963:* Arrived at Split for breaking up by Brodospas. *12.1963:* Demolition commenced.

71. LONDON (VII) (1951-1964)
O.N. 182559. 706g 267n. 201.0 x 36.2 x 12.9 feet.
Oil engine, 8-cyl., 2S.C.S.A., by British Polar Engines Ltd., Glasgow, 1290bhp.
3.1951: Built by Burntisland Shipbuilding Co. Ltd., Burntisland (Yard No. 336). *11.2.1954:* In collision in fog off South Foreland, Straits of Dover, with the Italian VOLODDA (4,673/15) while on passage from Bremen to Southampton. *29.7.1961:* Struck an unchartered rock spur and bottom damaged while on passage from Montreal to Baker Lake, an inlet off Hudson Bay, Canada. *9.1964:* Sold to Winsor Trading Co. Ltd., St. John's, Newfoundland and renamed WINSOR TRADER. *1967:* Sold to Topsail Shipping Co. Ltd., St. John's, Newfoundland and renamed TOPSAIL STAR. Tonnages now 1,205g, 706n. *1988:* Sold to Naviera Straule de R.L., San Lorenzo, Honduras, and later renamed SOPHIE EXPRESS. *1994:* Sold to other Honduras-flag owners and renamed PRINCESS TARRAH. Still in service.

LONDON (VII) *Dave Hocquard*

72. ANGUSBRAE (1951-1956)
O.N. 180066. 2,905g, 1,641n. 315.4 x 46.5 x 23.0 feet.
Triple, 3-cyl. by Central Marine Engine Works, West Hartlepool, 281hp.
12.1943: Built by William Gray & Co. Ltd., West Hartlepool (Yard No. 1159) for the Ministry of War Transport as EMPIRE BEACONSFIELD and managed by Constants (South Wales) Ltd., London. *12.1945:* Sold to Constants (South Wales) Ltd., (H. Constant, manager), London and renamed HAWKINGE. *12.1951:* Purchased by the Company and renamed ANGUSBRAE. *2.1956:* Sold to W. H. Müller & Co.'s Transport Maats. N.V., Rotterdam, Holland and renamed HISPANIA. *1960:* Sold to West End Corporation, Cefalinias, Greece and renamed DIA. *14.10.1964:* Foundered in position 44.12N, 08.38W after developing a leak while on passage from Antwerp to Bourgas, Bulgaria with a cargo of super phosphate

ANGUSBRAE entering Bristol from Archangel 1954 *George Wilson*

DUNDEE (VIII) *Fotolite incorporating Skyfotos*

73. DUNDEE (VIII) (1954-1967)
O.N. 182563. 1,781g, 884n. 251.4 x 43.1 x 18.9 feet.
Oil engine, 9-cyl., 2S.C.S.A., by British Polar Engines Ltd., Glasgow, 1,640bhp.
4.1954: Built by Burntisland Shipbuilding Co. Ltd., Burntisland (Yard No. 364). *1.1967:* Sold to Mediterranean Lines (1967) Ltd. (Ofer Bros. (Holdings) Ltd., managers), Haifa, Israel and renamed DORON. *1973:* Sold to Demetra Shipping Co. Ltd., Famagusta, Cyprus and renamed JUPITER. *1975:* Sold to Lefkas Shipping Co. Ltd., Famagusta and renamed PYLOS. *1977:* Sold to Pavilion Shipping Co., Famagusta and renamed KARMELLA. *1977:* Sold to Bronco (Marine) Co. Ltd., Limassol, Cyprus and renamed BRONCO but later VLYHO. *15.9.1978:* Foundered near Falconera Island after an engine room explosion while on passage from Chalkis, Greece to Tunis with a cargo of cement.

BROUGHTY (II) *Dave Hocquard*

74. BROUGHTY (II) (1955-1962)
O.N. 182564. 553g, 255n. 189.9 x 30.6 x 12.4 feet.
Oil engine 6-cyl., 2S.C.S.A., by British Polar Engines Ltd., Glasgow, 1,220bhp.
6.1955: Built by Scheepswerf ''Gideon'' v/h J. Koster Hzn, Groningen (Yard No. 234). *4.1962:* Sold to Channel Shipping Ltd., Jersey, name unchanged. *6.1963:* Sold to Stephenson Clarke Ltd., London, and converted to a liquefied gas carrier by Hawthorn Leslie (Shipbuilders) Ltd., Newcastle. Tonnages now 943g, 473n. *1.1964:* Renamed ABBAS. *2.1968:* Sold to Cia. di Navigazione ''Cossira'' S.p.A., Palermo, Italy and renamed CAP CERVO. *1972:* Sold to Cryomar Cia. di Navigazione, Palermo and renamed CRYOMAR. *1980:* Sold to Minos Tank Shipping Co., Piraeus, Greece and renamed MINOGAZ 1. *25.7.1986:* arrived at Perama, Greece. *9.1987:* In course of demolition at Perama.

KINGENNIE *G. E. P. Brownell/W.S.P.L.*

75. KINGENNIE (1958-1967) Tanker
O.N. 182566. 1,169g, 514n. 215.0 x 36.4 x 13.8 feet.
Oil engine, 7-cyl., 2S.C.S.A., by British Polar Engines Ltd., Glasgow, 1,120bhp.
5.1958: Built by George Brown & Co. (Marine) Ltd., Greenock (Yard No. 269). *3.1967:* Sold to Cambridge (Tankers) Ltd., London but management retained. *6.1972:* Sold to Seka S.A. Bunkering Stations, Piraeus, Greece and renamed AMALIA. *1983:* Sold to Sekavin Shipping Co., Piraeus, name unchanged. Still in service.

76. GOWRIE (V) (1959-1963)
O.N. 180694. 1,876g 965n. 289.4 x 44.4 x 18.4 feet.
Compound, 4-cyl., by builders, 1,200ihp.
1944: Built by Verschure & Co.'s Scheepsbouw en Machinefabriek, Amsterdam for Fisser & Van Doornum, Emden, as HENDRIK FISSER 5. *12.1945:* Recovered by Allied forces at Kiel in damaged condition, subsequently taken over by the Ministry of Transport, London, renamed EMPIRE GALBRAITH, and placed under management of Currie Line Ltd., Leith. *4.1946:* Sold to Currie Line Ltd., Leith and renamed HIGHLAND. *3.1959:* Purchased by the Company and re-named GOWRIE. *5.1963:* Sold to Cia. Naviera Algeo S.A., Greece and renamed HERMANOS. *9.1969:* Broken up at Vado, Italy, by Vado Alti Forni e Accieri.

GOWRIE (IV) *W.S.P.L.*

APPENDIX C – DUNDEE, PERTH & LONDON SHIPPING CO. LTD. – MANAGED VESSELS

1. BABYLON (1920-1920)
O.N. 144689. 1,596g, 989n. 311.6 x 42.3 x 14.6 feet.
Triple, 3-cyl., by T. Richardson & Sons Ltd., West Hartlepool, 249hp
1.1896: Built by Sir Raylton Dixon & Co., Middlesbrough (Yard No. 417) for Deutsche Dampfschiffahrts Ges. ''Hansa'', Bremen, Germany as RUDELSBURG. *10.1907:* Sold to A. C. de Freitas & Co., Hamburg, Germany and renamed BABYLON. *1910:* Sold to Deutsche Levante Linie, Hamburg, name unchanged. *8.1914:* Employed on ore trade within the Baltic. *11.10.1915:* Torpedoed by the British submarine E19 off Oland, Sweden and sank in shallow water. *4.5.1916:* Refloated and towed to Delfzijl for repair. *1.1920:* Owners taken over by Hamburg-Amerika Linie, Hamburg. *7.1920:* Vessel allocated to Great Britain and passed to The Shipping Controller, London with the Company as managers. *10.1920:* Sold to the Greek Government, name unchanged. *1923:* Sold to E. Tricoglou, Andros, Greece and renamed FILIA E. TRICOGLOU. *27.1.1926:* Stranded and sank on Siphantos Island, Greece while on passage from Sulina, Roumania to Sweden with a cargo of grain.

2. ROM (1920-1920)
O.N. 144692. 2,080g, 1,282n. 272.8 x 39.3 x 14.9 feet.
Triple, 3-cyl., by builders.
1905: Built by Flensburger Schiffsbau-Gesellschaft, Flensburg (Yard No. 249) for Robert M. Sloman jnr., Hamburg, Germany as ROM. *7.1920:* Vessel allocated to The Shipping Controller, London with the Company as managers. *11.1920:* Sold to James Cormack & Co., Leith and renamed ARNISTON. *28.3.1931:* Sank after being crushed by ice in the Gulf of Riga while on passage from Riga to Dundee and Leith with a cargo of timber.

3. CONIDA (1940-1945)
See Appendix B No. 63 under DRON.

4. GAUNTLET (1940-1946) Tug.
O.N. 98396. 149g, 12n. 100.0 x 19.6 x 11.4 feet.
Triple, 3-cyl., by builders, 75hp.
9.1891: Built by J. P. Rennoldson & Sons, South Shields (Yard No. 32) for Goole & Hull Steam Tug Co. Ltd., Goole as GOOLE No 8. *10.1899:* Sold to John Page, London and renamed GAUNTLET. *5.1902:* Transferred to Elliott Steam Tug Co. Ltd. (John Page, manager), London, name unchanged. *12.1924:* Sold to Victor A. Cappon, Dundee, name unchanged. *4.1937:* Transferred to V. A. Cappon Tugs Ltd. (V. A. Cappon, manager). *3.1940:* Management passed to the Company. *7.1946:* Arrived at Ghent for breaking up by Van Heyghen Freres. *8.1946:* Demolition began.

MENTOR *Struan. J. F. Robertson*

5. MENTOR (1940-1946) Tug.
O.N. 89701. 141g, 15n. 95.22 x 19.1 x 9.0 feet.
Compound, 2-cyl., by Rankin & Blackmore, Greenock, 50hp.
1883: Built by T. B. Seath & Co., Glasgow (Yard No.. 236) for Lancashire & Yorkshire and London & North Western Railway Companies, Fleetwood as BROCK. *1902:* Sold to G. E. J. Moody, Cleethorpes, name unchanged. *10.1903:* Sold to Lawson Steam Tug Boat Co. Ltd. (J. Lawson, manager), South Shields and renamed MENTOR. *6.1920:* Transferred to Lawson-Batey Tugs Ltd., South Shields, name unchanged. *2.1937:* Sold to V. A. Cappon Tugs Ltd. (V. A. Cappon, manager), Dundee, name unchanged. *3.1940:* Management passed to the Company. *7.1946:* Arrived at Ghent for breaking up by Van Heyghen Freres. *8.1946:* Demolition began.

6. LILLEAA (1940-1945)
O.N. 147527. 936g, 504n. 207.5 x 33.6 x 13.4 feet.
Oil engine filled, 8-cyl., 2S.C.S.A., by J. & C. G. Bollinders Co. Ltd., Stockholm.
1922: Built by Rennie, Ritchie & Newport Shipbuilding Co. Ltd., Wivenhoe, the company going into liquidation before completion. *7.1923:* Completed by Otto Andersen & Co., London for British United Investment Corporation (F. S. & A. A. Moller, managers), London as MAJONG. *11.1924:* Sold to G. Andersen, Bergen, Norway and renamed LILLEHORN. *4.1925:* Sold to Jonathan Dalziel, Glasgow, name unchanged. *5.1926:* Sold to Joseph W. Hobbs, Vancouver, name unchanged. *10.1926:* Transferred to Hobb Bros. Ltd. *11.1927:* Sold to Atlantic Pacific Navigation Co. Ltd. (G. M. Dean, manager), Vancouver, name unchanged. *9.1936:* Sold to Canadian Coast Lines Ltd., Halifax, name unchanged. *1.1938:* Sold to Atlantic Pacific Navigation Co. Ltd. (of Vancouver) which later went into liquidation. *6.1939:* Sold to D/S Hetland A/S (T. S. Basse, manager) Copenhagen, Denmark and renamed LILLEAA. *5.3.1941:* Taken over at Belfast by the Ministry of Shipping (later Ministry of War Transport), London, being managed by the Company. *10.1945:* Returned to the Danish Government and returned by them to D/S Hetland A/S (T. S. Basse, manager), Copenhagen. *2.11.1945:* Sank in a storm after engine breakdown in the Gulf of Bothnia while on passage from Kemi, Finland to Maesteved, Denmark.

GOWRIE (III) departing Blyth April 1946 *Laurence Dunn*

7. EMPIRE CAPE (1944-1945)
See Appendix B No. 62 under GOWRIE (III).

EMPIRE GARLAND *G. E. P. Brownell*

8. EMPIRE GARLAND (1945-1947)
O.N. 180609. 1,925g, 937n. 287.7 x 44.4 x 15.9 feet.
Compound, 4-cyl., by builders, 1,200i.h.p.
1944: Built by Stettiner Oderwerke A.G., Stettin for Deutsche Ost-Afrika Linie, Hamburg, Germany as NJONG. *5.1945:* Taken as a prize at Flensburg. *9.1945:* Taken over by the Ministry of War Transport, London, renamed EMPIRE GARLAND and managed by the Company. *2.1947:* Sold to General Steam Navigation Co. Ltd., London and renamed SHELDRAKE. *1958:* Sold to Johal Navigation Ltd., Monrovia, Liberia and renamed SALAMSTAR. *1961:* Transferred to the Greek flag and renamed AMBELOS. *1961:* Sold to Mrs M. Goumas, Piraeus, Greece and renamed MARMINA. *1968:* Sold to C. Raikos & F. Raikou, Piraeus and renamed FILIO. *15.6.1972:* Nikolaos Tzonis commenced demolition at Aspropyrgos, Greece.

9. EMPIRE CONISBOROUGH (1945-1946)
O.N. 180713. 1,237g, 686n. 225.4 x 34.7 x 13.6 feet.
Compound, 4-cyl., by Christiansen & Meyer, Harburg, 134hp.
1937: Built by Lubecker Flenderwerke A.G., Lubeck for Fisser & von Doornum Reederei G.m.b.H., Emden as MARIE FISSER 5.1945: Taken as a prize, in damaged condition, at Emden. *10.1945:* Allocated to the Ministry of War Transport, renamed EMPIRE CONISBOROUGH, and managed by the Company. *2.1946:* Allocated to the U.S.S.R. renamed and STEPAN SHAUMIAN. *1960:* Continued existence in doubt.

10. KINGENNIE (1967-1972) Tanker.
See Appendix B No 75.

APPENDIX D — DUNDEE SHIPPING CO. (1798-1806)
DUNDEE & PERTH SHIPPING CO. (1806-1826)

1. **LORD DUNCAN** in service 1798 — no details.

2. **LONDON PACKET** in service 1809 — no details.

3. **ROSE(I) (1802-1825)** Sloop.
29 reg. 28 x 14 x 6 feet.
6.1802: Built at Dundee for Dundee Shipping Co. *12.1825:* Sold to R. Anderson (of Newburgh), Perth. *5.1827:* Sold to J. Moffat & others, Lerwick. *1840:* Broken up.

4. **NEWCASTLE & BERWICK PACKET (1805-1826)** Sloop.
See Appendix A No. 2.

5. **BRIDPORT PACKET (1806-1826)** Smack.
See Appendix A No. 1.

6. **OSNABURGH (1806-1826)** Smack.
See Appendix A No. 3.

7. **LORD KINNAIRD (1806-1819, 1824-1826)** Smack.
See Appendix A No. 4.

8. **TAY (I) (1807-1826)** Sloop.
See Appendix A No. 5.

9. **DISPATCH (1808-1822)** Smack.
90 reg. 59 x 18 x 10 feet.
1805: Built at Bridport for John Richardson & Co., Perth. *1808:* Taken over by Dundee & Perth Shipping Co. *1819:* Re-rigged as a schooner. *1822:* Lost.

10. **DEFIANCE (1808-1826)** Smack.
See Appendix A No. 6.

11. **UNION (1808-1826)** Smack.
See Appendix A No. 7

12. **PERTH (I) (1809-1826)** Sloop.
See Appendix A No. 8.

13. **MARY (I) (1811-1826)** Sloop.
See Appendix A No. 9.

14. **AUGUSTA (1812-1825)** Sloop.
78 reg. 55 x 19 x 10 feet.
3.1812: Built at Dundee for Dundee & Perth Shipping Co. *8.1825:* Sold to George Anderson, Arbroath. *9.1828:* Sold to Colin Davidson, Inverness. *6.1846:* Sold to Alexander Ross, Inverness. *22.10.1853:* Driven ashore on Sharry Rocks, Lossiemouth while on passage from Sunderland to Inverness and became a total loss.

15. **ANNA (1813-1926)** Sloop.
See Appendix A No. 10.

16. **PERTH (II) (1816-1826)** Smack.
See Appendix A No. 15.

17. **DUNDEE (I) (1818-1826)** Smack.
See Appendix A No. 16.

18. **FISHERS (1820-1826)** Sloop.
See Appendix A No. 18.

19. JANE (1823-1826) Sloop.
See Appendix A No. 21.

20. LONDON (I) (1824-1826) Smack.
See Appendix A No. 22.

21. LIVERPOOL (1826 only) Sloop.
See Appendix A No. 23.

APPENDIX E — DUNDEE & PERTH UNION SHIPPING CO. (1819-1826)

1. LORD KINNAIRD (1819-1824) Smack.
See Appendix A No. 4.

2. MERSEY (I) (1819-1826) Sloop.
See Appendix A No. 17.

3. TAY (II) (1819-1825) Sloop.
87 reg. 60 x 19 x 10 feet.
5.1819: Built by Robert Strachan, Montrose for Dundee & Perth Union Shipping Co. *4.1825:* Sold to E. Edmond, Scarborough. *5.1826:* Sold to T. Scrivener and others, Bridlington. *12.1833:* Lost.

4. OLIVE (1822-1826) Smack.
See Appendix A No. 11.

5. COURIER (1823-1826) Smack.
See Appendix A No. 12.

6. ROBERT (1823-1825) Schooner.
88 reg. 62 x 19 x 11 feet.
1821: Built by John Calman, Dundee for John & James Thain, Dundee. *2.1823:* Acquired by Dundee & Perth Union Shipping Co. *1825:* Sold — no further record.

7. ELBE (1823-1826) Smack.
See Appendix A No. 13.

8. FORFARSHIRE (1823-1826) Smack.
See Appendix A No. 20.

9. FRIENDS (1823-1826) Sloop.
See Appendix A No. 19.

10. GEORGE Sloop.
In service in 1824 — no details.

11. GLASGOW (1825-1826) Sloop.
See Appendix A, No. 14.

APPENDIX F — DUNDEE & HULL SHIPPING CO. (1824-1857)

1. TAY (1825-1847) Schooner.
O.N. 7111. 82 reg. 56 x 17 x 11 feet.
1825: Built by John Calman, Dundee for Dundee & Hull Shipping Co. *1.1847:* Sold to A. B. Glenday & J. Millar, Dundee. *4.1850:* Sold to James Luke & others, Dundee. *6.1864:* Sold to William Nicoll, Dundee and lengthened to 75 feet, tonnage now 103. *30.11.1866:* Lost on Gaa Sands at the entrance to the Firth of Tay while inbound from Sunderland.

2. FAME (I) (1826-1827) Smack.
73 reg. 57 x 18 x 11 feet.
1787: Built at Whitby. *1806:* Registered at Dundee. *1.1826:* Purchased by Dundee & Hull Shipping Co. *1827:* Lost.

3. FIFE PACKET (1826-1830) Smack.
96 reg. 60 x 20 x 10 feet.
1807: Built at Bridport for John Richardson & Co., Perth. *1826:* Purchased by Dundee & Hull Shipping Co. *1830:* Lost.

4. HUMBER (1829-1844) Schooner.
O.N. 7120. 95 reg. 62 x 18 x 12 feet.
8.1829: Built by Thomas Adamson, Dundee for Dundee & Hull Shipping Co. *7.1844:* Sold to William Henderson, Dundee. *4.1850:* Sold to William Cramond & others, Dundee. *24.5.1890:* Sank after collision with s.s. BALLOCHBUIE (677/80) of Aberdeen, about 3 miles NE of Blyth, while on passage from Sunderland to Invergordon with a cargo of coal.

5. FAME (II) (1830-1848) Smack.
O.N. 7161. 86 reg. 60 x 18 x 11 feet.
12.1830: Built by D. & A. Brown, Dundee for Dundee & Hull Shipping Co. *3.1848:* Sold to James Mather, Dundee. *3.1851:* Sold to John Brown, Dundee. *10.10.1860:* Abandoned in the North Sea.

6. SHELAH (1843-1854) Schooner.
O.N. 17505, 129 reg. 71 x 20 x 12 feet.
9.1841: Built by R. & R. Sparrow, Wexford on their own account. *1.1843:* Purchased by Dundee & Hull Shipping Co. *5.1854:* Sold to James Stephen & others, Grangemouth. *5.1857:* Wrecked and dismantled.

7. QUEEN (I) (1842-1857) Schooner.
See Appendix A No. 46.

8. MARY (I) (1843-1844) Sloop.
See Appendix A No. 9.

9. ALBERT (1844-1855) Schooner.
O.N. 7228. 127 reg. 81 x 19 x 12 feet.
11.1844: Built by Robert Brown, Dundee for Dundee & Hull Shipping Co. *7.1855:* Sold to Searight & Co., Cape Town, South Africa. *2.1857:* Wrecked at Struys Bay, Cape Province.

10. QUEEN (II) (1854-1857) Iron screw steamer.
See Appendix B No. 11.

APPENDIX G — DUNDEE & NEWCASTLE STEAM SHIP CO. LTD. (1861-1891)

DUNDEE & NEWCASTLE SHIPPING CO. LTD. (1891-1917)

1. **DALHOUSIE (1861-1864)** Iron.
O.N. 29453. 198g, 156n. 144.5 x 19.0 x 10.4 feet.
Direct acting, 2-cyl., by builders, 60hp.
2.1861: Built by Gourlay Bros. & Co., Dundee (Yard No. 10) for Dundee & Newcastle Steam Ship Co. Ltd. *24/25.11.1864:* Wrecked at the mouth of the Firth of Tay on the south side of the Abertay Sands whilst inbound from Newcastle, with the loss of 33 persons including 20 passengers.

2. **PLADDA (1864-1890)** Iron.
O.N. 43691. 397g, 248n. 181.5 x 24.6 x 13.7 feet.
Direct acting, 2-cyl., by builders, 75hp.
9.1861: Built by Blackwood & Gordon, Port Glasgow (Yard No. 44) for Clyde Shipping Co., Glasgow. *12.1864:* Purchased by Dundee & Newcastle Steam Ship Co. Ltd., name unchanged. *1874:* New engine fitted, compound, 2-cyl, by Gourlay Bros. & Co., Dundee, 80hp. *13.12.1890:* Wrecked near Crail, Fife, while on passage from the River Tyne to Dundee with a cargo of coal, coke and general.

3. **TAY (1885-1889)**
O.N. 89092. 147g, 73n. 100.0 x 19.2 x 8.0 feet.
Compound, 2-cyl., by builders, 40hp.
4.1885: Built by Pearce Bros, Dundee (Yard No. 22) for Dundee & Newcastle Steam Ship Co. Ltd. *4.1889:* Sold to Brown & Tawse, Dundee, name unchanged. *1891:* Lengthened to 116.7 feet, tonnages now 177g, 56n. *5.1899:* Sold to Paton & Hendry (of Glasgow), name unchanged. *3.1911:* Sold to Robert Main (of Ayr), name unchanged. *5.1915:* Sold to The Ardrossan Salvage Co., Ardrossan, name unchanged. *12.1919:* Sold to Henry Hayward and Henry C. Mann (of London), name unchanged. *5.1920:* Sold to Sea Navigation Co. Ltd. (of London), name unchanged. *26.1.1921:* Sailed from Guernsey for Portsmouth with a cargo of granite and not heard of again.

4. **ALDERNEY (1891-1910)** Iron.
O.N. 72346. 422g, 262n. 175.0 x 25.2 x 19.5 feet.
Compound, 2-cyl., by John Shaw & Co., Newcastle, 90hp.
3.1875: Built by Wigham Richardson & Co., Newcastle (Yard No. 89) for London & South Western Railway Co., Southampton (Southampton-Havre/Channel Islands service). *4.1891:* Purchased by Dundee & Newcastle Shipping Co. Ltd., name unchanged. *5.1910:* Sold to Preston & Dublin Shipping Co. Ltd., Preston, name unchanged. *10.1913:* Sold to Levant Transport Co. Ltd. (H. Tyrer, manager), Liverpool and renamed NIGGEM. *10.1914:* Sold to Wilson & Reid, Belfast, name unchanged. *27.12.1914:* Foundered while on passage from Alexandria to Barcelona with a cargo of cotton and general. Crew landed on a sparsely populated region of North Africa near Sollum, and after trouble with tribesmen, trekked to safety across the Western Desert. The Master did not report the loss until 3rd May 1915.

5. **TAY & TYNE (1909-1917)**
See Appendix B No. 36.

APPENDIX H — KIRKCALDY STEAMSHIP CO. LTD.

1. RAVENSCRAIG (1899-1918)
O.N. 107039. 350g, 99n. 135.0 x 23.1 x 11.0 feet.
Compound, 2-cyl., by Cooper & Greig, Dundee, 50hp.
11.1899: Built by Dundee Shipbuilders' Co. Ltd., Dundee (Yard No. 128) for Kirkcaldy Steamship Co. Ltd. *5.1918:* Sold to Wear Steam Shipping Co. (1917) Ltd., (Thomas Rose, manager), Sunderland, name unchanged. *1.1922:* Transferred to Rose Line Ltd. (John H. Soppit, manager), Sunderland. *12.1925:* Manager became Thomas Rose. *7.1926:* Sold to Derwent Steam Shipping Co. Ltd. (Anthony & Bainbridge, managers), Newcastle, name unchanged. *17.9.1932:* Sank after collision with the steamer BARON POLWARTH (3661/29) when 2 miles from Sunk Light Vessel while on passage from Keadby to Chatham with a cargo of coal.

2. ROSYTH (I) (1903-1917)
See Appendix B No. 43.

ROSYTH (I) at Shoreham *I. W. Rooke*

APPENDIX I — THOMAS COWAN, GRANGEMOUTH

1. ITUNA (1886-1897)
O.N. 89655. 408g, 244n. 160.0 x 25.2 x 12.0 feet.
Compound, 2-cyl., by Hutson & Corbett, Glasgow, 70hp.
11.1884: Built by Dobson & Charles, Grangemouth (Yard No. 84) who went into liquidation before completion. Completed by Hutson & Corbett for London & Solway Steam Ship Co. Ltd., London as ITUNA. *7.1886:* Purchased by Thomas Cowan, name unchanged. *2.1895:* Transferred to Forth Steam Ship Co. Ltd. (Thomas Cowan, manager), Grangemouth, name unchanged. *7.1897:* Sold to J. Kielland, Drontheim, Norway, name unchanged. *1898:* Sold to A. W. Selmer, Drontheim, name unchanged. *1907:* Sold to C. Waage, Kopervik, Norway, name unchanged. *7.1.1908:* Stranded on Langeland coast near Rodbjerg while in ballast. *29.9.1908:* Refloated and taken to Christiania for repair. *3.1909:* On completion of repairs, sold to Acties. Fenris (C. A. A. Hirsch, manager), Moss, Norway and renamed FENRIS. *1913:* Sold to J. T. Ostbö, Stavanger, Norway, name unchanged. *1915:* Sold to Damps. Akties. Fenris (E. Lea, manager), Haugesund, Norway, name unchanged. *1916:* Sold to E. Evangen, Aalesund, Norway, name unchanged. *1917:* Sold to Ingvald Bjonnobos Rederi Akties, Christiansund, Norway, name unchanged. *1919:* Sold to Skibsactieselsk. Crescendo (T. Hals, manager), Christiania, Norway, name unchanged. *4.1920:* Sold to Joseph Gasan, Malta and renamed ITUNA. *26.3.1921:* Sank after striking a mine off Santa Maura, Greece, while on passage from Piraeus to Corfu and Malta with a cargo of flour.

2. BRUGES (1890-1894) Iron.
O.N. 90340. 576g, 340n. 170.3 x 29.1 x 11.7 feet.
Compound, 2-cyl., by J. W. & F. Wilson, Sunderland, 80hp.
11.1884: Built by Robert Thompson & Sons, Sunderland (Yard No. 143) for their own account (V. T. Thompson & Co. managers). *1889:* Sold to Tamar Steam Ship Co. Ltd., Plymouth, name unchanged. *10.1890:* Purchased by Thomas Cowan, name unchanged. *12.10.1894:* Sank after collision with the German steamer JOHANNA OELSSNER (931/89) off Hantsholmen while on passage from Dundee and London to Narva, Russia with a cargo of jute.

3. CAIRNGORM (1893-1898) Iron.
O.N. 87257. 1,108g, 692n. 240.6 x 32.9 x 15.6 feet.
Compound, 2-cyl., by W. Kemp, Glasgow, 98hp.
6.1883: Built by Dobie & Co., Glasgow (Yard No. 130) for R. & D. Cairns, Leith. *12.1892:* Transferred to D. Cairns, Leith, name unchanged. *10.1893:* Purchased by Thomas Cowan, name unchanged. *5.1897:* Transferred to Cairngorm Steam Ship Co. (Grangemouth) Ltd. (Thomas Cowan, manager), Grangemouth, name unchanged. *12.1898:* Sold to A. W. Selmer, Drontheim, Norway, and renamed ROWENA. *1911:* Transferred to Det. Selmerske Rederi, Trondhjem, name unchanged. *1915:* Sold to Damps. Akties. Blaafjeld (H. G. Martens, manager), Bergen, Norway and renamed BLAAFJELD. *1915:* Sold to Akties. Tom 1 (Ole Kopstad, manager), Bergen and renamed TOM 1. *1916:* Sold to Akties. Egero (Olsen & Ugelstad, managers), Christiania, Norway and renamed FALKEFJELL. *29.10.1916:* Torpedoed and sunk by UB 22 in position 55.42N 01.02E while on passage from Christiania to Hull with a cargo of timber.

4. NAROVA (1894-1911)
O.N. 90913. 949g, 493n. 213.0 x 32.0 x 12.3 feet.
Triple, 3-cyl., by builders, 99hp.
4.1894: Built by Ramage & Ferguson Ltd, Leith (Yard No. 126) for Narova Steam Ship Co. Ltd. (Thomas Cowan, manager), Grangemouth. *3.1911:* Sold to M. H. Bland & Co. Ltd., Gibraltar and renamed GIBEL YEDID. *13.7.1917:* Captured by U 48 when 150 miles W¾ N of Ushant and sunk by bombs placed on board by the U-boat crew.

5. RASONA (1896-1897)
O.N. 90915. 925g, 401n. 212.9 x 32.1 x 12.3 feet.
Triple, 3-cyl., by builders, 155hp.
3.1896: Built by Ramage & Ferguson Ltd., Leith (Yard No. 142) for Thomas Cowan. *3.1899:* Transferred to Rasona Steam Ship Co. Ltd., (Thomas Cowan, manager), Grangemouth, name unchanged. *20.2.1897:* Wrecked off St Ann's Head while on passage from Dublin to Burry Port, Carmarthenshire in ballast.

6. LOUGA (1898-1919)
See Appendix B No. 42.

7. PLOUSSA (1905-1916)
O.N. 119711. 1,001g, 512n. 218.3 x 33.1 x 14.2 feet.
Triple, 3-cyl., by builders, 155hp.
5.1905: Built by Ramage & Ferguson Ltd., Leith (Yard No. 199) for Thomas Cowan. *9.1916:* Sold to Antrim Iron Ore Co. Ltd., Belfast and renamed GLENTAISE. *8.1929:* Company taken over by Coast Lines Ltd., Liverpool and renamed ANTRIM COAST. *4.1933:* Sold to Scotto, Ambrosino, Pugliese Fils & Cie., Oran and renamed REGINA PACIS. *1937:* Sold to P. Cottaropoulos & G. Theophylactos, Marseilles, France and renamed PRADO. *8.1944:* Scuttled by German authorities at Marseilles. Later raised and broken up.

8. KOOLGA (1910-1918)
O.N. 129384. 1,110g, 564n. 232.1 x 33.9 x 14.9 feet.
Triple, 3-cyl., by builders, 188hp.
4.1910: Built by Caledon Shipbuilding & Engineering Co. Ltd., Dundee (Yard No. 213) for Thomas Cowan. *1918:* Sold whilst laid-up at Leith to The Aberdeen Steam Navigation Co. Ltd., Aberdeen, name unchanged. *10.1919:* Lay-up berth moved to Grimsby. *11.1919:* Brought into service. *10.1945:* Sold to Min Kiang Steamship Co. Ltd., Shanghai, China and renamed MIN YUNG. *11.1946:* Laid-up at Barry. *5.1947:* Sold to Cia. Maritima Sphika S.A., Panama and renamed BEATRIZ and resold to Cia. de Nav. Estoco S.A., Panama, name unchanged. *1.1952:* Sold to Kustenschiffahrt A.G., Basle, Switzerland and renamed GALLUS. *5.7.1953:* Arrived at Hamburg and in *9.1953* purchased by Eisen & Metall K.G. Lehr & Co., and broken up by Walter Ritscher.

APPENDIX J — ABERDEEN, NEWCASTLE & HULL STEAM CO. LTD.

J1. ABERDEEN & NEWCASTLE STEAM NAVIGATION CO. (1844-1866).

1. **VELOCITY (1844-1849)** Wooden Paddle.
215g, 149n. 118.4 x 18.4 x 11.4 feet.
Engine by Greenhead Foundry Co., Glasgow.
5.1821: Built by William Denny, Dumbarton for Aberdeen & Leith Steam Yacht Co., Aberdeen. *10.1825:* Sold to Aberdeen, Leith & Clyde Shipping Co., Aberdeen, name unchanged. *1835:* Re-engined by I. & W. Napier, Glasgow. *7.1844:* Sold to W. Duthie, Aberdeen, name unchanged; Lengthened by Alexander Duthie & Co., Aberdeen to 145.0, tonnages now 266g, 171n. *9.1844:* Acquired by Aberdeen & Newcastle Steam Navigation Co., name unchanged. *25.10.1848:* Stranded on Aberdeen Pier and became a total loss.

2. **VICTORIA (1848-1864)** Iron Paddle.
O.N. 6836. 210g, 153n. 158.5 x 19.9 x 10.2 feet.
Engine of 100hp.
11.1848: Built by Tod & McGregor, Glasgow (Yard No. 52) for Aberdeen & Newcastle Steam Navigation Co. *5.1864:* Sold to Aberdeen, Tyne & Hamburg Steam Navigation Co., Aberdeen, name unchanged. *10.1864:* Sold to W. Bailey & W. Leetham, Hull, name unchanged. *15.12.1865:* Arrived at Lisbon, Portugal and transferred to Empreza Luzitania (Bailey & Leetham, managers), Lisbon, name unchanged. *1873:* Believed broken up.

3. **PRINCESS ALICE (1865-1866)** Wooden Paddle.
O.N. 17233. 405g, 255n. 165.6 x 27.0 x 13.8 feet.
Engine of 150hp.
1843: Built by Tod & McGregor, Glasgow (Yard No. 36) for Preston & Wyre Railway Harbour & Docks Co., Fleetwood. *1850:* Passed to Lancashire & Yorkshire Railway Co., Fleetwood, name unchanged. *12.1854:* Transferred to Lancashire & Yorkshire and London & North Western Railway Companies, name unchanged. *1855:* Sold to F. Kemp & others, Fleetwood, name unchanged. *9.1858:* Sold to J. Holmes & H. Earle, Liverpool, name unchanged. *10.1860:* Sold to I. Hodgson, Whitehaven, name unchanged. *3.1861:* Sold to T. Jackson & others, Whitehaven. *1.1865:* Acquired by J. B. Adam on behalf of Aberdeen & Newcastle Steam Navigation Co., name unchanged. *10.1866:* Transferred to Aberdeen, Newcastle & Hull Steam Co. Ltd., name unchanged. *3.2.1874:* Sold at Bayonne, France, presumably for breaking up.

J2. ABERDEEN, GRIMSBY & HULL STEAM PACKET CO. (1855-1863) ABERDEEN & HULL STEAM NAVIGATION CO. (1863-1866)

1. **ABERDEENSHIRE (1855-1865)** Iron.
O.N. 6910. 220g, 150n. 136.0 x 20.6 x 11.5 feet.
Engine by Inglis & Co., Glasgow, 50hp.
1855: Built by William Simons & Co., Renfrew, Glasgow (Yard No. 79) for Aberdeen, Grimsby & Hull Steam Packet Co. *1863:* Owners became Aberdeen & Hull Steam Navigation Co. *1865:* Sold to Rawson & Robinson, Hull, name unchanged. *1871:* Lengthened to 171.2 feet, tonnages now 345g, 215n. *1879:* Engine compounded by Earle's Co., Hull. *27.5.1895:* Capsized and sank at Berville, at entrance to River Seine, while on passage from Hull to Rouen, France, with a general cargo.

2. **PHAROS (1861-1866)** Wooden Paddle.
O.N. 7841. 270g, 186n. 143.2 x 21.7 x 14.8 feet.
Engine of 160hp.
5.1846: Built by William Fairbairn & Son, Millwall, London for Commissioners of Northern Lights, Granton. *9.1861:* Acquired by Aberdeen, Grimsby & Hull Steam Packet Co., name unchanged. *1863:* Owners became Aberdeen & Hull Steam Navigation Co., *10.1864:* Lengthened to 171.6 feet, tonnages now 328g, 243n. *10.1866:* Transferred to Aberdeen, Newcastle & Hull Steam Co. Ltd., name unchanged. *6.1877:* Sold to Thomas Williamson, Barrow and broken up.

3. LA PLATA (1864-1866) Iron.
O.N. 24392. 372g, 253n. 160 x 25.0 x 13.0 feet.
Engine of 90hp.
1854: Built by John Laird, Birkenhead (Yard No. 105) for South American General Steam Navigation Co., Liverpool. *4.1859:* Sold to H. T. Watson, Goole, name unchanged. *12.1864:* Acquired by Aberdeen & Hull Steam Navigation Co., name unchanged. *10.1866:* Transferred to Aberdeen, Newcastle & Hull Steam Co. Ltd. *10.1867:* Sold to J. Taylor, Middlesbrough, name unchanged. *1868:* Sold to C. E. Muller, Middlesbrough, fitted with new engine of 60hp, tonnages now 351g, 198n, name unchanged. *18.8.1868:* Wrecked off Flamborough Head while on passage from Middlesbrough to Rotterdam.

J3. ABERDEEN, NEWCASTLE & HULL STEAM CO. LTD. (1866-1940)

1. PHAROS (1866-1877)
See this Appendix under J2.2 above.

2. LA PLATA (1866-1867)
See this Appendix under J2.3 above.

3. PRINCESS ALICE (1866-1874)
See this Appendix under J1.3 above.

4. JAMES HALL (1870-1888) Iron.
O.N. 60705. 346g, 184n. 174.0 x 24.0 x 13.3 feet.
Compound, 2-cyl., by builders, 65hp.
4.1870: Built by Hall, Russell & Co., Aberdeen (Yard No. 171) for Aberdeen, Newcastle & Hull Steam Co. Ltd. *10.1888:* Sold to Aberdeen, Leith & Moray Firth Steam Ship Co. Ltd., Aberdeen, name unchanged. *23.1.1904:* After collision with the s.s. LUDDICK (430/98) drifted ashore near Donmouth, Aberdeen and became a total loss.

5. ALEXANDER PIRIE (1873-1905) Iron.
O.N. 65102. 460g, 250n. 180.0 x 26.0 x 14.0 feet.
Compound, 2-cyl., by builders, 90hp.
11.1873: Built by A. Hall & Co., Aberdeen (Yard No. 282) for Aberdeen, Newcastle & Hull Steam Co. Ltd. *12.1905:* Sold to A. Coulouthros, Andros, Greece and renamed NICHOLAOS. *1909:* Sold to G. Katrakis, Piraeus, Greece, name unchanged. *1923:* Broken up.

6. NORTHERN CITY (1873-1875) Iron.
O.N. 65100. 274g, 190n. 155.0 x 21.7 x 12.0 feet.
Compound, 2-cyl., William King & Co., Glasgow, 50hp.
10.1873: Built by John Fullerton & Co., Paisley (Yard No. 15) for M. I. Wilson, Liverpool as CARNFORTH. *11.1873:* Acquired by Aberdeen, Newcastle & Hull Steam Co. Ltd. and renamed NORTHERN CITY. *23.1.1875:* Struck a rock near Johnshaven, Forfarshire while on passage from Hull to Aberdeen with 165 tons of general cargo and nine passengers. Refloated after 10 minutes and proceeded on voyage but water gained in her hold and put out the boiler fires. Vessel finally sank 8 miles from Aberdeen.

7. MARY JAMIESON (1875-1878) Wooden brigantine.
O.N. 70444. 206g, 197n. 119.0 x 25.5 x 12.6 feet.
6.1875: Built by Redway & Son, Dartmouth for Aberdeen, Newcastle & Hull Steam Co. Ltd. *4.1878:* Sold to Peterhead Cod Fishery Co., Peterhead, name unchanged. *21.7.1890:* Wrecked on Opobo Bar, Nigeria while on passage from Opobo to Rotterdam with a cargo of palm kernels.

8. COUNTESS OF ABERDEEN (1878-1894) Iron.
O.N. 77445. 580g, 291n. 200.1 x 26.8 x 13.9 feet.
Compound, 2-cyl., by builders, 180hp.
2.1878: Built by Barrow Shipbuilding Co. Ltd., Barrow (Yard No. 52) for Aberdeen, Newcastle & Hull Steam Co. Ltd. *15.4.1894:* Ran ashore during fog near Cove Bay, Kincardineshire, while on passage from Hull to Aberdeen with a general cargo. Fire later broke out and she became a total loss.

EARL OF ABERDEEN *A. Duncan*

9. EARL OF ABERDEEN (1889-1915)
O.N. 94527. 734g, 326n. 210.0 x 30.2 x 14.8 feet.
Triple, 3-cyl., by builders, 200hp.
1.1889: Built by Hall, Russell & Co., Aberdeen (Yard No. 259) for Aberdeen, Newcastle & Hull Steam Co. Ltd. *10.1915:* Sold to Leith, Hull & Hamburg Steam Packet Co. (J. Currie & Co., managers), Leith and renamed BRITANNIA. *18.10.1917:* Sailed from Middlesbrough for St. Malo with a cargo of pig iron and not heard of again — uncertain whether loss due to weather or enemy action.

10. GLEN TILT (1894-1898) Iron.
O.N. 84367. 453g, 276n. 165.5 x 23.0 x 12.4 feet.
Compound, 2-cyl., by builders, 62hp.
11.1882: Built by Hall, Russell & Co., Aberdeen (Yard No. 242) for Aberdeen Glen Line Steam Ship Co. Ltd., Aberdeen. *7.1894:* Acquired by Aberdeen, Newcastle & Hull Steam Co. Ltd., name unchanged. *17.7.1898:* Wrecked at Kettleness near Whitby, while on passage from Hull to Stockton-on-Tees with a cargo of wheat and maize.

11. NORWOOD (1895-1917)
O.N. 104509. 798g, 348n. 220.8 x 30.2 x 15.1 feet.
Triple, 3-cyl., by builders, 205hp.
4.1895: Built by Hall, Russell & Co., Aberdeen (Yard No. 286) for Aberdeen, Newcastle & Hull Steam Co. Ltd. *11.2.1917:* Sailed from Middlesbrough for Aberdeen and presumed mined in the North Sea.

12. LUDDICK (1898-1924)
O.N. 108658. 530g, 184n. 167.7 x 26.1 x 10.4 feet.
Compound, 2-cyl., by Ross & Duncan, Glasgow, 73hp.
11.1898: Built by R. Williamson & Son, Workington (Yard No. 118) for Aberdeen, Newcastle & Hull Steam Co. Ltd. *1924:* Sold to British Lines Ltd., London, name unchanged. *1925:* Sold to Continental Lines Ltd., London and renamed CONTINENTAL FREIGHTER. *1928:* Sold to Freighter Steam Ship Co., London, name unchanged. *19.11.1930:* Sank in the River Scheldt after collision, while on passage from Rumpst to Shoreham with a cargo of bricks. *4.12.1930:* Refloated and beached. *8.12.1930:* Refloated and docked at Antwerp. Believed later declared a constructive total loss and abandoned to the Belgian Government who sold her to E. Herbosch for breaking up.

13. HIGHLANDER (1916-1939)
O.N. 137187. 1,216g, 618n. 243.3 x 34.9 x 15.2 feet.
Triple, 3-cyl., by builders, 214hp.
2.1916: Built by Caledon Shipbuilding & Engineering Co. Ltd., Dundee (Yard No. 241). *10.1929:* Management transferred to Dundee, Perth & London Shipping Co. Ltd. *10.1939:* Sold to The North of Scotland & Orkney & Shetland Steam Navigation Co. Ltd., Aberdeen, name unchanged. *1.8.1940:* Damaged in air attack 10 miles SSE of Girdleness but brought two aircraft down with her anti-aircraft fire. *8.1940:* Renamed ST. CATHERINE. *14.11.1940:* Sunk in air attack near the South of Outer Buoy, Aberdeen Swept Channel, with the loss of one passenger and 14 crew.

14. KILDRUMMY (1924-1937)
See Appendix B No. 56.

ABOYNE

15. ABOYNE (1937-1946)
O.N. 165246. 1,020g, 386n. 248.7 x 37.7 x 15.1 feet.
Triple, 3-cyl., by J. G. Kincaid & Co. Ltd., Greenock, 264hp.
2.1937: Built by Caledon Shipbuilding & Engineering Co. Ltd., Dundee (Yard No. 364). *6.1943:* Taken over for service as a convoy rescue ship. *7.1945:* Returned to owners. *10.1946:* Sold to Clyde Shipping Co. Ltd., Glasgow and renamed ARKLOW. *1949:* Sold to The Ulster S.S. Co. Ltd. (G. Heyn & Sons Ltd., managers), Belfast and renamed FAIR HEAD. *1954:* Sold to Palgrave, Murphy (Shipowners) Ltd., Dublin and renamed CITY OF HAMBURG. *1958:* Sold to Hellenic Mediterranean Lines Ltd., Piraeus, Greece and renamed LIGURIA. *1960:* Sold to T. & F. Athanassiades, Piraeus and renamed THOMAS A. *4.6.1963:* Abandoned off Sicily after fire broke out in her cargo while on a voyage from Galatz, Romania, to Liverpool with timber. Later beached at Scalambri but became total loss.

MANAGED VESSEL

16. EMPIRE SEAWORTHY (1945-1946)
O.N. 180381. 522g, 300n. 142.6 x 27.1 x 16.0 feet.
Oil engine, 4-cyl., 2S.C.S.A., by British Polar Engines Ltd., Glasgow.
11.1945: Built by Goole Shipbuilding & Repairing Co. Ltd., Goole (Yard No. 445) for the Ministry of War Transport (managers Aberdeen, Newcastle & Hull Shipping Co. Ltd.). *1946:* Sold to Middle East Coastal Services Ltd., Famagusta, Cyprus and renamed SIDIBARRANI. *1951:* Sold to Straits Steamship Co. Ltd., Singapore and renamed SEMENYIH. *1967:* Sold to Sharikat Perkapalan Kris Sdn. Berhad (Manfield & Co. Ltd., managers), Labuan, name unchanged. *12.1971:* Hong Huat Hardware Co. Pte. Ltd. commenced demolition at Singapore.

APPENDIX K — V. A. CAPPON TUGS LTD. (1913-1946)

1. GRANGE (1913-1915, 1923-1929) Iron—Paddle tug.
O.N. 82332. 125 g, 45n. 100.0 x 18.1 x 9.4 feet.
Lever, 1-cyl., by J. P. Rennoldson & Son, South Shields, 70hp.
1880: Built by Joseph T. Eltringham, South Shields (Yard No. 86) for Clyde Shipping Co., Glasgow as FLYING DUTCHMAN. *2.1892:* Sold to Forth Towing Co. Ltd., (William Buchan, manager), Grangemouth and renamed GRANGE. *10.1895:* Transferred to Grangemouth & Forth Towing Co. Ltd. (Andrew A. Mackay, manager), Grangemouth, name unchanged. *3.1913:* Purchased by Victor A. Cappon, name unchanged. *1914:* Hired by the War Department. *1.1915:* Sold to the Admiralty. *3.1923:* Repurchased from the Admiralty. *1.1929:* Broken up at North Queensferry.

2. CONQUEROR (1913-1917) Iron—Paddle tug.
O.N. 89619. 177g, 16n. 123.5 x 20.1 x 10.1 feet.
Lever, 2-cyl., by builders, 120hp.
1884: Built by Hepple & Co., North Shields (Yard No. 386) for William Sandford, London as CONQUEROR. *9.1889:* Sold to Soc. Anon. du Remorquage Boulonnais, Boulogne, France and renamed CONQUERANT. *1896:* Sold to Soc. Nouvelle du Remorquage Boulonnais, Boulogne, name unchanged. *4.1905:* Sold to Rosa & William Lennard (Benjamin I. Davies, manager), Middlesbrough and renamed CONQUEROR. *10.1910:* Sold to John W. W. Woodward & James Nicholson of 2 Shore, Leith, port of registry and name unchanged. *7.1913:* Purchased by Victor A. Cappon, name unchanged. *1916:* Hired by the Admiralty for service as a Dockyard tug. *2.1917:* Sold to R. Redhead & Son Ltd., Newcastle, name unchanged. *1919:* Returned to owners. *8.1929:* Owners' title became Redhead & Dry's Tugs Ltd., Newcastle, name unchanged. *5.1944:* Sold to France, Fenwick Tyne & Wear Co. Ltd. (Frank Dawson, manager), Newcastle, name unchanged. *5.1956:* Sold to the British Iron & Steel Corporation for £2,150 and allocated to J.J. King & Co. Ltd., Gateshead for breaking up.

3. TYNEDALE (1917-1923) Iron—Paddle tug.
O.N. 89812. 99g, 10n. 94.0 x 17.0 x 9.2 feet.
Lever, 1-cyl., by R. B. Finlay & Son, North Shields, 38hp.
10.1885: Built by Lawson & Eltringham, South Shields for William Reed, North Shields as TYNEDALE. *3.1895:* Passed to John & Elspeth Reed on death of William Reed. *2.1897:* Sold to Joseph Gray, South Shields, name unchanged. *1.1901:* Sold to James I. Minto, Leith, name unchanged. *11.1917:* Purchased by Victor A. Cappon (in association with Joseph Gray until 5.1922). *6.1923:* Broken up at Montrose.

4. VICT (1921-1937) Iron—Twin-Screw tug.
O.N. 144701. 73g, 10n. 80.2 x 16.8 x 8.2 feet.
Compound, 2 x 2-cyl., Amos & Smith, Hull, 35hp.
1889: Built by Head & Barnard, Hull for service on inland waterways. *4.1921:* Purchased by Victor A. Cappon (in association with Joseph Gray until 5.1922), name unchanged. *9.1937:* Broken up at Granton.

5. GAUNTLET (1924-1940)
See Appendix C No. 4

6. MENTOR 1937-1940
See Appendix C No. 5

APPENDIX L — COQUET SHIPPING CO. LTD. (ANTHONY & BAINBRIDGE, managers), NEWCASTLE (1946-1956)

1. COQUETDALE (1946-1951)
See Appendix B No. 56 under KILDRUMMY.

2. COQUETSIDE (1947-1951)
O.N. 180607. 1,058g, 585n. 219.7 x 34.9 x 14.2 feet.
Triple, 3-cyl., by A. Borsig G.m.b.H., Berlin, 109hp.
1923: Built by Nüscke & Co. A.G., Stettin for Westdeutsche Schiffahrts A.G., Düsseldorf, Germany as RHENANIA. *1924:* Sold to Kolner Reed., A.G. (Edmund Halm & Co., managers), Cologne, Germany and renamed MARTHA HALM. *1926:* Sold to Angf.Aktieb.Bore, Abo, Finland and renamed BORE VII. *18.12.1936:* Wrecked at Manninklub, south of Kotka, Finland while on passage from Abo to Kotka in ballast. Declared a constructive total loss and sold to Aug. Bolten Wm. Miller's Nachfolger, Hamburg, Germany, repaired and renamed GOTAALV. *1938:* Sold to Schulte & Bruns, Emden, Germany and renamed BERNHARD SCHULTE. *3.3.1941:* Sunk off the Lofoten Islands but later raised, repaired and returned to service. *5.1945:* Seized by Allied Forces at Flensburg. *7.1945:* Transferred to the Ministry of War Transport (Monroe Bros. Ltd., Liverpool, managers), and renamed EMPIRE CONGO. *3.1946:* Owners now Ministry of Transport. *24.2.1947:* Purchased by Coquet Shipping Co. Ltd. and renamed COQUETSIDE. *3.1951:* Sold to Casimiro Cosulich, Genoa, Italy and renamed DENEB. *1958:* Sold to Nautica S.p.A., Cagliari, Italy, name unchanged. *13.10.1966:* S.p.A. Cantiere Navali del Golfo commenced demolition at La Spezia, Italy.

3. COQUETDYKE (1952-1956)
O.N. 169238. 635g, 333n. 181.5 x 30.0 x 13.5 feet.
Oil engine, 4S.C.S.A., 6-cyl., by N. V. Werkspoor, Amsterdam.
8.1952: Built by Bodewes Scheepswerven N.V., Martenshoek (Yard No. 396) for Coquet Shipping Co. Ltd. *1.1956:* Sold to Zillah Shipping Co. Ltd., (W. A. Savage Ltd., managers), Liverpool and renamed EARLSFIELD. *7.1967:* Transferred to Coast Lines Ltd., Liverpool and sold to R. S. Briggs & Co. (Shipping) Ltd. (Briggs Shipbrokers & Agents Ltd., managers), London, name unchanged. *1969:* Renamed KATIE H. *3.1971:* Sold to Seabright Shipping Ltd. (managers as before), name unchanged. *7.3.1972:* In collision with the Belgian fishing vessel ZEEPAREL (139/68) and sank about 8 miles north of Noord Hinder Light vessel, while on passage from Rotterdam to London.

COQUETDYKE as EARLSFIELD *G. E. P. Brownell/W.S.P.L.*

APPENDIX M — JOHN WILSON (1949-1951)
LOCKETT WILSON LTD. (1951-1954)
LOCKETT WILSON LINE LTD. (1954-1968)

1. WILMAS (1949-1951) Twin-screw barge.
O.N. 183037. 126g, 65n. 97.5 x 20.4 x 7.3 feet.
Oil engines (2), each 4-cyl., by J. & Co. G. Bolinders N.V., Alblasserdam.
1916: Built by Osbourne, Graham & Co., Sunderland for unknown owners for service on inland waters. *6.1949:* Acquired by John Wilson and James R. Massey, London and named WILMAS. *10.1949:* John Wilson now sole owner. *4.1951:* Sold to French owners — no further record.

WILMAS at St. Valery, Somme

2. PARKSTONE (1951-1951)
O.N. 165627. 200g, 128n 108.4 x 21.7 x 7.9 feet.
Oil engine, 4S.C.S.A., 4-cyl. by Appingedammer Brons Motorenfab., Appingedam; new oil engine fitted 11.1948: 4S.C.S.A., 5-cyl., by Blackstone & Co., Stamford, 200bhp.
11.1929: Built by J. Meyer's Schoopshouw Maatschappij N.V., Zalt-Bommel (Yard No. 552) for H. Mulder, Voorburg, Holland as APOLLINARIS III. *1933:* Owners now titled N.V. Scheepvaart Maats. Schouwen (H. Mulder, manager). *2.1937:* Sold to John Carter (Poole) Ltd., Poole and renamed PARKSTONE. *5.1948:* Sold to I. P. Langford (Shipping) Ltd. (of Gloucester), name unchanged. *1.1950:* Peter Lockett acquired a half interest in the vessel. *5.1951:* John Wilson purchased half of Peter Lockett's holding. *9.1951:* Owners became Nevill Long & Co. Ltd. of Liverpool, name unchanged. *10.1951:* Sold to Benjamin Ackerley & Co. Ltd., Liverpool, name unchanged. *4.1954:* Sold to Thomas Watson (Shipping) Ltd., Rochester and renamed LADY SONIA. *7.1961:* Sold to Intercon Coasters Ltd., Rochester, name unchanged. *10.1963:* Sold to M. W. Hardy & Co. (Mercantile) Ltd, London, name unchanged. *5.1966:* Sold to Peter Williams (of Cardiff), name unchanged. *4.1968:* Sold to Herb Ship Ltd. (of Bude), name unchanged. *5.1968:* Sold to Alan E. B. Jones (of Portsmouth), name unchanged. *5.1971.* Sold to Thomas J. Bowen (of Southampton), name unchanged. *11.1972:* Sold to James H. Haywood (of Portsmouth), name unchanged. *1.1977:* Sold to Edgell Wharf (Services) Ltd., Southampton and broken up.

PARKSTONE

3. DUNAVON (1951-1954)
O.N. 128110. 235g, 88n. 125.3 x 21.1 x 8.8 feet.
Compound, 2-cyl., by Alexander Hall & Co. Ltd., Aberdeen, 56hp; fitted in 1952 with oil engine: 2S.C.S.A. 6-cyl., made in 1942 by British Polar Engines Ltd., Glasgow.
9.1908: Built by Alexander Hall & Co. Ltd., Aberdeen (Yard No. 445) for Robert Rix & Sons Ltd., Hull as SPURNPOINT. *4.1919:* Sold to Elvedon Shipping Co. Ltd., (Ernest G. Griffin, manager), Cardiff, name unchanged. *4.1920:* Sold to Scorrier Steam Coasters Ltd., (John H. Woods manager), Cardiff, name unchanged. *8.1927:* Sold William J. Ireland, Liverpool and renamed QUICKTHORN. *3.1931:* Sold to Buchan & Hogg, Grangemouth and renamed DUNAVON. *6.1941:* Owners became Dunavon Steamship Co. (Buchan & Hogg Ltd., managers), Grangemouth. *12.1945:* Sold to William R. Metcalf, Falmouth, name unchanged. *6.1951:* Purchased by John Wilson & Peter Lockett, London, name unchanged. *6.1953:* Owners became Lockett Wilson Ltd. *5.1954:* Sold to Arlesford Trading Co. Ltd., London, name unchanged. *9.7.1955:* Arrived at Llanelli, Carmarthenshire to be broken up by Rees Shipbreaking Co. Ltd.

4. MORION (1951-1951).
O.N. 180369. 410g, 190n. 142.2 x 27.0 x 8.5 feet.
Oil engine, 2S.C.S.A., 6-cyl., by Petters Ltd., Loughborough, 275bhp.
1.1945: Built by Goole Shipbuilding & Repairing Co. Ltd., Goole (Yard No. 432), having been laid down as CHANT 39, later renamed FABRIC 39, and finally launched *13.11.1944* as EMPIRE FANG for the Ministry of War Transport, London. Placed under the management of William Robertson, Glasgow. *7.1946:* Sold to William Robertson (later William Robertson Shipowners Ltd.), Glasgow and renamed MORION. *8.1951:* Purchased by John Wilson and Peter Lockett, name unchanged. *10.1951:* Sold to Nevill Long & Co. Ltd. (Benjamin Ackerley & Co. Ltd., managers (of London)), port of registry and name unchanged. *5.1952:* Renamed LONGBOAT. *10.1954:* Sold to Gerard Harvey (of Quebec), port of registry and name unchanged. *8.1956:* Fitted with new oil engine, 4S.C.S.A., 6-cyl. by Blackstone & Co. Ltd., Stamford, 324bhp. *5.1963:* Transferred to Maritime Harvey Ltee, Quebec, Canada. *4.1972:* Sold to Edgar Lavoie et freres, Quebec, name unchanged. *9.1972:* Renamed DE LAVOYE. *10.1972:* Sold to Joseph A. Lavoie, Quebec, name unchanged. *11.1975:* Transferred to Lavoie, Lavoie et Fils Inc., Quebec. *4.1978:* Sold to Vapores Orinoco S.A., Panama, name unchanged. *1979:* Transferred to Honduras flag with owners unspecified. Continued existence uncertain.

5. ROSELYNE (1952-1953)
O.N. 169088. 313g, 143n. 141.7 x 21.5 x 9.1 feet.
Oil engine, 2S.C.S.A., 5-cyl., by Crossley Bros. Ltd., Manchester, 275bhp.
8.1943: Built by R. Dunston Ltd., Thorne, Doncaster (Yard No. 394) for the Ministry of War Transport, London as EMPIRE TOWNSMAN, and placed under the management of Osborn & Wallis Ltd., Bristol. *12.1946:* Sold to W. D. Tamlyn, Plymouth and renamed ROSELYNE. *2.1952:* Purchased by Lockett Wilson Ltd., name unchanged. *1.1953:* Sold to Fowey Harbour Commissioners, Fowey, converted to a hopper barge and renamed LANTYAN. *5.1957:* Sold to Dale Sand & Gravel Co. Ltd. (of London), name unchanged. *6.1964:* Sold to Seaborne Aggregates Co. Ltd. (P. E. Penfold, manager) (of London), name unchanged. *12.1965:* Sold to Amey Marine Ltd. (P. E. Penfold, manager), Southampton and renamed PEN ARUN. *6.1972:* Sold to Charles A. Brindle (of Cowes), name unchanged. *1.1974:* Sold to Dale Sand & Gravel Co. Ltd. (of London), Guernsey and renamed SIR CEDRIC. *1.1975:* Sold to Martin J. Minter-Kemp (of St. Ives), name unchanged. *4.1975:* Sold to Roselyon Shipping Co. Ltd., Padstow, name unchanged. *1977:* Sold to Societe Pte. Derrien-Bichue (of Lannion), France, name unchanged. Still in service.

6. PURBECK (1952-1959)
O.N. 164874. 199g, 121n. 99.7 x 24.0 8.1 feet.
Oil engine, 2S.C.S.A., 6-cyl., by Atlas-Diesel A/B, Stockholm.
6.1936: Built by Charles Hill & Sons Ltd., Bristol (Yard No. 244) for John Carter (Poole) Ltd., Poole. *4.1952:* Purchased by John Wilson & Peter Lockett, name unchanged. *1.1955:* Transferred to Lockett Wilson Ltd. *2.1956:* Transferred to Lockett Wilson Line Ltd. *3.1959:* Sold to Cerebos Ltd., London, name unchanged. *4.1961:* Sold to Alan J. Brush Ltd., Maldon, name unchanged. *1970:* Broken up at Mistley, Essex.

PURBECK *John G. Callis*

7. CORTACHY/CONCORDE (I) (1953-1961)
See Appendix B No. 59 under CORTACHY

8. CLICHY (1954-1961)
See Appendix B No. 55 under CLOVA

9. CROMBIE (1954-1960)
See Appendix B No. 60

10. VENDOME (1960-1968)
O.N. 301255. 344g, 173n. 136.0 x 24.0 x 10.5 feet.
Oil engine, 4S.C.S.A., 6-cyl., by Lister Blackstone Marine Ltd., Dursley, 396bhp.
7.1960: Built by Brazen Island Shipyard Ltd., Polruan Bay, Fowey (Yard No. 2) for Lockett Wilson Line Ltd. *5.1968:* Sold to Thomas Watson (Shipping) Ltd., Rochester and renamed LADY SORCHA. *7.1971:* Sold to John A. Osborne, Plymouth, Montserrat, Leeward Islands, West Indies, name unchanged. *20.8.1975:* Sank South of Castries, St. Lucia after collision with the m.v. WHITSHOAL II (3,643/43) while on passage from Trinidad to Montserrat.

VENDOME *Dave Hocquard*

11. VAUBAN (1962-1968)
O.N. 182569. 370g, 158n. 137.9 x 23.6 x 9.4 feet.
Oil engine, 4S.C.S.A., 6-cyl., by Lister Blackstone Marine Ltd., Dursley, 467bhp.
11.1962: Built by Brazen Island Shipyard Ltd., Polruan Bay, Fowey (Yard No. 3) for Lockett Wilson Line Ltd. *11.1968:* Sold to J. J. Prior (Transport) Ltd., London, name unchanged. *12.1968:* Sold to Coppack Bros. & Co., Connah's Quay, name unchanged. *4.1971:* Sold to Cornish Shipping Ltd., Plymouth, name unchanged. *1980:* Intended sale to Bell Ships (Union Transport (London) Ltd., managers) not completed although the new name LA BELLE CAROLE was painted-up. *5.1981:* Ceol Mor Shipping Ltd., Hull appointed managers and renamed ROLSTON. *11.1982:* Sold to Chartborder Ltd. (Wilship Maritime Services Ltd., managers), Hull, name unchanged. *30.11.1985:* Laid-up at Hull. *8.1986:* Sold to Terence Rayner (of Bradford), name unchanged. *27.7.1987:* Demolition commenced at Barrow-on-Humber by New Holland Shipyard Ltd.

VAUBAN leaving Jersey *Dave Hocquard*

APPENDIX N — CHANNEL SHIPPING LTD. (1955-1968)

1. ERROL (II)/GROUVILLE (I) (1955-1964)
See Appendix B No. 58 under ERROL (II).

GROUVILLE (I) *Dave Hocquard*

2. GOREY (I) (1956-1963)
O.N. 160497. 349g 149n. 136.0 x 24.0 x 10.0 feet.
Oil engine, 2S.C.S.A., 4-cyl., by N. V. Krom, Amsterdam; new oil engine fitted 1950, 2S.C.S.A., 4-cyl., by British Polar Engines Ltd., Glasgow.
6.1928: Built by Charles Hill & Sons Ltd., Bristol (Yard No. 170) for Shell Mex Ltd., London as the tanker SHELL MEX 8. *12.1931:* Transferred to Shell Mex & B.P. Ltd., London and renamed SHELBRIT 4. *5.1952:* Renamed SHELL DRIVER. *9.1956:* Purchased by Channel Shipping Ltd. and converted to dry cargo. *3.1957:* Renamed GOREY. *7.1963:* Sold to W. J. Sutton & R. L. Morrish, Hull and renamed CHARGER. *1.1966:* Sold to Overseas & General Brokerage & Finance Co. Ltd., London, name unchanged. *12.1970:* Broken up in the United Kingdom.

3. GRANTEZ (1956-1957) Twin-screw
O.N. 163394. 377g. 118n. 135.0 x 25.1 x 11.4 feet.
Oil engines, 2S.C.S.A., each 5-cyl., by L. Gardner & Sons Ltd., Manchester.
10.1933: Built by Rowhedge Ironworks Co. Ltd., Rowhedge (Yard No. 5484) for National Benzole Co. Ltd., as BEN HENSHAW. *11.1956:* Purchased by Channel Shipping Ltd., and converted to dry cargo. *2.1957:* Renamed GRANTEZ. *11.1957:* Sold to Ashmead (Padstow) Ltd., Padstow, name unchanged. *6.1959:* Converted to a sand dredger, fitted with oil engines made in 1944, 4SCSA, each 12-cyl., by Davey, Paxman & Co. Ltd., Colchester, 900bhp. *7.7.1970:* Stranded in the River Camel off Padstow and broke her back — later broken up in Padstow Harbour.

4. FAUVIC (1959-1962)
O.N. 300427. 485g, 233n. 155.0 x 27.7 x 10.5 feet.
Oil engine, 4S.C.S.A., 6-cyl., by Klöckner-Humboldt-Deutz, Cologne.
1951: Built by Foxhol N.V., Foxhol (Yard No. 89) for E. G. Smith (E. Wagenborg's Scheepvaart & Expeditiebdr. N.V.), Oestwold, Holland as FRIEDA. *11.1959:* Purchased by Channel Shipping Ltd., and renamed FAUVIC. *3.1962:* Sold to Western Shipping Ltd. (Channel Shipping Ltd., managers), Plymouth and renamed MELEDOR. *23.4.1965:* Sank in the River Seine near Yainville after collision with Norwegian m.v. FRIERFJORD (5,243/44) while on passage from Fowey to St. Etienne du Rouvray, near Rouen, with a cargo of china clay.

FAUVIC *W.S.P.L.*

5. CLARY (1960-1961)
O.N. 181516. 215g, 103n. 123.0 x 23.0 x 8.7 feet.
Oil engine, 4S.C.S.A., 4-cyl., by Humboldt-Deutzmotoren A.G., Cologne-Deutz, 250bhp.
1938: Built by Scheepswerven Gebr. van Diepen, Waterhuizen (Yard No. 834) for Maria Litmeyer, Haren a/d Ems, Germany as HERMANN LITMEYER. *5.1945:* Taken as a prize at Nyborg, Denmark. *5.1946:* Taken over by the Ministry of War Transport, London, renamed EMPIRE CONDEE and placed under the management of Great Yarmouth Shipping Co. Ltd. *3.1947:* Sold to Alfred E. F. Thomson (later Plym Shipping Co. Ltd.), Plymouth and renamed CONDEE. *4.1950:* Sold to William H. Müller & Co. (London) Ltd., London and renamed AISNE. *3.1960:* Purchased by Channel Shipping Ltd. and renamed CLARY. *2.1961:* Sold to Shipping & Trading Co. Ltd. (of Gibraltar), name and port of registry unchanged. *3.1964:* Put into Valencia, Spain with engine trouble. *22.1.1966:* Partially flooded while lying at Algeciras, Spain. *1975:* Sold to Manuel Garcon (of Tangier), Panama and renamed MARIE ELIZABETH. *20.2.1976:* Suffered severe fire damage whilst loading at Barcelona, Spain, for Casablanca, Morocco, beached in Barcelona Harbour, and abandoned by her owners.

CLARY as AISNE *G. A. Osbon*

CLICHY *Dave Hocquard*

6. CLICHY (1961-1964)
See Appendix B No. 55 under CLOVA.

7. PONTAC (1961-1962)
O.N. 164156. 311g, 149n. 130.7 x 24.6 x 9.0 feet.
Oil engine, 2S.C.S.A., 5-cyl., by British Auxiliaries Ltd., Glasgow, 325bhp.
12.1934: Built by Goole Shipbulding & Repairing Co. (1927) Ltd., Goole (Yard No. 305) for Great Yarmouth Shipping Co. Ltd., Yarmouth as LOWESTOFT TRADER. *11.1961:* Purchased by Channel Shipping Ltd. and renamed PONTAC. *5.1962:* Sold to Nicolaos Zoulias & Nicolaos Ninos, Piraeus, Greece and renamed MILOS. *1964:* Sold to G. & A. D. Andrias, Piraeus and renamed VASSILIOS LITOCHORON. *1973:* Sold to N. Perris, Piraeus, name unchanged. *1976:* Sold to Kefal Navigation Co. Ltd., Limassol, Cyprus, name unchanged. *1979:* Renamed SAN ANTONIO. *1986:* Deleted from "Lloyd's Register". Vessel's continued existence in doubt.

8. BROUGHTY (II) (1962-1963)
See Appendix B No. 74.

9. GOREY (II) (1963-1968)
O.N. 305721. 427g, 252n. 153.9 x 24.7 x 10.3 feet.
Oil engine, 4S.C.S.A., 8-cyl., by N. V. Werkspoor, Amsterdam.
1949: Built by N. V. Scheepswerf Delfzijl v/h Gebr. Sander, Delfzijl (Yard No. 184) for William H. Müller & Co. N.V., Rotterdam, Holland as MARNE. *9.1963:* Purchased by Channel Shipping Ltd. and renamed GOREY. *10.1968:* Sold to Grandport Shipping Ltd., Panama, name unchanged. *1970:* Sold to Hadjioannou Bros., Piraeus, Greece and renamed HADJIOANNOU. *1976:* Sold to Billymar Ltd., Limassol, Cyprus and renamed KAPTANGIROGIS. *1977:* Sold to Hadjioannou Bros., Limassol and renamed SAINT GEORGE I. *11.12.1977:* Wrecked at Alikes, NE of Zakinthos Island, while on passage from Laurium, Greece to Koper, Yugoslavia with a general cargo.

ROTTUM arriving at Jersey *Dave Hocquard*

10. ROTTUM/CONCORDE (II) (1963-1968)
O.N. 305722. 452g, 246n. 150.9 x 26.2 x 11.8 feet.
Oil engine, 4S.C.S.A., 6-cyl., by N.V. Appingdammer Bronsmotoren, Appingedam.
1957: Built by Barkmeyer Scheepswerf N.V., Vierverlaten (Yard No. 149) for H. P. Veling & Co. (later transferred to Redreij "Rottum"), and managed by Kamp's Scheepsvaart en Handelmaatschappij N.V., Groningen, Holland. *10.1963:* Purchased by Channel Shipping Ltd., name unchanged. *2.1965:* Renamed CONCORDE. *10.1968:* Transferred to subsidiary company J. G. Renouf & Co. Ltd., Jersey, name unchanged. *11.1970:* Sold to Metcalf Motor Coasters Ltd. (T. J. Metcalf, manager), London and renamed DAVID M. *5.1973:* Sold to Cornish Shipping Ltd. (S. William Coe & Co. Ltd., mangers), Liverpool and renamed POLMEAR. *4.1974:* Sold to Sea Island Marine Ltd. (of Bridgend, Glamorgan), London and renamed SIM VENTURE. *8.1975:* Sold to Ripmeester & Co. B.V., Rotterdam, Holland and renamed CILICIA. *1976:* Sold to A. A. D. Sawalhi, Beirut, Lebanon and renamed SUS 2. *1976:* Sold to Mohamed Ali Mohamed Dib Al Sawalhi, Beirut and renamed MIYSAR. *1978:* Renamed CONCORDE I. *1979:* Sold to Afifi & Co. Ltd., Beirut and renamed AFAF. *1980:* Renamed ABOUD ABDO. *25.2.1981:* Ran ashore at Abu Kashura,, 5 miles east of Rosetta, Egypt while on passage from Iskenderun, Turkey to Alexandria, Egypt and became a total loss.

11. ERROL (III) (1964-1965)
O.N. 182099. 499g 278n. 161.1 x 28.5 x 9.8 feet.
Oil engine, 2S.C.S.A., 6-cyl., by A/B Atlas-Diesel, Stockholm, 540bhp.
4.1946: Bult by Kalmar Varv, Kalmar (Yard No. 353) for Rederi A/B Ruth (L. Glücksman, manager), Gothenburg, Sweden as RUTH. *1947:* Sold to Rederi A/B Diana (Tore Ulff, manager), Stockholm, Sweden and renamed DELILAH. *10.1948:* Sold to Imperial Chemical Industries Ltd., London, registered at Glasgow and renamed LADY ANSTRUTHER. *12.1964:* Purchased by Channel Shipping Ltd. and renamed ERROL. *3.1965:* Sold to Marine Salvage Ltd. (of London), name unchanged. *1.1966:* Sold to Overseas & General Brokerage & Finance Co. Ltd., London, name unchanged. *6.1967:* Sold to Savas Bros., Volos, Greece and renamed MARIA S. *1972:* Sold to G. Siskopoulos & Co., Thessalonika, Greece and renamed VASILIOS S. *1978:* Sold to Blizzard Shipping Co. Ltd., Limassol, Cyprus and renamed NINO. *1979:* Reported foundered in the Mediterranean.

ERROL (III) *Dave Hocquard*

12. GROUVILLE (II) (1964-1968)
O.N. 305737. 384g 192n. 160.8 x 24.6 x 10.9 feet.
Oil engine, 4S.C.S.A., 8-cyl., by N. V. Werkspoor, Amsterdam.
1947: Built by Haarlemsche Scheepsbouw Maatschappij N.V., Haarlem (Yard No. 497) for William H. Müller & Co. N.V., Rotterdam, Holland as ESCAUT. *12.1964:* Purchased by Channel Shipping Ltd. and renamed GROUVILLE. *9.1968:* Sold to Marine Enterprises (Malta) Ltd. (Maltese National Lines Ltd., managers), Valletta, Malta and renamed RACHEL PACE. *3.1969:* Managers became owners and renamed MALTESE TRADER. *5.1971:* Sold to Nikoloas Xanthopoulos, Panama and renamed NATASA. *1972:* Sold to Albina S.A., Panama and renamed ANNA I. *1972:* Sold to Interglobal Navigation & Shipping S.A., Panama and renamed PANAGIOTIS. *1974:* Renamed ANNA MARIA. *1974:* Sold to Rolen Marine Co. Ltd., Limassol, Cyprus and renamed LEILA. *1976:* Sold to Badra Shipping Lines Ltd., Limassol and renamed RANIA B. *1983:* Renamed BRAVO 2 on sale to unspecified owners. *1.1985:* Damaged by stranding whilst laid up at Limassol. Refloated and broken up.

GROUVILLE (II) *G. H. Somner Collection*

APPENDIX O — WESTERN SHIPPING LTD., PLYMOUTH (1962-1969)

1. MELEDOR (1962-1965)

See Appendix N No. 4 under FAUVIC.

2 TREVISCOE (1962-1969)

O.N. 304822. 494g, 281n. 154.3 x 27.6 x 12.0 feet.
Oil engine, 4S.C.S.A., 8-cyl., by N. V. Werkspoor, Amsterdam, 500bhp.
7.1952: Built by Scheepswerf "Voorwaarfs" N.V., Martenshoek (Yard No. 160) for Spliethoff's Bevrachtingskantoor N.V., Amsterdam, Holland as LIJNBAANSGRACHT. *1962:* Purchased by Western Shipping Ltd. and renamed TREVISCOE. *1969:* Managers became W. D. Tamlyn & Co. Ltd., Plymouth. *1974:* Sold to Alba Shipping Co. Ltd., (Gillie & Blair Ltd., managers), South Shields, and renamed BEAULY FIRTH. *11.1974:* Sold to A. E., J. J. & H. Le Bond, South Shields, registered at Cork, with name unchanged. *1976:* Sold to Adinda Shippping Co. S.A., Panama and renamed GABRIELLE. *1977:* Renamed MICHELINE. *1979:* Sold to Compania Naviera Panasabine S.A., (I.T.F.A., P.V.B.A., managers), Panama and renamed SABINE 1. *1980:* Sold to Compania Naviera Panakarine S.A., Panama and renamed KARINE. *12.12.1980:* Arrived at Ostend in a damaged condition after being in collision with the Belgian m.v. FEDERAL OTTAWA (21,661/80) on the previous day. *9.5.1983:* Arrived at Bruges for breaking up.

TREVISCOE at Charlestown, Cornwall *Dave Hocquard*

APPENDIX P — DAVID C. THOMAS (1873-1885), DAVID C. THOMAS & SON (1885-1913), BRUSSELS STEAM SHIP CO. LTD., (1913-1967)

1. **CITY OF GHENT (1873-1891)** Iron.
O.N. 63145. 204g, 125n. 135.9 x 20.4 x 9.7 feet.
Diagonal direct acting, 2-cyl., by builders, 40hp — new engine fitted 1881, compound, 2-cyl., by Windas & Dunsmore, London, 40hp.
1.1871: Built by Thomas Charlton, Grimsby (Yard No. 5) for Edward Banister & Co., Grimsby. *6.1872:* Sold to Grimsby Steam Ship Co. Ltd., Grimsby, name unchanged. *4.1873:* Purchased by David C. Thomas, name unchanged. *1885:* Transferred to David C. Thomas & Son. *6.1891:* Sold to Samuel Crowell (of Halifax, Nova Scotia), name unchanged. *11.1898:* Managers became Pickford & Black (of Halifax N.S.). *10.1910:* Sold to Pickford & Black Ltd., Halifax, N.S., name unchanged. *8.9.1911:* Sold to City of Ghent Co.. Ltd. (Pickford & Black Ltd., managers), Halifax, N.S., name unchanged. *4.1912:* Sold to W. A. Beattie (of Picton), name unchanged. *7.1916:* Sold to Theodor Shipping Co. Ltd., Newcastle, name unchanged. *5.9.1916:* Stopped and seized by UB 18 and sunk by time-bomb when 18 miles SE of Cape Barfleur, France, while on passage from River Tyne to Rouen with a cargo of coke.

2. **CITY OF BRUSSELS (I) (1873-1879)** Iron.
O.N. 67318. 236g 143n. 131.2 x 20.0 x 10.9 feet.
Compound, 2-cyl., by Pattison & Atkinson, Newcastle, 40hp.
2.1872: Built by Edward Lindsay, Newcastle for Robert Fell & Co., Newcastle as ADJUTANT. *8.1873:* Purchased by David C. Thomas and renamed CITY OF BRUSSELS. *22.11.1879:* Sank in Middle Gat, River Scheldt after collision with the s.s. RIO TEJO (639/65) while on passage from Brussels to London with a general cargo.

3. **CITY OF VERVIERS (1875-1902)** Iron.
O.N. 70736. 267g, 169n. 135.3 x 22.2 x 10.2 feet.
Compound, 2-cyl., by builders, 30hp.
6.1875: Built by J. Readhead & Co., South Shields (Yard No. 112) for David C. Thomas. *1885:* Transferred to David C. Thomas & Son. *7.1902:* Sold to J. R. Stewart & Co., London, name unchanged. *6.7.1903:* Stranded at Llandulas; subsequently refloated and towed to Tranmere and broken up.

4. **CITY OF BRUSSELS (II) (1880-1915)** Iron.
O.N. 76384, 2-cyl., by Kincaid, Donald & Co., Greenock, 67hp.
7.1880: Built by R. Chambers jnr., Dumbarton (Yard No. 14) for David C. Thomas. *1885:* Transferred to David C. Thomas & Son. *1913:* Transferred to Brussels Steam Ship Co. Ltd. *10.1915:* Sold to Hugh Flinn, Liverpool, name unchanged. *2.1920:* Renamed BRUSSELS. *12.1920:* Transferred to Hugo Flinn on the death of his father. *5.7.1922:* Stranded on Shoreham Bar while on passage from Caen to Shoreham with a cargo of basic slag. Later refloated and broken up at Southampton.

5. **CITY OF LONDON (I)/CITY OF LIEGE (1891-1928)**
O.N. 99031. 351g, 182n. 135.3 x 23.6 x 11.0 feet.
Triple, 3-cyl., by North Eastern Marine Engineering Co. Ltd., Newcastle, 50hp.
12.1891: Built by Schlesinger, Davis & Co., Newcastle (Yard No. 162) for David C. Thomas & Son. *1913:* Transferred to Brussels Steam Ship Co. Ltd. *11.1927:* Renamed CITY OF LIEGE. *10.1928:* Sold to Hercht Pfeiffer Ltd., London, name unchanged. *5.1929:* Sold to Metal & Iron Corporation Ltd., London and renamed INGELO. *1931:* Sold to Hugo Köster, Rostock, Germany and renamed AXEL. *1936:* Owners became Köster & Seeling, Rostock. *10.1.1940:* Sank off Kieler Förde, Baltic Sea after collision with Hitler's yacht GRILLE, then serving as a mine patrol vessel.

6. CITY OF CHARLEROY (I) (1902-1928)
O.N. 115908. 368g, 198n. 135.0 x 23.6 x 11.9 feet.
Triple, 3-cyl., by A. Rodger & Co., Glasgow, 62hp.
10.1902: Built by Mackie & Thomson, Glasgow (Yard No. 277) for David C. Thomas & Son. *1913:* Transferred to Brussels Steam Ship Co. Ltd. *2.1928:* Sold to James C. Newman, London, name unchanged. *8.1930:* Sold to Humphrey D. Lea, London, name unchanged. *5.1932:* Sold to Herbert Rowland, London, name unchanged. *2.1933:* Sold to Arthur Waterson (of Bangor) and renamed EILANDE. *25.2.1933:* Wrecked on Black Middens, River Tyne while outward bound to Par, Cornwall with a cargo of coal.

7. PRINCE LEOPOLD/CITY OF MALINES (1913-1925)
O.N. 123657. 375g, 148n. 135.0 x 23.6 x 11.9 feet.
Triple, 3-cyl., by MacColl & Pollock Ltd., Sunderland, 78hp.
5.1905: Built by Mackay Bros., Alloa (Yard No. 1) for Anglo-Belgian Prince Line (Thomas Ellis, manager), London as PRINCE LEOPOLD. *6.1913:* Transferred to Brussels Steam Ship Co. Ltd. (Thomas Ellis, manager), London. *2.1920:* Renamed CITY OF MALINES. *12.1925:* Sold to Great Yarmouth Shipping Co. Ltd., London, name unchanged. *10.1947:* Sold to Wirral Steam Ship Co. Ltd., London, name unchanged. *1.1948:* Renamed WIRRAL BANK. *2.1951:* Sold to Norman Dakin, London, name unchanged. *9.1952:* Broken up at Grays, Essex by Thomas W. Ward Ltd.

8. PRINCE CHARLES/CITY OF BRUSSELS (III) (1913-1923).
O.N. 120546. 373g, 160n. 135.0 x 23.6 x 11.9 feet.
Triple, 3-cyl., by MacColl & Pollock Ltd., Sunderland, 65hp.
5.1905: Built by Mackay Bros., Alloa (Yard No. 2) for Anglo-Belgian Prince Line (Thomas Ellis, manager), London as PRINCE CHARLES. *6.1913:* Transferred to Brussels Steam Ship Co. Ltd. (Thomas Ellis, manager). *3.1920:* Renamed CITY OF BRUSSELS. *11.1923:* Sold to Dampfschiffahrts Ges. "Gaida", Riga, Latvia and renamed NAIGA. *1928:* Sold to Lübeck-Oslo Linie G.m.b.H., Lübeck, Germany and renamed HOLSTENTOR. *10.12.1944:* Capsized and sank 7 miles west of Falkenberg, Sweden.

9. CITY OF BRUSSELS (IV) (1925-1940)
O.N. 148707. 629g, 357n. 175.1 x 28.6 x 15.9 feet.
Triple, 3-cyl., by William Beardmore & Co. Ltd., Glasgow, 88hp.
11.1925: Built by Burntisland Shipbuilding Co. Ltd., Burntisland (Yard No. 136) for Brussels Steam Ship Co. Ltd. *13.5.1940:* Seized at Brussels by German authorities on occupation of Belgium, after having previously shot down two German aircraft at Willebroek on her passage to that port. *1942:* Taken into German naval service as a flakship, renamed VIPER and stationed at Bayonne, France. *23.8.1944:* Scuttled at Bayonne — later raised and broken up.

CITY OF LONDON (II) *W.S.P.L.*

10. CITY OF LONDON (II) (1927-1962)
O.N. 149965. 668g, 310n. 175.1 x 28.6 x 15.9 feet.
Triple, 3-cyl., by William Beardmore & Co Ltd., Coatbridge, 88hp.
12.1927: Built by Burntisland Shipbuilding Co. Ltd., Burntisland (Yard No. 145) for Brussels Steam Ship Co. Ltd. *1962:* Company taken over by Dundee, Perth & London Shipping Co. Ltd. in association with George Gibson & Co. Ltd. *8.1962:* Sold to Stamatios & Nicolaos Leriotis, Piraeus, Greece and renamed AGIOS IOANNIS. *1963:* Sold to G. I. Thomas, Piraeus and fitted with an oil engine, 2S.C.S.A., 5-cyl. by Harland & Wolff Ltd, Belfast, 500bhp, name unchanged. *1967:* Sold to Apostolos Katapodis, Piraeus, name unchanged. *1971:* Sold to Dionyssios Stavrou & Co., and later George Stavrou-Nicolaos Zoulias & Co., Piraeus, name unchanged. *1.12.1973:* Run ashore 6 miles NW of Cavo Mandello near Karistos, Greece after developing a leak while on passage from Sitia, Crete to Volos, Greece and became a total loss.

11. CITY OF CHARLEROY (II) (1942-1947)
O.N. 163204. 869g, 457n. 197.7 x 30.7 x 12.1 feet.
Triple, 3-cyl., by builders, 131hp.
9.1933: Built by J. Lewis & Son Ltd., Aberdeen (Yard No. 128) for John Kelly Ltd. (William Clint, manager), Belfast as ROSAPENNA. *3.1937:* Sold to P. Hawksfield & Son Ltd., Dover and renamed KATHLEEN HAWKSFIELD. *9.1942:* Purchased by Brussels Steam Ship Co. Ltd. and renamed CITY OF CHARLEROY. *4.1947:* Sold to Williamstown Shipping Co. Ltd. (Comben, Longstaff & Co.), London and renamed CHESTERBROOK. *11.1950:* Sold to William Robertson Shipowners Ltd., Glasgow and renamed GIRASOL. *1.1958:* Transferred to Gem Line Ltd (William Robertson Shipowners Ltd., managers). *6.1958:* Sold to Ubaldo Gennari fu Torquato & Cia, Ancona, Italy and renamed HIERAX. *7.1971:* Societa Industrie Varie commenced demolition at La Spezia, Italy.

12. CITY OF BRUSSELS (V) (1947-1964)
O.N. 181606. 691g, 362n. 172.0 x 30.2 x 14.9 feet.
Triple, 3-cyl., by builders, 130hp.
4.1947: Built by J. Lewis & Sons Ltd., Aberdeen (Yard No. 195) for Brussels Steam Ship Co. Ltd. *1962:* Company taken over by Dundee, Perth & London Shipping Co. Ltd. in association with George Gibson & Co. Ltd., Leith. *7.1964:* Sold to Barbamihalis Corporation, Panama and renamed BARBAMIHALIS. *1966:* Sold to Cia. de Navegacão Baltir Ltda., Panama fitted with an oil engine, 4S.C.S.A., 8-cyl. by Klöckner-Humboldt-Deutz, Cologne, 800bhp, and renamed CAPITAO BISMARCK. *1969:* Sold to "Ancora" Soc. de Navegacão Aveirense S.a.r.L., Panama and renamed AVEIRO. *24.9.1969:* Laid-up at Bilbao, Spain. *1971:* Reverted to ownership of Cia. de Navegacão Baltir Ltda. and previous name. *7.1971:* Broken up in Spain.

CITY OF BRUSSELS (V) *W. H. Brown*

COMPANY MANAGERS/MANAGING DIRECTORS FROM 1826

1. **JAMES NICOLL**
   Joint manager (with Thomas Matthew) from 1826 until he retired in March 1838.

2. **THOMAS MATTHEW**
   Joint manager (with James Nicoll) from 1826, and sole manager from 1838 until his death in 1842.

3. **THOMAS MEARNS**
   Interim manager appointed in 1842 on the death of Thomas Matthew.

4. **GEORGE MILLS**
   Interim manager appointed in 1843. Described as "lately shipbuilder and naval architect of Glasgow".

5. **ROBERT MARSHALL**
   Appointed manager in 1844. Had risen to be manager of Dundee & Arbroath Railway Co. before joining the Company. Resigned in March 1852 on being appointed manager of West India Royal Mail Steamship Co., London. Was instrumental in sending LONDON (II) on a cruise to Hamburg in 1845, and erecting workshops at the west end of Earl Grey Dock. Died in June 1884.

6. **THOMAS COUPER**
   Appointed manager in 1852. Previously manager of Dundee & Hull Shipping Co. Introduced the first screw steamer LONDON (IV) into the fleet in 1856. Disposed of sailing schooners in 1863. Retired because of ill health in August 1879 and died on 18th February 1880.

7. **JAMES W. KIDD**
   Appointed manager in 1879. From 1869 had been responsible for the London office of the Company. Retired because of ill health in 1915 but made managing director in recognition of his services. Retired from the Board in October 1918.

8. **RALPH C. COWPER**
   Appointed manager in 1917. Started career with George Gibson & Co. of Leith. In 1910 became manager of Aberdeen, Newcastle & Hull Steam Co. Ltd. Died 30th July 1947 at his home in Fort Street, Dundee, aged 75.

9. **JOHN R. COWPER**
   Appointed General Manager in 1947 on the death of his father Ralph C. Cowper. Opened trading to the Great Lakes. Retired in 1966 because of ill health. Died in 1967.

10. **JAMES M. CHALMERS**
    Appointed Managing Director in 1967. Joined the Company in 1935. Became Chief Accountant in 1953. Became Secretary in 1962. Retired in 1987.

11. **ALASDAIR D. CHALMERS**
    Appointed Managing Director in 1987 on the retirement of his father James M. Chalmers.

ACKNOWLEDGEMENTS

For help in the preparation of this history I am greatly indebted to many individuals and not least to the unknown person who many years ago ensured that the Minute Books of the Company since its inception in 1826 were not destroyed. They contained a wealth of information and detail that I could never have found anywhere else. I am grateful to the Dundee City Archives for allowing me access to the earlier books now in their care, and to Mr. James M. Chalmers, managing director of the Company until 1987, for giving me the freedom to delve into the later Minute Books still held at East Dock Street. I cannot thank Mr. Chalmers enough for allowing me to ask him many, many questions — his memory on shipping matters going back some 50 odd years was invaluable. Being put in touch with Captain Sandy Campbell M.B.E. and Captain George Wood was also another stroke of fortune. Their contributions on life at sea and of certain incidents and voyages in which they and their ships were involved has added a further dimension to the story. For the details of the Channel Islands ''connection'' I had the willing help of Dave Hocquard and Mr. George Le Moine, both Jersey residents.

Over many years the late Mr. John Ingram, a reporter on the staff of the Dundee Courier and Advertiser and also the Evening Telegraph, kept notes on local shipping matters. On his death some years ago it was fortunate that all this material was passed by his widow to the Dundee Central Library. The notes, now nicely bound in a volume, were gladly made available to me and proved most useful — I am indebted to the staff of that library for their help. The nearby McManus Galleries have been most helpful in locating pictures and indeed had a photograph commissioned of the painting of Captain William Speedy specially for this book.

Illustrations have come from many sources and where that is known suitable acknowledgement has been made. I am most grateful to Roy Griffin, Cliff Parsons and Tony Smith of the World Ship Photo Library for tracking down those pictures within the Society's archives. Many other individuals — too numerous to mention by name — sent photographs and other material from amongst their collections and I much appreciate their interest.

Sincere thanks are due to the Central Record team for their efforts to ensure that the fleet lists were as accurate as they can be, to the staff of the Public Records Office, Kew, Surrey for producing many records that I requested over a long period of time, to the Guildhall Library, City of London and Miss Jenny Wraight for finding record cards and other material for me to study, and to Mrs. I. M. Bladen and Mr. J. N. Hopkins of the Department of Trade, Cardiff for producing ships' record files and providing me with details of the service of the late Captain Sandy Campbell M.B.E.

The front cover was designed by Purewell Signwriters, Christchurch, Dorset and the back cover is a reproduction of the cover of a Company brochure issued in 1938.

INDEX OF NAMES

Ships' names in BLOCK LETTERS are those carried when the vessel was owned or managed by the Dundee, Perth & London Shipping Co Ltd group of companies.

Ship's name	Built	List
CONCORDE (II)	1957	N 10
Concorde I	1957	N 10
Condee	1938	N 5
CONIDA	1936	B 63
Conqueror	1884	K 2
Conquérant	1884	K 2
Continental Freighter	1898	J312
COQUETDALE	1924	B 56
COQUETDYKE	1952	L 3
COQUETSIDE	1923	L 2
CORTACHY	1934	B 59
Countess of Aberdeen	1878	J3 8
COURIER	1816	A 12
CROMBIE	1934	B 60
Cryomar	1955	B 74
Dalhousie	1861	G 1
DAME	1807	A 26
DART	1836	A 38
David M	1957	N 10
David P	1911	B 50
De Lavoye	1945	M 4
Deedale	1924	B 56
DEFIANCE	1807	A 6
Delilah	1946	N 11
Deneb	1923	L 2
Dia	1943	B 72
Dispatch	1805	D 9
Doron	1954	B 73
Dotterel	1934	B 52
DRON	1936	B 63
Dunavon	1908	M 3
DUNDEE (I)	1818	A 16
DUNDEE (II)	1834	B 2
DUNDEE (III)	1883	B 26
DUNDEE (IV)	1885	B 27
DUNDEE (V)	1911	B 34
DUNDEE (VI)	1919	B 40
DUNDEE (VII)	1934	B 52
DUNDEE (VIII)	1954	B 73
EAGLE	1858	B 14
Earl of Aberdeen	1889	J3 9
Earlsfield	1952	L 3
EDINA	1939	B 66
Eilande	1902	P 6
ELBE	1816	A 13
Empire Bard	1942	B 66
Empire Beaconsfield	1943	B 72
EMPIRE CAPE	1945	B 62
Empire Condee	1938	N 5
EMPIRE CONISBURGH	1937	C 9
Empire Congo	1923	L 2
Empire Fang	1945	M 4
Empire Galbraith	1944	B 76
EMPIRE GARLAND	1944	C 8
EMPIRE SEAWORTY	1945	J316
Empire Taw	1921	B 45
Empire Townsman	1943	M 5
ERROL (I)	1920	B 51
ERROL (II)	1936	B 58
ERROL (III)	1946	N 11

Ship's name	Built	List
Escaut	1947	N 12
Esperanza	1854	B 11
Evelyn Manor	1920	B 51
Fabric 39	1945	M 5
FAIR CITY	1904	B 32
Fair Head	1937	J315
FALCON	1854	A 45
Falkefjell	1883	I 3
Fame (I)	1787	F 2
Fame (II)	1830	F 5
FAUVIC	1951	N 4
Fenris	1884	I 1
Fife Packet	1807	F 3
Filia E Tricoglou	1896	C 1
Filio	1944	C 8
Finistère	1875	B 22
FISHERS	1820	A 18
Flying Cormorant	1908	B 65
Flying Dutchman	1880	K 1
Flying Swallow	1905	B 64
Fordmac	1939	B 66
FORFARSHIRE	1823	A 20
FORTH	1830	A 29
Frederick Hughes	1936	B 58
Frieda	1951	N 4
FRIENDS	1821	A 19
Gabrielle	1952	O 2
GALA	1939	B 61
GALLIA	1865	B 20
Gallus	1910	I 8
GANNOCHY	1937	B 69
Gaspesia	1909	B 44
Garmoyle	1904	B 39
GAUNTLET	1891	C 4
George	—	E 10
GEORGE DUNCAN	1847	A 44
Georgios	1937	B 57
Gerasimos A	1934	B 59
Gibel Yedid	1894	I 4
GIPSY	1805	A 27
Girasol	1933	P 11
GLAMIS	1936	B 54
GLASGOW	1816	A 14
Glen Nor	1935	B 55
Glen Tilt	1882	J310
Glentaise	1905	I 7
Goole No 8	1891	C 4
GOREY (I)	1928	N 2
GOREY (II)	1949	N 9
Gotaalv	1923	L 2
GOWRIE (I)	1909	B 33
GOWRIE (II)	1909	B 41
GOWRIE (III)	1941	B 62
GOWRIE (IV)	1939	B 66
GOWRIE (V)	1944	B 76
Grange	1880	K 1
GRANTEZ	1933	N 3
GROUVILLE (I)	1936	B 58
GROUVILLE (II)	1947	N 12

Ship's name	Built	List
Njong	1944	C 8
NORTH INCH	1904	B 39
NORTH SEA	1881	B 24
North Voyageur	1909	B 44
Northern City	1873	J3 6
Norwood	1895	J311
OLIVE	1814	A 11
Orehoved	1935	B 55
OSNABURGH	1800	A 3
Panagiotis	1947	N 12
Parkstone	1929	M 2
Pen Arun	1943	M 5
PERTH (I)	1809	A 8
PERTH (II)	1816	A 15
PERTH (III)	1834	B 3
PERTH (IV)	1890	B 30
PERTH (V)	1915	B 35
PERTH (VI)	1937	B 57
Pharos	1846	J2 2
Pladda	1861	G 2
Ploussa	1905	I 7
Polmear	1967	N 10
PONTAC	1934	N 7
Portelet	1918	B 37
Prado	1905	I 7
Prince Charles	1905	P 8
Prince Leopold	1905	P 7
Princess Alice	1843	J1 3
Princess Tarrah	1951	B 71
PURBECK	1936	M 6
QUEEN (I)	1842	A 46
QUEEN (II)	1854	B 11
Quickthorn	1903	B 43
Quickthorn	1908	M 3
Rachel Pace	1947	N 12
Rania B	1947	N 12
Rasona	1896	I 5
Ravenscraig	1899	H 1
RED SEA	1889	B 28
Regina Pacis	1905	I 7
Rhenania	1923	L 2
Robert	1821	E 6
ROE	1835	A 37
Rola	1936	B 54
Rolston	1962	M 11
ROM	1905	C 2
Romylia	1936	B 54
Rosalind	1911	B 38
Rosapenna	1933	P 11
Rose (I)	1802	D 3
ROSE (II)	1828	A 25
Roselyne	1943	M 5
ROSYTH (I)	1903	B 43
ROSYTH (II)	1911	B 50
ROTTUM	1957	N 10
Rowena	1883	I 3
Rudelsburg	1896	C 1
Ruth	1946	N 11

Ship's name	Built	List
Sabine 1	1952	O 2
St Catherine	1916	J313
Saint George I	1949	N 9
St Ronaig	1921	B 46
Salamstar	1944	C 8
SAMSON	1857	B 13
San Antonio	1934	N 7
Scantic	1934	B 60
Scorpion I	1946	B 68
SCOTIA (I)	1861	B 15
SCOTIA (II)	1862	B 16
SCOTIA (III)	1875	B 22
Sea Union	1935	B 55
Semenyih	1945	J316
Shelah	1841	F 6
Shelbrit 4	1928	N 2
Sheldrake	1944	C 8
Shell Driver	1928	N 2
Shell Mex 8	1928	N 2
Sidibarrani	1945	J316
Sim Venture	1957	N 10
Sir Cedric	1943	M 5
SIR WILLIAM WALLACE	1830	B 1
SOLICITOR	1849	A 43
Sophie Express	1951	B 71
SOVEREIGN	1828	A 24
Springhaven	1937	B 69
Spurnpoint	1908	M 3
STAR	1831	A 32
Slathis A	1881	B 25
Stepan Shaumian	1937	C 9
Stolida	1936	B 54
Stowmead	1933	N 3
Stronshira	1904	B 39
Sus 2	1957	N 10
SWAN	1830	A 30
SWIFT	1838	A 39
TAY (I)	1807	A 5
Tay (II)	1819	E 3
TAY (III)	1830	A 31
Tay (D & H)	1825	F 1
Tay (D & N)	1885	G 3
TAY & TYNE	1909	B 36
Tayfirth	1904	B 32
Teresa	1911	B 38
Thomas A	1937	J315
TID	1800	A 28
Titan	1805	B 19
Tom 1	1883	I 3
Topsail Star	1951	B 71
Toryu Maru	1889	B 28
Trade Mariner	1935	B 55
TREVISCOE	1952	O 2
Tynedale	1885	K 3
UNION	1807	A 7
Valfiorita	1915	B 35
Valzell	1935	B 53
Vasilios	1937	B 57
Vasilios S	1946	N 11

Ship's name	Built	List
Vassilios Litochoron	1934	N 7
VAUBAN	1962	M 11
Velocity	1821	J1 1
VENDOME	1960	M 10
Vict	1889	K 4
VICTORIA	1849	A 42
Victoria (A & N)	1848	J1 2
Victoria	1865	B 20
Volta	1883	B 26
Vlyho	1954	B 73
W	1891	B 49
Wah Chung	1911	B 38
War Wensum	1919	B 40
WHITE SEA	1881	B 25
Wilmas	1916	M 1
Winsor Trader	1951	B 71
Wirral Bank	1905	P 7
YENDIS	1911	B 50
ZENOBIA	1847	A 41
Zygos 1	1936	B 54

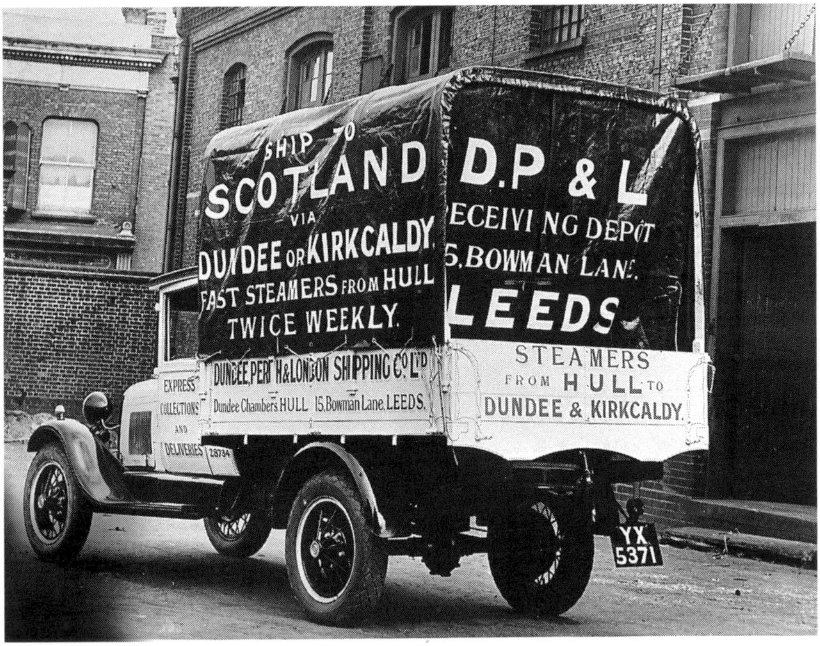

A Company vehicle in the 1920s